STATE, SOCIETY
AND INFORMATION TECHNOLOGY IN ASIA

State, Society and Information Technology in Asia

Alterity Between Online and Offline Politics

Edited by

ALAN CHONG

S. Rajaratnam School of International Studies, Singapore

and

FAIZAL BIN YAHYA

Institute of Policy Studies, Lee Kuan Yew School of Public Policy, National University of Singapore, Singapore

Routledge

Taylor & Francis Group

LONDON AND NEW YORK

First published 2014 by Ashgate Publishing

Published 2016 by Routledge
2 Park Square, Milton Park, Abingdon, Oxon OX14 4RN
711 Third Avenue, New York, NY 10017, USA

Routledge is an imprint of the Taylor & Francis Group, an informa business

British Library Cataloguing in Publication Data
A catalogue record for this book is available from the British Library

The Library of Congress has cataloged the printed edition as follows:

State, society and information technology in Asia : alterity between online and offline politics / by [edited by] Alan Chong and Faizal Bin Yahya.
pages cm
Includes bibliographical references and index.
ISBN 978-1-4724-4379-3 (hardback)
1. Internet--Social aspects--Asia. 2. Information technology--Social aspects--Asia. 3. Asia--Politics and government--21st century. I. Chong, Alan. II. Yahya, Faizal, 1965-

HN655.2.I56S73 2014
302.23'1095--dc23

2014023028

ISBN 9781472443793 (hbk)

Contents

List of Figures and Tables

Figures

Tables

List of Contributors

Nasya Bahfen is a senior lecturer in the School of Media Film and Journalism at Monash University in Melbourne, Australia. Her research interests cover the intersection between online media, internationalization and diversity, with a specific focus on the Muslim world and southeast Asia. Her academic publications span the areas of communication technology and digital media studies as well as organizational, interpersonal and intercultural communication. They have appeared in journals such as *Islam and Christian–Muslim Relations*, *Australian Journalism Review*, *Pacific Journalism Review* and *Cross Cultural Management*. She is currently working on an Australian Research Council Grant study on cyber-racism and community resilience. Nasya Bahfen can be contacted at nasya.bahfen@monash.edu.au.

Alan Chong is Associate Professor at the S. Rajaratnam School of International Studies in Singapore. He has published widely on the notion of soft power and the role of ideas in constructing the international relations of Singapore and Asia. His publications have appeared in *The Pacific Review*; *International Relations of the Asia-Pacific*; *Asian Survey*; *East Asia: an International Quarterly*; *Politics, Religion and Ideology*; the *Review of International Studies*; the *Cambridge Review of International Affairs* and *Armed Forces and Society*. He is also the author of *Foreign Policy in Global Information Space: Actualizing Soft Power* (Palgrave, 2007). He is currently working on several projects exploring the notion of 'Asian international theory'. His interest in soft power has also led to inquiry into the sociological and philosophical foundations of international communication. In tandem, he has pursued a fledgling interest in researching cyber security issues. He has frequently been interviewed in the Asian media and consulted in think-tank networks in the region. He can be contacted at: iscschong@ntu.edu.sg.

Pui Yee Choong was a Senior Research Analyst at the S. Rajaratnam School of International Studies in Singapore. Her research interests are on social and political affairs in Malaysia, identity politics, social movements and religious mobilization. Her publications have appeared in *Peace and Policy* and *The Roundtable*. One of her most recent publications is a book chapter in Electoral Dynamics in Malaysia: Findings from the Grassroots (ISEAS and SIRD). In addition to that, she has also authored multiple op-eds in regional papers and news portals such as *Asia Times*, *The Straits Times*, *The Diplomat*, *The Edge* and *Today*. She has also been interviewed in the Asian media and international media on the electoral and social movement issues in Malaysia. She can be contacted at: nalika.puiyee@gmail.com.

Kay Hearn is an Adjunct Lecturer at Edith Cowan University in Western Australia and her main area of research is Internet management in the People's Republic of China. She has published on the official and official discourses played out on environmental and HIV activism in the PRC via, online gaming in China. Her work has been published in *Journal of Current Chinese* and *Continuum: Journal of Media and Cultural Studies.* She also has research interests in the relationship between cyber security, international relations and hacking. She has presented her findings at the *Australian Information Warfare and Security Conference* in 2009 and 2008. In addition Kay's work has also explored the use of the Internet and social media during times of crisis. She can be contacted at k.hearn@ecu.edu.au.

Byoung Won Min is Associate Professor at Ewha Womans University in Seoul, Korea. His main research interests are on international relations theory, information technology and politics, security studies, and complex systems and networks. He has published a lot of articles in *Journal of International and Area Studies*, *Review of International and Area Studies*, *Korean Political Science Review*, *Peace Studies*, *Korean Journal of International Studies*. The books he published include; *The Political Economy of Collective Intelligence* (2011, co-authored), *World Politics of Transformation* (2007, co-authored), and *International Politics in Complex Systems* (2005). He can be contacted at: byomin@ewha.ac.kr.

Fernando Paragas is an Assistant Professor at the Wee Kim Wee School of Communication and Information at the Nanyang Technological University, Singapore. His research focuses on the intersections among mediated communication, international migration, and message design. His current research focuses on the antecedents of mediated learning. He completed his PhD degree in Mass Communication at Ohio University as a Fulbright fellow. Dr Paragas earned his MA in Urban and Regional Planning, for which he received a Dean's Medallion, and BA in Communication Research, where he received the 1996 Best Undergraduate Thesis Award, at the University of the Philippines (UP), Diliman Campus. He has received awards from UP, the Corporate Communication International and the Asian Federation of Advertising Associations – *Newsweek Magazine*. He can be contacted at fparagas@ntu.edu.sg.

Joefe B. Santarita is an Assistant Professor and currently the College Secretary of the Asian Center, University of the Philippines. His research interests focus on South Asian political economy, ancient Indian influences, diasporic experiences, as well as contemporary business communities in the Philippines. Two of his projects were successfully published as book chapters in the Institute of Southeast Asian Studies' 'Rising India and Indian Communities in East Asia' and 'Negotiating Identity: Sikhs in Southeast Asia' aside from several research results that appeared in journals and proceedings. Recently, he is working on a study about the rise of Indian Information Technology Enabled Services' companies in the Philippines. He can be contacted at joefes@yahoo.com.

Kwoh-Jack Tan is an Associate Research Fellow at the S. Rajaratnam School of International Studies. He is also a PhD candidate at the University of New South Wales in Sydney, Australia. His main research interests are in analyzing international relations from postcolonial perspectives, Singapore's foreign policy, and the power capabilities of small states. He is also interested in postcolonial critiques of disciplinary International Relations, and the constructions of 'the international' from everyday life. His recent commentaries have appeared in *The Straits Times* (Singapore), *TODAY* (Singapore), *The Nation* (Thailand) and *The Diplomat*. He can be contacted at: iskjtan@ntu.edu.sg.

Faizal Bin Yahya is a Research Fellow at the Institute of Policy Studies, Lee Kuan Yew School of Public Policy, National University of Singapore and his main research interests are on human capital flows, state owned enterprises (SOEs), small and medium enterprises (SMEs) knowledge based industries, regional trade and economic linkages. His recent three books are; *The Migration of Indian Professionals to Southeast Asia* (co-authored) (Routledge, December 2010), *Economic Cooperation between Singapore and India: An Alliance in the Making?* (Routledge, May 2008), *New 'Temples' of India: Singapore and India Collaboration in Information Technology Parks* (Brill, October 2008). In addition, he has published more than 30 peer reviewed journal articles and book chapters. Faizal Bin Yahya can be contacted at faizal.yahya@nus.edu.sg.

Acknowledgements

Discussions on this book project were initiated in 2009 just after the Global Financial Crisis (GFC) of 2008. This financially seismic event not only threw the entire global financial system into disarray but societal and political dynamics as well. Things were never to be the same after the GFC and one pronounced new trend saw the reinvigoration of the State for regulatory and management oversight in countering the excesses of market forces. While the intrusiveness of State intervention appeared in North America and Europe as a drastic return to the past, in Asia it was more of the same. From another direction, the editors were also inspired by a series of scholarly volumes published between 2001 and 2012 which aimed to discuss assorted responses around the globe to the promise of 'information society' or 'networked society'. The penetration of personal computers, laptop computers, smart phones, iPads and iPhones heralded a visually arresting landscape of seemingly technologically enhanced politics and society. Yet realities on the ground appeared to defy the promise of inexorable liberalization through the proliferation of information technology (IT). Civil society was empowered by the personalized broadcast capabilities of Internet-based social media and the phenomenon of citizen bloggers and hackers, who could equally turn on both their own governments and foreign adversaries, hogged news headlines. In Asia, the 'offline' State and its associated apparatuses proved remarkably durable in the face of IT-empowered citizenry. In cases such as China, Malaysia, South Korea, and Singapore, governments 'negotiated' the political impacts of IT to thwart large scale political liberalization. Even in the more politically open Philippine and Indian contexts, the needs of enhancing the call centre industry reinforced businesses' clamour for government to prepare and maintain a hospitable infrastructure for their profitable operations. When it came to promoting the IT-connected global city, Kuala Lumpur, Taipei and Singapore were not shy about employing *dirigiste* propaganda techniques. Each city only differed in degree of governmental intervention. In the meantime, Asians were also experimenting 'online' with forms of identity driven and economically inspired forms of fledgling virtual communities as the cases of the Muslim student diaspora, the mobile phone and Web-savvy Filipino expatriate community, and the Malaysian oppositional movements demonstrate. Set against this backdrop of the cross-cutting complexity of the politics and political economy of the Asian region, this book argues that the IT-facilitated capitalist order ought to be studied through the full range of its subterranean transboundary impacts.

Early approaches to possible contributors to this volume started during the Sixth International Conference of Asian Scholars (ICAS) at Daejeon in South Korea in 2009. Given the complexity and evolving nature of the topics covered in this volume, it took quite some time for the manuscript to be reviewed and published. In this regard, we convey our heartfelt gratitude to our fellow contributors for their patience, willingness and hard work to see this book project through to completion. Perhaps, given the dynamism and flux of the Asian region, and especially in the areas of social media, information technology, politics and society, it should not have been surprising to some that it has taken quite a while to get such a pioneering volume published.

The co-editors would like to thank their respective institutions, the Institute of Policy Studies and the S. Rajaratnam School of International Studies, for granting them multiple stretches of research time to complete this book project. They would also like to thank the Institute of International Affairs of Seoul National University for allowing Byoung Won Min, the author of Chapter 7, to reproduce substantive sections of his own journal article, 'Government Biting Back [at] Civil Society: Regulations of Information Technologies and Media in South Korea', *Journal of International and Area Studies* (South Korea) Volume 20, number 1 (2013), pages 111–124, in English for the purpose of his contribution to this volume.

On a personal note, co-editor Alan Chong would like to thank Cherian George, Fernando Paragas, both the Undergraduate and Masters students taking the various incarnations of the course 'The International Politics of Communication' at the Faculty of Arts and Social Sciences at the National University of Singapore, as well as at the Wee Kim Wee School of Communication and Information at the Nanyang Technological University, for their feedback and inspiration for investigating the political impact of IT on Asian politics. Lee Il Woo, Associate Research Fellow in the Rajaratnam School's Military Studies Programme, also deserves special mention for assisting Alan Chong with the bulk of the preparation of the index to this book at the eleventh hour. His help was crucial in getting this book to production on time.

Faizal Bin Yahya would like to thank his wife Rita and their children Aiman, Ezra, Ezriel and Nina for their understanding, support and love throughout this book project.

Finally, we hope that this book project will contribute to shaping the larger narrative about the development of one of the largest and most diverse regions in the world – Asia – and provide an avenue for its marginal and subterranean interests to be seen and heard. It would also be gratifying to us should the book spur further discussions and work in this multidisciplinary field.

Alan Chong
Faizal Bin Yahya

Introduction

State, Society and Information Technology in Asia: Alterity between Online and Offline Politics

Alan Chong and Faizal Bin Yahya

In the first two decades of the twenty-first century, the precise contours of the Internet's impact upon society and politics remain unclear. The dominant, and western-oriented, paradigm was largely laid out by American Vice-President Al Gore's statement to the International Telecommunication Union in 1994, in tandem with the intellectuals associated with the vision of the Information Society (Webster, 1995). These thinkers of the 1990s predicted that the arrival of computers networked across sovereign borders and physical barriers would be a liberating force producing a global dialogue of liberal hues. In Gore's memorable words, the information superhighway comprises,

> networks of distributed intelligence – [which] will allow us to share information, to connect, and to communicate as a global community. From these connections we will derive robust and sustainable economic progress, strong democracies, better solutions to global and local environmental challenges, improved health care, and – ultimately – a greater sense of shared stewardship of our small planet. (Gore, 1994)

The more quixotic among these visions predicted that the so-called Third World states would leapfrog the various stages of industrialization undergone by Western Europe and North America (Krishna and Madon, 2003). This book argues that this dominant paradigm needs to be supplemented by the perspective of alterity in Information Technology's (IT) impact. In particular, we wish to draw upon Asian cases to demonstrate an alterity that can be understood as *a condition of privileging the hitherto marginal and subterranean aspects of a capitalist world order through the capabilities of information and communications technologies*. This alterity offers an explanatory alternative to the paradigm of inevitable material upliftment and political liberalization of societies planet-wide.

Ironically, most mainstream scholarship treating the impact of IT on Asian polities and societies neglect the findings of the media modernizers of the 1960s. Under the shadow of the Cold War and the worldwide trends of decolonization, American researchers and Peace Corps volunteers were in urgent need of a framework for comprehending the frictions impeding the embrace of modern mass media in the developing world. The 'orthodoxy' of the time predicted that once the teeming illiterate and semi-literate populations of the postcolonial states encountered radio and television in tandem with the reading habits oriented towards mass circulation newspapers, they would aspire to improve themselves occupationally, and in their scale of ambition. Through these individual pathways to the liberation of mental horizons, and the demonstration of attractive alternative modes of work and lifestyles, the poor of the developing world would inexorably yearn to uplift themselves from poverty (Milikan, 1967). These idealistic modernizers quickly realized that thick local contexts, usually referred to euphemistically as 'culture', either filtered the effects of modern mass media or severely impeded latter's potential. Stories of that era of miscommunication were thus rampant along the following lines: Congolese soldiers encountering the Disney character of Donald Duck for the first time reacted angrily to the pictures on the big screen thinking that the cartoon was making a mockery of their intelligence; the men of a northern Nigerian village were indifferent to public announcements about the need to boil water for drinking since they had habitually left it to the women to perform household chores, and since the women could not understand the logic of boiling to kill lethal bacteria, they did not bother changing their daily habits either; additionally, many villagers in the developing world showed no reaction at all to public health documentary screenings that showed close-ups of the lice that spread typhus since they understood that these insidious creatures could never possibly grow that big! (Schramm, 1967, pp.21–23). As a result, communication researchers came to the very simple conclusion that 'communication … has no life of its own. Human beings and society breathe life into it' (Schramm, 1967, p.27).

Alterity therefore calls for scholars and observers to pay attention to the unique social and political uses being made of IT in the service of particular offline and online *causes that are filtered by pre-existing social milieus*. The result is that Asian social and political IT usage and adaptations may yet produce very different impacts from those envisaged by the dominant modernizing and liberalizing paradigm. Many of the chapters in this volume will in fact suggest that Asian IT modes actually produce a highly-elitist, techno-savvy social strata that might increasingly become socially divorced from their local Asian origins due to the need to integrate their lives and draw comfortable incomes from global flows of information that connect only modernities. A few authors have nonetheless challenged this trend of elitist inevitability by suggesting that IT is empowering grassroots public opinion in Asia in very novel ways that conflate state-society and elite-mass relations. But even when empowerment is evident through IT usage, the result is often an ambiguous degree of democratization without achieving liberal democracy within the state. Within the scope of this book, IT will be interpreted in the broadest sense possible so as to accommodate the widest range of technologically-assisted mobilization of politics and political economy. IT encompasses the industrial manufacture of high-speed computing chips and their business environments; the integration of computer formats into mobile phone technologies; the adapted functions of computers themselves; the employment of social media, and blogs on the Internet for political causes; and the deployment of these technologies for myriad political, economic and social uses to both control and liberate. The latter usage of IT includes the political economy of business processes that arise from IT development, and the facilitation of new industries such as telephone call centres. These 'digital modernities' are probably hybridized ones that will reflect a western-flavoured cosmopolitan worldview, but at the same time, enable more traditional social and political causes such as Islamic youth, humanistic civil society groups, migrant workers and ethno-religious movements to empower their presence in defiance of state-produced stereotypes that constrain their offline progress. Some chapters will also argue that there is a heavy dose of creative old-fashioned state-driven propaganda that erects the ideational and infrastructural skeletons for the construction of IT hubs.

This book takes as its starting point the fact that IT has been one of the key drivers of economic development, but that its influence on political and societal development has also raised concerns in various Asian countries about its unexpected functions and impacts. However, since the Chinese, the Hong Kongers, Japanese, Koreans, Malaysians, Singaporeans, and Taiwanese have developed their economic miracles based on IT patterns, these techno-platforms have not lost their staying power and centrality within the developmental strategies of these newly industrializing economies. In fact, it was the worldwide economic interdependence generated by their position in the world IT economy that frequently enabled 'contagion' across electronically-linked stock markets, as well as laying the backbone of their recovery from each financial crisis. Complex Asian production chains for multinational corporations were made possible due to the allure and expeditiousness of high-speed communications networks connecting networked production teams. With the advent of business process outsourcing (BPO) and the Internet, whole sectors of data entry and call centre businesses were virtually created overnight in India, the Philippines, Singapore and more recently, in Cambodia. Furthermore, given the fact that English was the operating language of the majority of western-based multinational corporations, Indian IT professionals helped in no small part to generate 'Brand India' out of the stultifying shadow of Nehruvian socialism that used to characterize the Indian economy.

Asia also matters as a potentially rich sociological and political repository of encounters with information policy. The rhetoric of Microsoft Corporation and its likes, along with the neoliberal rhetoric of international financial institutions such as the World Bank, IMF and WTO, seem to presuppose that the principles deriving from freedom of information are the only philosophy relevant to the new techno-economic order. Asian practice however offers guidance on information from a different bearing – *how far does intensified information flow approximate increased wisdom?* Yet, however 'modern' Asian governments might seem in terms of their constitutional trappings and media organizations, information is still regarded in many official quarters as an abstraction that should be controlled according to the intellectual maturity of their citizen audiences. The view from the summits of officialdom is such that information should flow only to those who can aid the sacred cause of collective national progress. Discordant voices are healthy, but up to a point. One might object that this is a simplistic picture that ignores the legions of media-savvy Aung San Suu Kyi supporters across Asia and the gumption of Chinese, Malaysian, and Vietnamese bloggers who undermine authoritarian accounts of political perjury allegedly committed by the political Opposition. This is a fair criticism in so far as one can accept that the vast swathe of Asian populations cutting across huge barriers of ethnicity, class, religion and income brackets understand the practice of democracy uniformly. Most Asian governments, including some of the most democratic in Taiwan, Japan and South Korea have at one point or another attempted to correct media portrayals of policies and politicians' images. Likewise, it should be queried, as some of the contributors to this book do, whether the arrival of the Asian IT miracle economy is necessarily an outcome foreshadowed completely by the 'information societies' of the First World Americans, British and the French. Asia is likely to take some time to work out its myriad interpretations of its 'modernities' according to assorted syncretic local criteria of information utility even as it embraces imported high technology designs. These differentiated modernities pose the question of how much dissonance exists between the online architecture of IT and the offline politics that condition it. We label this disjuncture 'alterity'.

Alterity is thus possible whenever one compares say Chinese and Korean information policies and consumer uses of the Internet vis-à-vis the examples emanating from the USA and Western Europe. *The Asian connected society, or insofar as it can be termed a nascent information society, is likely to be differentiated from the rest of the world.* This book offers the first cut in examining the multiple dimensions of Asian difference in the sociology and politics of IT. It is worthwhile noting that one can identify four pre-existing political trends gleaned from both the existing literature and empirical trends of information and communication technology acculturation within Asia. These suggest that advanced electronic media will not be embraced in smooth unilinear fashion throughout Asia. Consequently, in the penultimate sections of this introductory chapter, the idea of alterity in 'offline politics' will supply an umbrella for comprehending the Asian encounter with IT.

The Psychological Politics of Mediating Incremental Progress

It is an often forgotten fact that the newspaper, the radio, television and Internet were all invented in the territory of the cultural 'West'. While it is a matter of historical record that the Chinese had invented their version of printing chronologically before Johannes Gutenberg's movable type technology, the former did not develop the newspaper. This historical contrast points to a disparity in the cultural embrace of modern communications that potentially extends into philosophical debates about the origin and ownership of modernization.

Gerald Sussman and John Lent, two important scholars of communication politics in the developing world, argue that realistically grounded inquiry into communication implementation in non-western regions ought to begin by 'asking who gains, who pays, and who bears the burdens of their [communication technology] usage and suggesting how Third World countries can better domesticate the stakeholder arrangements' (1991, p.x). Dependency should therefore not only be construed in terms of a materialist framework, it is also about the construction of mindsets along lines of material development conceived in a different historical and cultural context. Indeed most pragmatic-minded technologists would prefer that culture, a seemingly amorphous concept, remains marginal to planning for the improvement of a universal humankind. Yet, in most national contexts, culture is lived as a way of life shaped by particularistic attitudes towards social structures, unequal opportunities, harmonization of change with pre-existing authorities, as well as a balance between human initiative and mechanical representation. Such is the case with the initial employment of computers in various social and economic sectors in the states of the ASEAN (Association of Southeast Asian Nations) region (Talisayon, 1990, pp.152–156). Pedagogy, bureaucratic cultures and rural-urban income divides jointly mattered in determining the rate of IT usage. Resistance to computer penetration in society is often not simply overcome by throwing money at the problem and installing ever larger quantities of hardware in remote population centres (Raboy *et al.*, 2010).

Research on Indian and Sri Lankan citizens' use of mobile phones have revealed that the driving purposes of acquisition of electronic communications lies mainly in factors of cost; convenience of access; need for calling upon relatives' remittances from abroad; as well as the relative ease of keeping in contact with relatives and friends. The last factor was particularly important for rural populations who value cheaper and more convenient substitutes for arduous long distance travel for personal communication (Zainudeen, 2008, pp.52–57). Ironically, the surveys showed that the preferences for landline telephones and mobile phones were shaped in both countries by cost structures and perceptions of their reasonableness. There was little thought given by users to lofty considerations of advancing society collectively into an 'information society' where the vast majority of workers become symbolic analysts. These trends warn that IT usage revolves around the unpredictability of mindset accommodation, instead of assuming that transformations would occur in self-evident fashion once people came into contact with the new communication technologies (Miard, 2012, p.126). More recent research reveals that an assortment of social temptations has amplified the social demand for mobile phones that can access the Internet, swap pictures and 'brand' their possessors as attractive socialites. This has, in turn, chipped away at Indian society's traditional class and caste barriers (Doron and Jeffrey, 2013).

Pre-existing studies of telecommunications in China have also drawn attention to the need to comprehend the backdrop to the embrace of hitherto alien technologies in certain societies (Baark, 1997, ch.1; Lee, 1997). It is not simply a historical question relating to how electronic communications were adopted into popular use. The Chinese experience in the nineteenth century suggested that the impression provided by the import of the electric telegraph was connected to the wider debate about the relative superiority of western gunboats and mechanized firepower. The scientific demonstration of the prowess of the West was inevitably bound up with the question of whether Chinese values were outmoded and inferior in an absolute sense in relation to foreign ones. Additionally, there was the philosophical debate over the extent of acclimatization to western ideas. It vexed the late Qing Dynasty reformers, led by Zeng Guofan (1811–1872), when they pondered the question: 'could the Chinese people, and the learning and knowledge that provided the foundation of their civilization, be in need of further development?' (Summarized in Baark, 1997, p.1).

Of course, the young generations of modernizing Asia often forget that their forebears had struggled to rationalize their worldviews with the new technology, as well as getting adjusted to the revolutionary pace of life the technology introduced. Even today, when academic observers treat the mobile phone, iPhone, iPad, laptop computer and Internet access as symbols of the modernizing and democratizing Asian middle classes, they forget that these symbolic uses have carried with them social and political disruptions in their train. The Internet spreads rumours of malfeasance in Chinese local government, or of cover-ups of health epidemics and food safety scandals, and consequently, these random bits of alarming piecemeal information are seized upon by uninformed citizens eager to take matters into their own hands as pre-emptive measures in the absence of a more responsive government (Huang 2013). In some ways, electronic communication technologies intensify 'speed' in human reaction, escalating emotions and thought processes into heightened anxieties and less discriminating reflexes. Futurist Alvin Toffler had warned of this particular aspect of technological speed overwhelming human senses in his book *Future Shock* (1970) even though it was abstractly addressed to a modern readership. Future shock stemming from rapid telecommunications might just as easily help explain the kinks in Asian communications usage today. Witness the recurring controversies over YouTube political revelations, blog exposés, purported slander by journalists and civil society against Asian royalty, and the exaggeration of political guilt when police and military actions are captured on Facebook gossip and other podcasts over Sino-Vietnamese, Sino-Japanese and Sino-Korean incidents at sea.

Political Conditions, Governmental Intervention and the Fostering of Connected Businesses

The development of every new technology is almost always financially supported by some wealthy interest that would in turn seek the cover of political patronage. This was very much the story of every electronic technology from the telegraph to the Internet. Some studies have even applied 'universal' economic theory to the explanation of the trajectory of telecommunications and IT development. Eli Noam argues for instance that,

> demand is a function of price and benefits, both of which are in turn functions of the size of the network ... This suggests the need, in some circumstances, to subsidize the early stages of the network – up to the critical mass point n_1 – when the user externalities are still low but cost shares high. These subsidies could come either from the network provider or its membership as a start-up investment, or from an external source such as a government as an investment in 'infrastructure', a concept centred around positive externalities. (Noam, 1994, p.23)

Sussman and Lent (1991) have cogently argued that this is a fair description as well of the Third World's experience in 'wiring' their societies into the Information Age. Their edited volume had surveyed telecommunication developments from the 1960s through the 1980s in India, Malaysia, the Philippines, and Singapore and concluded that infrastructural installation and usage coincided with elite designs for material development and the economic manoeuvres for sustaining their primacy in their respective territories. It is understandable if one dismisses this sort of depiction as a neo-Marxist research bias. Yet the fact of the matter is that electronic communications require hefty start-up funding for building the 'hardware', as well as the commitment to follow through by attracting the 'software' of profitable uses from the general public or business consumers. In the Developed Economies, private enterprise has mostly replaced the hand of government in driving Internet utilities, but in Asia the hand of governments is still very much in the picture as it seeks to significantly shape the preferences of the private sector (Beal, 2003). This will in fact be further vindicated by the various chapters examining the political economy of IT in Singapore, Malaysia, South Korea, India and the Philippines.

In Asia, the story of India's embrace of IT became a vehicle for assertions of national authenticity in designing development strategies that shifted from governmental steerage towards private sector dominance. For several decades since gaining independence in 1947, a Ministry of Communications had presided over the pace and budget for telecommunications within the rubric of socialist-influenced central planning. Up till 1985, when attempts at reforming the communications sector began, the budgetary share of telecommunications stagnated at 2–3 per cent of the total national budget. A report on the history of Indian telecommunications commented ruefully on this statistic: 'With no access to any other sources of funds, this permitted very moderate growth of the sector' (Sethi, 2006, p.6). After India's economic reforms of 1991, it was the private sector that ushered in the extended boom which the Indian telecommunications market experienced from the 1990s onward. By 2006, the Indian government allowed up to 100 per cent foreign direct investment in the following niches within telecommunications: Internet service provision; infrastructure provision relating to Internet Protocol; electronic mail services; voice mail services; and telecommunications manufacturing (Sethi, 2006, p.17).

In a major study of the multidimensional India-Singapore IT collaboration that commenced in the 1990s, Faizal Yahya had argued that India had looked to the Southeast Asian city-state to help it modernize its infrastructure (2008a, ch.1). The Singaporean partner represented a unique mix of state capitalism and national capital that was simultaneously associated with assorted First World multinational companies. This Singaporean 'brand' in IT collaboration had been built upon the Republic's record of building infrastructure for profitable economic hubs at home and elsewhere in Asia, and this had in turn earned its government-linked companies such as Temasek Holdings, and its subsidiaries such as Ascendas and the Sembawang Group, invaluable reputations as premium providers of high technology business infrastructure. In these ways, the injection of a Singaporean input into India's IT sector assisted the latter in acculturating to the ways and means of a global IT economy that integrated California to the Pacific Rim economies, Israel in the Middle East, Western Europe and Mexico. Indian IT talent abroad was enhanced in value as India's domestic economic liberalization gained in pace, while Indian IT entrepreneurs operating software companies and institutes of technology could ride on an important Asian brand name – Singapore Incorporated – to introduce their products and services to markets beyond both national economies (Yahya, 2008b, ch.4). Of course, Singapore's role in catalyzing both the upgrading of Indian IT facilities and the expansion of Indian IT business abroad should not be overstated either. The Singaporean role in Indian IT simply illustrated the political conditions that allowed the private sector at home and abroad, along with the collusion of government-linked companies, to drive a successful revenue and brand-generating national IT industry. The current reputation of Indian IT firms such as Tata Consultancy Services, Infosys Systems Limited, Satyam Computers and Wipro attest to the role of political leeway in contributing to the flourishing of IT capitalism.

In the chapters that will follow, some authors will reinforce the theme that IT progress did not arise simply from the motions of an 'invisible hand'. More importantly, IT capitalism required political willpower in tandem with private capital's willingness to trust governments' ambitions. The chapters by Yahya, Santarita, Chong and Min in this volume reveal that the entrenched legacies of governmental intervention in the building of IT infrastructure in India, the Philippines, Malaysia, Singapore, South Korea and Taiwan remained very much in the forefront, even if the IT project was dedicated towards inviting private sector and civil society participation in the post-construction phase. The chapters by Yahya and Santarita offer explanations from a largely policy-oriented perspective on how a developmental state approach had contributed to the emergence of India and the Philippines as 'economic powerhouses' in IT Enabled Services. One does not normally associate these two Asian states with what Chalmers Johnson (1982) described as a 'plan rational state', that is, a state that incorporates the private sector in a masterplan to develop its own vision of the collective economic good within a globally competitive environment. To be fair, as Yahya's sole authored chapter on the political economy of data security in the Business Process Outsourcing

(BPO) industry in India points out, the sincerest intentions of the state have been unable to police against IT security slippages. These security slippages include the leaking of passwords through employee misdemeanours and other money skimming schemes activated by insiders in the BPO sector. As Yahya points out, it required the backlash from adverse publicity to prod the Indian government to introduce legislation to curb future recurrences of criminality in the IT-related and BPO services. On the other hand, India's private sector IT firms continually clamour for New Delhi to stay its hand in over-regulating their highly profitable growth trajectory (Aggarwal, 2012).

In Japan, IT Enabled Services have also revealed that the developmental state is potentially too extended for its host economy's own good. Research on Japan's telecommunications liberalization since the mid-1980s also revealed that the new post-liberalization market-driven players have also found cause to rollback the former monopolist Nippon Telegraph and Telephone's (NTT) entrenched infrastructural advantages in optical fibre and broadband cables as well as NTT's political coziness with the Ministry of Internal Affairs and Communications. These contestations took various forms including lawsuits and foreign business pressures (Taplin and Wakui, 2006). As a result, there are multiple avenues for tension between governments, business and civil society when IT usage does not develop in conformity with the state's original and instrumental priorities. The point to be noted from the Asian experience in the politics and political economy of IT is that values and interests contest, or overlay with simple neoliberal prescriptions for IT modernization. The Asian state appears in most cases to zealously guard its ultimate right to assert sovereignty even as it promotes online economic connectivity and tolerates grassroots democratization by netizens on social media. This volume calls attention to these inconvenient truths that defy the neat economic and scientific theorizing of market friendly network expansion predictions espoused by certain early literatures on telecommunications modernization in the Asia-Pacific (Cowhey, 1994; Noam, 1994).

Internet Community between Nationalism and Cosmopolitanism

The Internet in Asia is heavily politicized by its parallels with the political contestations endemic to global politics. As we have argued in the preceding subsection, IT implementation did not take place according to a linear policy pattern. Logics of liberalizing IT markets and the rollback of governmental monopolies in communications required political will and calculated risk-taking by elites. In the process, values were contested and new constituencies with stakes in the post-liberalization communications landscape emerged. According to Cuthbert and Hoover (1991), for instance, telecommunications penetration in the Eastern Caribbean region was liberally exploited by principally American media businesses who promised the poor island economies the wealth of the relevant technology possessors along with the programming content that could be run on this very technology. In this way, the embrace of the infrastructure facilitated American cultural imperialism. This was an issue that perennially featured in discussions of Third World global communications discussions ever since the New World Information and Communication Order was placed onto the developmental agenda in the early 1970s by many governments in Africa, Latin America and even in the Asia-Pacific.

In fact, value disputes have increasingly come to dominate debate on the increased possibilities of IT usage in Asia. Some governments such as North Korea adopt outright postures of suspicion towards the possibilities of widespread computer and Internet access, while India, Malaysia, Singapore, Thailand and South Korea have tried to moderate delinquent uses of the Internet while seeking to enlarge their economies' presence on the information superhighway. China is interestingly experimenting with a mix of authoritarian controls on online vocabulary, Net patrolling and insulating a Chinese version of the Internet to reflect domestic political order. Kay Hearn's chapter explores this dimension in significant detail. China's netizens, who are often the younger generation benefitting from three decades of post-Mao reforms, have nonetheless revealed the brutally candid face of online nationalism over events such as the accidental bombing of the Chinese embassy in Belgrade by NATO (1999) and the aerial accident with the US Air Force EP-3 reconnaissance plane over the southern Chinese coast (2001). Chinese netizens often appear to mount retaliatory public opinion 'offensives' over remarks by foreign leaders which are deemed as 'insensitive' to the prestige of an emerging Chinese superpower. Given the nature of China's political system, the external observer often suspects that the sheer volume of netizens' criticism of foreign interference and arrogance towards the Chinese nation is tolerated, even fanned, by subtle official acquiescence. In early 2013, a report by *The New York Times* alleged that the Chinese military was purposively employing trained 'hacktivists' to ferret American industrial secrets (Wong, 2013).

Online nationalism in Singapore and South Korea also carries this chameleonic quality of appearing spontaneously pro-regime, although on some issues, these very netizens turn on their own elected governments through satire and bluntness. Singapore has signally applied traditional libel and sedition laws against netizens whose published comments had been deemed by the state to impugn the standing of elected officials or threaten inter-racial discord (Rodan, 1998; Kluver, 2004). Thailand too had disrupted YouTube services between 2006 and 2008, and again in 2012, on the grounds that videos derogatory towards the Thai monarchy had been posted on the popular media site. Malaysia too had also been making the news for curbs on netizen activity ever since the Asian Financial Crisis of 1997–8. Prime Minister Mahathir bin Mohamad had attributed his country's economic woes to a conspiracy among Western and Jewish bankers to 'talk down' Malaysian economic fundamentals, henceforth recovery required strict vigilance in censoring Web postings. It was not a sheer coincidence that Premier Mahathir was also seeking to denigrate his recently-sacked finance minister and former Deputy Prime Minister Anwar Ibrahim by instituting a 'net patrol' on all sites hosted on sovereign

Malaysian territory (Richardson, 1998). The list of inward-oriented and domestically disciplined IT policies goes on to include how India and the Philippines are also attempting to preserve their shares of the lucrative call centre business.

Asian governments and large sections of their societies are treating IT infrastructure as twenty-first century equivalents of railroads and telegraph networks that could be placed squarely under nationalist control. This flies in the face of erstwhile American Vice-President Albert Gore's quixotic declaration of 'universal service' within an envisioned 'global information society' at the International Telecommunication Union conference in Buenos Aires in 1994 (Gore, 1994). Gore's declaration has occupied a place in the short history of the Internet that spells unfulfilled promise in the case of Asia. Some scholars have suggested that IT could in fact foster regional integration in Northeast Asia on the basis of the interoperability of third generation and next generation mobile communications, digital television and broadcasting, open source software and even exploring the next generation Internet (Ure, 2008). These technical dimensions of cooperation make sense if IT is wholeheartedly geared towards the betterment of the material welfare of the ordinary citizen regardless of race and nationality. But nationalism appears redoubtable for the present, and if Beijing's IT policies in the early 2000s are any gauge, IT is being made to conform forcibly to the logic of politics rather than being allowed a free flowing evolution towards liberalizing and unpredictable directions.

In spite of governmental steerage of online nationalism, non-state, civil society groups in Asia are also independently tuning the Internet towards their own needs. The chapter by Paragas studies the embrace of mobile phones as an extension of familial controls by husbands and wives separated from the Philippine homeland by overseas work commitments. Mobile phones facilitate long distance assurance of families' well-being and enable psychological admonitions from afar. They also ease the availability of remittances back to the Philippines. Wealth flows almost directly back to the families of the expatriate Filipinos. Likewise, the chapter by Bahfen draws attention to the fact that Internet blogs and email have facilitated a reaffirmation of Islamic identity amongst Muslim youth from Malaysia, Indonesia and Singapore studying abroad in Australia. This burgeoning sense of online community defies both the standard fundamentalist religious frame and the secularization narrative. It appears that the Internet opens itself to open ended social uses according to variants of community.

Virtual Cultures as Political Subcultures

Increasingly, Asia's Internet users also constitute varieties of subcultures, some of whom are appendages of the mainstream political factions of offline politics, while many others have constituted themselves into circles of political autonomy. The latter occasionally ally themselves with the offline political mainstream, but often these social circles that have grown up around particular uses of the

Internet provide interest articulation outlets to segments of society that might, under ordinary circumstances, be too apathetic to even organize themselves as full-fledged members of civil society with formal physical premises and standing memberships. Manuel Castells in his book *The Internet Galaxy* (2001) has for instance identified four different web cultures that are interdependent: the techno-meritocratic culture, the hacker culture, the virtual communitarian culture, and the entrepreneurial culture. It is worth quoting at length how Castells elaborates this interdependence among the four:

> Together they contribute to an ideology of freedom that is widespread in the Internet world. However, this ideology is not the founding culture because it does not interact directly with the development of the technological system: freedom has many uses. *These cultural layers are hierarchically disposed: the techno-meritocratic culture becomes specified as a hacker culture by building rules and customs into networks of cooperation aimed at technological projects. The virtual communitarian culture adds a social dimension to technological sharing, by making the Internet a medium of selective social interaction and symbolic belonging. The entrepreneurial culture works on top of the hacker culture, and on the communitarian culture, to diffuse Internet practices in all domains of society by way of money-making. Without the techno-meritocratic culture, hackers would simply be a specific countercultural community of geeks and nerds.* Without the hacker culture, communitarian networks in the Internet would be no different from many other alternative communes. Similarly, without the hacker culture, and communitarian values, the entrepreneurial culture cannot be characterized as specific to the Internet. (Castells, 2001, p.37; italics mine)

Much more research needs to be undertaken to demonstrate whether there is indeed a full-scale duplication within Asia of this ostensibly western-derived architecture of virtual culture. Castells treats the Internet ideology of freedom as an overarching assumption for his book and argues through intelligent conjecture and generic news observation that the Internet can be empowering for human endeavour if the technology can be fully comprehended by humankind as a whole. Yet it is also telling that Castells left open-ended, the question of what substantive community might come to mean in the Internet era; he observed rhetorically that,

> you perceive the world analyzed in this book [*The Internet Galaxy*] very differently if you are an Internet entrepreneur or a school teacher. Our professional, social, ethnic, gender, geographical, cultural differences lead to very different consequences in the relationship of each one of us to the network society. (2001, p.281)

Indeed, as the assorted chapters by Min on South Korean Internet users, Bahfen on Muslim student diasporas, Tan on Singaporean netizens, and Choong on Malaysian political grassroots on social media will show, the transformations of community facilitated by the Internet may ultimately be less than profound. They may instead mirror the imperfections of offline political contentions, and even accentuate polarization with less guarded language put out in online chatrooms, blogs and social networking sites. Ironically, the Internet may provide a channel for ostracized offline interests that may be religious, racial or ideological in orientation, thereby enlarging the offline arena for political contestation into the online sphere.

A more helpful theoretical insight may be that offered by Steven Jones who argues more cautiously that virtual culture should be comprehended through 'a discontinuous narrative space'. Jones explains that cyberspace is literally both an imagined and imaginary space. Narratives are 'artefacts of community and may represent a good portion of what communities do to maintain and reproduce themselves over time' but on their own do not constitute community (Jones, 1997, p.15). In fact, to fully elaborate virtual culture as a community with its definitional trappings of being a habit, way of dressing, speaking, achievement and particular worldview, one has to resort to Benedict Anderson's arguments about paying attention to the pre-existing mental furniture of associating the narratives to one's actually lived life. It is in this way that 'imagined community' becomes meaningful (Anderson, 1991). Therefore, Jones warns that,

> the Internet serendipitously brings to us, in our living rooms and offices, a sense of connectedness, but it is an aimless connectedness, a kind which reassures that between 'us' and 'them' there may be some common ground after all. And, once reassured, anything more brings us too close to having to go 'out there'. (1997, p.17)

In most Asian contexts, one is likely to find that virtual community is often an extension of terrestrial politics and governance. Certain activities, like putting up firewalls for protecting citizen sensibilities from going wayward as defined by the government of the day, or encouraging computer hacking as an expression of patriotism against an insolent external power, are experimental halfway forms of virtual community more common in Asia. Research on Singapore's Internet politics have pointed out the emergence of significant offline drivers to the curbs and resistance to those very curbs on Internet campaigning (Rodan, 1998; Kluver, 2004). The contributions by Hearn and Tan in this volume echo this perspective and go on to suggest that clues to the operation of online culture relate closely to how state-society relationships play out offline. Ongoing research on the post-9/11 sources of Internet radicalization of Islamic terrorists have also begun to probe at the nexus between youthful susceptibility, popular culture formats, Internet navigational proficiency, and the strength of one's Islamic beliefs. Interrogations of terrorists arraigned in Australia, Britain and Singapore have revealed that the Internet was a significant facilitator of material that influenced their attitudes towards their religion as well as towards non-believers (Bergin *et al.*, 2009). In this regard, Bahfen's chapter reveals, by contrast, that the Internet can alternatively be used to reaffirm mainstream, non-violent Islamic identities.

Finally, the fact that China is occupying a prominent position in this book's coverage needs some additional explanation. China's domestic state-society relations, as well as its relations with the wider global community, are being tested by its policies towards Internet use by its citizens as well as foreign residents within its sovereign territory. It seems quite evident that the authorities in Beijing regard sovereignty as an ideal that ought to be implemented in as absolute a manner as possible even in governing the employment of IT. In this regard, the territorial and demographic size of China in the Internet age serves as an experimental vehicle for preserving knowledge monopolies under the rubric of a one-party state within a developmental context. It would be interesting, for instance, to observe the outcome of the stability of such a regime when performance legitimacy, especially in the economic realm, is weaker in comparison to ideological legitimacy. Regime stability can be questioned when the mismanagement of public corporations becomes widely known, corruption threatens the viability of government-run banks, high officials are publicly shamed and subjected to public investigations, or when viral outbreaks and food safety scares tarnish the image of the ruling party. Understandably, the Internet was not even created when the first totalitarian regimes appeared in world history, but the invention of new media technologies that cater to mass dissemination of information have had an impact on regime stability at various times. The Catholic Church had found its political hegemony eroded by the invention of the Gutenberg printing press, while the commercialization of radio technology ironically facilitated the emergence of Hitler's Germany. Likewise, China's ordering of a hierarchical society under the wing of the Chinese Communist Party and its ideological cloak of 'Socialism with Chinese Characteristics' will have to contend with the subcultures that are likely to emerge with increasing use of computers and the Internet among both its white collar workforce and youths of schooling age.

Down the line, China's restive minorities in its landlocked provinces, as well as disgruntled rural populations that have been mistreated by exploitative local bureaucracies, may occasion subversive uses of the Internet to draw attention to their plight. More research needs to be conducted to survey how far dissent within China has migrated online and 'offshore' out of China's sovereign jurisdiction. The emotional fallout from the Tiananmen Incident of June 1989, along with the negative publicity the Chinese leadership endured over separatist rioting in Tibet in the run-up to the Beijing Olympics of 2008, have already forewarned Beijing over the politically centrifugal effects of dissident expression on the Internet. The recurring riots involving Uighur minorities in Xinjiang will likely serve as another test of the degree of either Internet openness, or closure.

As mentioned earlier in this introduction, China's approach to the Internet has tended to adopt stridently nationalist blinkers. As early as 2000, Chinese officials conducted one of their largest crackdowns on Internet cafes throughout the country. This was done to eliminate citizen exposure to politically undesirable influences, as well as to install special software on Internet cafe computers to scan for undesirable material in the future. In 2003, China made global news headlines by being among the first four state and intergovernmental actors in requiring Microsoft Corporation to reveal the source codes of its popular Windows software. The other three sovereignty conscious actors were interestingly NATO, Russia and Britain. Like these latter three, Beijing feared that Microsoft Windows could stealthily provide hostile foreign governments 'backdoor' access to state secrets. This was a veiled reference to the US, the national host of Microsoft (IHT, 2003). In July 2004, following private cellphone texting of allegations of official cover-ups in dealing with the SARS viral epidemic in 2003, as well as various corruption cases, the Chinese authorities forced telecommunications companies to install software and hardware to filter out and delete 'harmful' vocabulary and undesirable messages altogether. Since then, it had emerged that Web companies like Google and Yahoo had cooperated with Beijing in blocking certain searches and identifying 'miscreants' for prosecution. In 2005, it was a huge moment of irony that western IT security firms such as Cisco, Nortel Networks, Sun Microsystems and 3COM had been publicly named as having supplied China equipment for web filtering (Mackinnon, 2005). These practices may of course be far less alarming in the wake of the large tranche of revelations about American cyber espionage activities worldwide brought out from 2013 onwards by Edward Snowden, a former intelligence contractor for the US National Security Agency. In August 2014, it was reported that Beijing banned its government agencies from procuring anti-virus software from US-based Symantec Corporation and Russia-based Kaspersky Lab on the grounds that Snowden's revelations were guiding a new policy of relying more on domestic software vendors as a hedge against foreign espionage. It was also reported that Microsoft's Windows 8 operating system was also precluded from Chinese procurement due to concerns about possible backdoor penetration of China's IT systems (Finkle, 2014). Meanwhile, China's netizens seem to have found ways to obviate official controls in launching cyber-attacks, online protests and blogging against American and Japanese targets whenever nationalist fervour spikes over particular incidents. Whether this hints at some level of official tolerance for informal diplomatic retaliation remains to be researched; meanwhile Beijing continues to encourage research and investment in dual use IT. The recent allegations of Chinese cyber espionage worldwide between 2010 and 2013 are surely a consequence of training citizens for dual use IT (BBC, 2013).

More recently, the events of the so-called 'Arab Spring' in the Middle East seems to have inspired a fresh wave of defiance of Beijing's Internet controls amongst Chinese bloggers and democracy activists overseas. The imitative 'Jasmine Revolution' launched by the latter aims to treat the virtual calls for demonstrations in mainland China as having succeeded by proxy in triggering the spikes in police presences in major Chinese cities. The 'Jasmine Revolution' is in effect a virtual collective demonstration for democracy (Goodman, 2011). At the time of writing, the most recent instance of political alterity against the Chinese state involves a self-appointed Internet vigilante publicizing abuses committed by Chinese bureaucrats regardless of the provinces in which they occur.

Through specific case studies, Hearns' chapter in this volume follows up on Gudrun Wacker's (2003) pioneering research on censorship and the Internet in the emerging Chinese superpower. Evidently, there is much to be comprehended about the textures of the politics of IT implementation, cyberpolitics as that realm of politicking taking place completely within the Internet, and their interplay or control from terrestrial politics. Glimpses of the untidy politics in these Asian cases suggest a research agenda that inquires into the 'othering' and 're-othering' of the medium of IT.

Scrutinizing the *Alterity* within Information Society in Asia

In 1989, Manuel Castells defined the field of the 'informational city' as 'the relationship between new information technologies (IT) and the urban and regional processes' (Castells, 1989, p.2). He envisioned that in time to come, IT would transform the relationships between production, society and space. Subsequently, from 1996 onwards, he published a three part volume that addressed 'informational capitalism' as a mode of development in which the main source of productivity is the qualitative capacity to optimize the combination and use of factors of production on the basis of knowledge and information. Aside from the obvious economic implications of IT, Castells did admit he had not fully thought through the implications of the interaction between communication technologies, social life and residential patterns. In 2007, Castells co-published another book, *Mobile Communication and Society: a Global Perspective* which attempted to probe at the social and political impact of what he terms the diffusion of 'mobile communication technologies' into every conceivable aspect of human life. He and his co-authors could not reach a holistic and integrated conclusion to their inquiry. Instead, they called attention to the multimodal, time dispersing and nomadic possibilities afforded by cellphone voice communication and cellphone-enabled multimedia messaging capabilities. People's lifestyles were becoming generically transformed by IT, but the exact causalities and interplays with pre-existing political behaviours remain under-explored at this time (see also Miard, 2012).

Admittedly, Castells was not the first sociologist or geographer to call attention to the multidimensional impact of information and communications technologies on political, social and economic landscapes. We can refer to the earlier and contemporary works of Marshall McLuhan, Ithiel de Sola Pool, Peter Drucker, Daniel Bell, and Kenichi Ohmae in this regard. Nonetheless, this fledgling body of literature on IT's socially transformative impact leads us to commission this project to explore the IT mode of development in as many dimensions as possible using Asia as a case study for making tentative observations about informational modes and any possibilities for pre-theorizing. We are specifically interested in investigating a range of power possibilities that involve creating alternative value chains, wealth transfers, the propaganda as value creation, and the empowerment of new political and economic actors that operate below the radar of global economic intelligence agencies. We list some possibilities in the following sub-paragraphs that may be tantamount to offering an account of socio-political *alterity* to 'informational capitalism' that is no less critical in explaining the transformations of space, power and fortunes in a globalizing world. In reiteration, *this alterity can be understood in terms of privileging the hitherto marginal and subterranean aspects of a capitalist world order through the capabilities of information and communications technologies*. In this regard, we do not exclude IT-associated forms such as:

- communications-facilitated diasporas' cultural or religious networks;
- electronically-derived remittance cultures among white-collar and blue-collar expatriate workers;
- the impact of intra-IT industry (r)evolutions;
- the role of propaganda in globalizing informational cities;
- hackers, techno-elites, virtual communitarians and entrepreneurs as fledgling global citizens.

These communicational phenomena are clearly 'network formations' and influence the development of a range of activities such as identity formation, innovation, production and management. In the networked enterprise characterized by strategic alliances, there is room for unlimited expansion and dynamic innovation. We are inspired by Latham and Sassen's call to investigate 'digital formations' that generate conversations and knowledge spaces that are inexorably 'transnationalizing … a growing range of local or national relations and domains, as well as the formation of new ones' (2005, p.3). Likewise, we are cognisant of Bach and Stark's interest in exploring 'recombinatory logics' in the world of the Internet whereby social use of the Internet is focussed not only on the patterns of links but also upon the interactions that produced those patterns in the first place. Such are the dimensions of the 'new geographies of association' produced by IT (2005, p.41). Yet, this volume put together by Latham and Sassen conjecturing the future transformations afforded by IT neglects the significance of allowing actual diverse case studies from the ground to speak for the possibilities of change. There are in fact a smattering of Eurocentric cases, and a single chapter on 'Information Technology and State Capacity in China'. In many ways, this reflects the pervasiveness of the 'digital divide' afflicting even academic mindsets in producing knowledge concerning the two-thirds of humanity popularly known as the 'Developing World'.

We are focusing on Asian case studies for a number of reasons, a few of which have been flagged out in the opening sections of this introduction. Firstly, given the relatively uninterrupted growth of states in the Pacific Rim, notwithstanding the Asian Financial Crisis of 1997–8, it is likely that societies there will be standard-bearers of a rival version of twenty-first century modernity. Western case studies, while important, will increasingly be unable to serve as representative explorations of different modernities. Secondly, the emergence of populous industrializing 'giants' of the likes of India and China are likely to have a say in determining the shape of an 'informational capitalism' that might elide the imputed positive link between democratic states and economic creativity. Thirdly, Asia's transformation is not easily captured by stock market indices and national economic data. It may well be that micro-actors like diasporas, expatriates and unofficial social movements are significant drivers of change through their creative exploitation of IT. Most existing studies of Asian media tend to be omnibus volumes treating Asian political communication within the crosshairs of authoritarianism and poverty (McCargo, 2003; Rodan, 2004; Sen and Lee, 2007). Others concern themselves with the overall state of vulnerability afflicting political journalism in the Asia-Pacific as an entry point into discussion of Web-based reporting controversies (Atkins, 2002; Busch and Rentzow-Vasu, 2008). The single most important probe to date of the politics of IT in Asia is the book edited by Ho Kong Chong, Randolph Kluver and Kenneth Yang titled *Asia.com: Asia Encounters the Internet* (2003). This volume delivers a broad-brush survey of the Asian scene utilizing umbrella themes such as information inequality, surveillance and social control, piracy and intellectual property rights. There are nine fairly in-depth country studies of civil society use of the Internet but these do not appear to speak to any attempt at pre-theorizing Web politics in the region. Instead, the editors emphasize the limits of their exploration of their wonderment towards Asian 'first encounters' with the Internet. The editors note that 'Asian governments, businesses, and individuals have embraced the Internet for primarily economic reasons, and, in so doing, have opened the gates to a wide variety of unanticipated consequences'. In that vein they caution that,

> as Asia encounters the Internet, then, both Asia and the Internet are changed. Asia's long history, unique socio-political configurations, and, yes, Asia's values, will ultimately help to shape the technological phenomenon known as the Internet, through the evolving of a set of regulatory mechanisms and policies surrounding the Internet. (Ho *et al.*, 2003, pp.16–17)

This is precisely where this book takes off. The authors represented in this volume are interested in probing at Asian socio-political configurations arising from IT usage, or in anticipation of intensified Internet cultures. We also hope to scrutinize the character of governmental policies, including ideological drivers, behind attempts to govern the Internet from national jurisdictions. In many ways, we pay attention to the alterity of how grounded political realities, many of them rooted in a pre-IT era, have metamorphosed to shape the nature of IT deployment. In a number of cases, pre-IT political ways have retarded the libertarian premises of IT as perceived in the West. Instead, certain authoritarian states have grafted a sophisticated authoritarian streak onto grand plans for IT development. In most of the chapters that follow, the authors deliberately call attention to the trends defying the inexorable, so-called 'democratizing' effects of IT.

In the following chapters, we have deliberately asked the contributors to offer reflections upon the following questions in relation to the alterity between the online and offline politics of IT:

1. To what extent do online causes, programmes and businesses rely upon the backbone of offline political processes?
2. Conversely, do offline political and social formations exert a disproportionate impact upon online networks?
3. Additionally, how do the offline progeny of online networks and industries impact the wider governance of IT-connected societies and governments?
4. What is the shape of IT-revolutionized social and political entities in Asia?

In consequence, the chapter contributions have been clustered into two broad subsections of exploration.

Social Politics of IT

Due to its ubiquity and accessibility, Asian societies have taken to IT in a significant way, but not one that has been anticipated by their governments. In the first section of chapters that follow, the examination of IT's impact and usage by Asians will pose an empirical challenge to existing understandings of media-society relations in various Asian states. The various authors have either directly or indirectly tackled the question of whether IT mostly drove social and political change, or if it was in converse, that is, change occurred because IT facilitated what were pre-existing social and political currents predisposed to transforming the *status quo*.

Nasya Bahfen's chapter dealing with Islamic Internet identities among three national groups of Southeast Asian students proposes that Islamic identities amongst young people have mostly been driven by pre-existing beliefs and aspirations to maintain their faith. In particular, one of her findings reveals that the Internet served as a highly preferred medium for consolidating the faith amongst the students who mostly found themselves to be a minority in their chosen place of higher education, specifically Australia. These student users not only employed the Internet to locate information about their faith, they found email useful for asserting their identity in terms of presenting Islamic views via online discussions connecting their fellow Islamic adherents in Australia with their fellow believers in their countries of origin. Bahfen's use of survey data makes these points with enormous clarity. Interestingly, she contends that the embrace of the Internet in Southeast Asia and Australia by these Islamic communities reflects both the fluid nature of religious identity as an ongoing process and the dependence of alterity on relationships with both other human beings and technology. Alterity can be seen in the effects of offline political, social and cultural processes on their online communication, through the construction of imagined Muslim communities and in the output of news and information received by Muslim audiences online.

The following chapter by Fernando Paragas titled 'Migrants, Mobiles and Money: Alterity and the Confluence of Three Transnational Flows' investigates the sociology of IT use as it is framed by long distance emotional and financial communication via the mobile phone. The centre-piece of Paragas' study is the Filipino expatriate diaspora. The very existence of this diaspora as the key driver of the 'remittance economy' is itself a form of alterity – the often underpublicized pillar of a globalized Filipino economy. According to Paragas, this alterity in migrant work can only be elaborated through the intersections of labour flows, communication flows through mobile telephony, and monetary flows through remittances. These flows are important because as the demographics of the migrant workforce have changed, so have the communication technologies they use to communicate with their partners and the means with which they send money from host to home countries. Mobile telephony has evidently displaced the telegraphic transfer, letter and landline telephone for keeping in touch with loved ones back home and directing their finances according to the flows of remittances to them. Additionally, the use of the mobile phone in conjunction with Facebook facilitates workers' mobilization in their various countries of temporary domicile on assorted social causes such as the inadequate policing of foreign workers' rights in their workplaces and other political attempts at disenfranchizing Filipino expatriates in the host country. Paragas finds that there is strong alterity in social media usage because of the different levels of infrastructures across home and host countries, nuanced alterity in migrant worker mobilization (strong in politics but weak in economics) and weak alterity in remittances (because of weak economic discussion and weak online presence of the key corporate stakeholders).

Kwoh-Jack Tan's chapter 'Blogging Singapore: Control and Excess between Offline and Online Worlds' introduces the reader into more political territory in terms of media-society relations in a national context. Singapore is of course the most 'wired' society in Southeast Asia, and possibly the top three Asia-wide in terms of Internet penetration per 1,000 count of population. It also poses the unusual confluence of a soft authoritarian democracy grappling with the freedoms associated with Internet use. As Tan puts it, the ruling People's Action Party's 'dominance over offline spaces has not automatically translated into a similarly robust control over online spaces – the process of contestation and re-contestation remains an ongoing, dynamic and complex one'. After examining a number of episodes where bloggers and website administrators encountered brushes with the law since 2001, Tan suggests that ultimately the negotiations between government and netizens revolve around a typically Singaporean culture of excess, a term borrowed from the work of Yao Souchou, which refers to 'an all-consuming anxiety, grounded in the ruling party's particular telling of "the Singapore Story", that both paralyzes and serves as a spur to action in order to avert national collapse – a kind of excess which underpins its impulses to control'. Nonetheless, the policy of the Singaporean government cannot be regarded as purely authoritarian since it has frequently pushed the line that it always regulates the Internet with a 'light touch'. Moreover, the Singaporean netizen-activist has developed ingenious ways of getting around the 'out-of-bounds markers' by biding their time, dressing up serious issues in humorous analogies, conducting independent journalistic inquiry whose results are published directly onto blogs within minutes and hours before the main printed dailies, or bandwagoning with civil society protests offline. Yet, this is done under the shadow of the vaunted 'culture of excess' where even middle of the road bloggers are mindful of disrupting socio-political harmony in a country that had witnessed traumatic race riots as recently as the 1960s. That said, Tan finds that the Singapore case echoes much of what bloggers elsewhere have been able to achieve by merely reporting 'alternative news' and tempting governments to respond to these 'unexpectedly' mediatized events and issues. This is clearly a case of Internet alterity liberating political spaces incrementally, in negotiated paces, rather than revolutionary ones.

Finally, we explore a slice of the social politics of IT in Malaysia with Choong Pui Yee's take on the synergistic relationship between grassroots political movements and the desire to pursue the democratization of Malaysia's hegemonic dominant party democracy online. Through three small case studies of fledgling new media initiatives, ranging from campaigns for clean elections, to legal education, to satire via YouTube videos, Choong suggests that new media has facilitated the lively presence of alternative voices in Malaysian politics. Yet, these have remained mostly loud voices on social media. When it comes to translating online effervescence into offline actions, the record is far more modest. Riot police will have to be contended with and the dominant ruling coalition's electoral machine will have to be challenged at the ballot box, amongst other demographic factors. Choong's case study reiterates strong circumstantial evidence that democratization via new media is a tangible product of alterity in IT usage. Perhaps, this is all that can be expected of IT alterity, serving mostly as a productive irritant against hegemonic frames of offline governance. This is something the Malaysian study shares in common with the preceding chapters on Muslim students on the Internet, Filipino diasporic mobile phone and Facebook linkages, and Singaporean civil society activism online.

Governmental Steering and Policy Alterity

The final cluster of chapters necessarily deals with the role of Asian governments in steering public IT usage and integrative IT roles in business operations. As the following chapters will reveal, there are complex roles that governments undertake in fostering information society, not all of which accord with liberal freedoms or untrammelled capitalism. From the perspective of many Asian governments, financially and intellectually vulnerable populations and economies should either be led or be boldly cajoled to emulate the habits of the twenty-first century. Modernization is often interpreted by official quarters as a project too important to be left to either happenstance, or worse, updated neo-colonial influences from the West. For authoritarian developmental states such as China and

Singapore, it is also imperative that the benefits of joining the IT age should not be embraced at the expense of political stability, which in turn is often interpreted to mean preserving the longevity of dominant party regimes. Even in relatively more democratic Malaysia, Taiwan and South Korea, the imprint of centrally-directed developmental planning for economic uses of the Internet and wider IT applications is evident.

Taking on a combative and contested line of exploration of government and IT relationships, Kay Hearn's chapter addresses the links between nationalism, government sanction and cyberattacks in the People's Republic of China (PRC) through what she terms as a 'centre/margin' analysis. She employs this framework since hacking constitutes a virtual form of interaction between the Chinese Communist Party (CCP), as the central authority of the PRC, and other groups such as democracy dissidents and other nation-states. Hearn assumes that Internet time and space are dependent upon networks of interpersonal association. The Internet facilitates both and can also be used to challenge networks, physically through hacking, and organizationally through the development of oppositional networks. In the context of modern China it is important to look at the way in which the Internet has been utilized by both state and non-state actors, and in order to understand China's adaptation to a changing media environment. Social media is an environment that the government actively seeks to mould, and which at the same time forces it to deal with forms of use that they actively seek to discourage in the name of national stability. Hearn illustrates this perspective through explorations of China's legal framework for IT use, the role of the military in cyberwarfare, cyber-interactions over Taiwanese politics and foreign relations, the Tibet question and the motivations of nationalist hackers. In short, Hearn's contribution demonstrates that the medium of the Internet actually becomes an arena for enacting contestation within State-Society relations and between States and Non-state Web Actors as a form of dialogical interaction. Hearn concludes that this sort of communication does not inevitably deliver greater democratization to the PRC.

Continuing with the theme of intense governmental intervention to adapt IT as a booster to economic growth and political enhancement, Alan Chong's chapter subjects the influential 'global cities' literature to a political reality test on the grounds that any reinvention of urban metropolises into IT-connected hubs of information and economic flows tends to be an outcome of successful propaganda issued from a particular set of socio-political interests. Although Chong accepts that the global city is a product of late twentieth century transnational processes involving capitalism, information and communications technology, and technocratic government, he argues that this happy conjunction came into existence as a result of the deliberate operation of what he terms a 'global city foreign policy'. This phrase refers to 'the realm of promotional activity designed to attain for the city a significant degree of connectedness with cross-border flows of finance, production and information so as to achieve a commanding position in the global capitalist economy to extract surpluses from these very flows'. Unfortunately, the study of the global city's *foreign policy* has been marginalized in scholarly accounts of both globalization and foreign policy analysis. Chong explains that the foreign policy of a global city has gained in political importance due to the advance of informational capitalism. With the exception of well-publicized Japanese cities such as Tokyo and Osaka, other Asian cities in the categories of the 'newly first world' and 'developing' contexts have innovated in operating multifaceted foreign policies that construct their prosperity as connected, value-adding nodes in borderless informational capitalism. Three Asian cities (Taipei, Kuala Lumpur and Singapore) serve as illustrations of the 'foreign policy of a global city' since they are all aspirants to the status of a twenty-first-century Asian definition of capitalist modernity. Furthermore, they represent the continuum between the 'newly first world' and the 'developing'. Chong's chapter therefore argues that this fledgling global city foreign policy is manifested through a form of complex alterity that can be analyzed as the *propaganda of enlargement and integration* via the cases of Taipei, Kuala Lumpur and Singapore.

Next, Byoung Won Min's chapter introduces the reader to the South Korean context where he draws attention to the sharp political currents that operate beneath the progressive linear image of South Korea being one of Asia's top three most-connected industrialized societies. His chapter title is deliberately provocative: 'Biting Back Against Civil Society: IT, Media and Communication Regulations in South Korea'. It suggests that the government in Seoul is intent on exercising paternalism against an unruly Internet-savvy civil society. Min notes a huge irony in South Korea's status as an OECD developed country. These tangible statistics of material progress have not taken into account the flourishing social activism of Korean citizens that have become a symbol of the transformative power of IT in the political arena. The candlelight demonstration in the spring of 2008 against the government-led negotiations for importing beef that was rumoured to be contaminated by Mad Cow disease was regarded by governing elites as another case of recalcitrant social movements operating under the cover of a democratizing Korea. This seems to have led the South Korean government, which is currently helmed by a revived coalition among conservatives, towards a showdown against the 'smart mobs' who have equipped themselves with sophisticated IT-based technologies and democratic aspirations. Min introduces two cases in his chapter about this struggle between the Korean government and the civil society. They will show how the Korean government has been troubled by the contradictions posed by IT-related policies and regulations – the clash between efficiency and public accountability, or what Min terms the competition between principles of 'efficiency' and 'publicity'. The first case was about the establishment of the Korea Communications Commission (KCC) in 2008, which was to be an independent regulatory body for the information and communication sectors. The second case deals with the controversy surrounding the new media law passed in 2009 that allowed big companies and capital owners to hold shares in broadcasting industries. In both cases, the Korean government had accelerated institutional arrangements and legislation regarding the new IT-based social communication mechanisms. The core question posed in these cases would be: 'How well does the Korean government keep the balance between the two contradictory principles of efficiency and public accountability (publicity)?' The answer, Min argues, is 'not very well'. It seems that the Korean government has been biased toward the logic of efficiency rather than toward the logic of publicity.

The final two chapters that deal with governmental steering are contributed by scholars of IT-connected businesses. As such, their approach towards the question of IT alterity takes on a more descriptive, problem-solving tone in accounting for the role of government in starting up what they term Information Technology Enabled Services (ITeS). Their task is to explain the strong hand of governmental steerage even though the private sector is often touted as the driving force behind the Indian and Philippine ITeS industries. Joefe B. Santarita's chapter treating the inputs underpinning the successful entrenchment of the call centre and data processing businesses in India and the Philippines details how their respective governments supplied both hard and soft infrastructures to foster a conducive operating environment for MNCs to contract their services locally. The familiar developmental problems of inadequate start-up infrastructure had to be tackled head on in order for both countries to produce IT-driven centres of excellence overnight amidst national economic landscapes of uneven growth and highly varied levels of efficiency. Santarita specifically details how both governments implemented unusually expeditious changes in educational, technological and manpower policies to accommodate and complement the industry's rapid growth. In some ways one might observe echoes in India and the Philippines of the bureaucratic authoritarian developmental state that had overseen the success of the East Asian 'tiger economies' of the 1980s and 1990s.

Finally, Faizal Bin Yahya's chapter throws light on another significant dimension of governmental steerage of ITeS – the need to police the reputation and viability of the ITeS industries. Yahya has chosen to focus specifically on the Business Processing Outsourcing (BPO) dimension of ITeS to make his case. As he puts it, the Indian state has in recent years been challenged by highly publicized concerns, aired by both domestic public opinion and foreign clients, over data management and the overall security of Indian BPO companies. Yahya consequently argues that given a string of publicized security lapses committed either wilfully or accidentally by Indian IT workers in BPO operations, the Indian government had little choice but to provide assurances in terms of tightening up vetting requirements for IT personnel and encouraging internal self-policing measures by BPO contracting firms in India. The alterity in all this lies clearly in the fact that the security and efficiency of IT businesses is ultimately heavily dependent on governments 'ordering' the operating environment in terms of a corrective function, so as to preserve the respectability and attractiveness of IT-facilitated outsourced work.

The Politics and Sociology of Embracing IT: The Persistence of Alterity in the Asian Experience

Consequently, through this book-length exercise of exploring the alterity produced by IT-modernizing Asia, the following general conclusions about the nature of Asian information society may be drawn from the present study. Firstly, alterity is about *dissonance in values during the process of applying IT to develop the Asian society and economy*. Pre-electronic media values have grown entrenched in mindsets concerning the way Asian societies have operated. After all, electronic information and communication technologies have been an import from western societies. Given the proliferation of social, occupational and politically subversive uses of the Internet in Malaysia, Singapore, South Korea, Japan, China and India over the past five years, the Asian experience should illuminate the pitfalls and potentials of getting Asian populations to embrace electronic communications technologies. Some scholars may dispute the presence of a singular Asian experience given the variety of socio-political conditions in Asia, but surely, societies that are more accustomed to traditional non-IT media will encounter some form of contest of values when IT becomes part of everyday use. On a more optimistic note, one might assert that IT may induce a value shift – perhaps embracing more 'westernized values' such as liberalism and faceless networking.

Secondly, alterity in the cases of diasporic communication and the roles of the developmental state in fostering communication modernization may well reveal the *centrality of authoritarian politics in determining the extent of embrace of electronic media* within transnational and national contexts. Communities are enabled in solidarity, arising from the need to police themselves for or against existing authorities and knowledge communities. Contrary to the initial optimism put out by the initial wave of cyber-analysts in the early 1990s, computers, IT and satellite technologies in Asian contexts are often rendered widespread due to directed political agencies. The Asian state is, in this regard, enacting a role not widely envisioned in North America, or Europe for that matter. Diasporas too employ computer-mediated communication as a means of enhancing the virtual identity of their exclusively imagined nationality. Finally, the two chapters dealing with IT Enabled Services highlight the often under-acknowledged, and mutually interactive, reliance on the steering role of government to keep the knowledge based economy reputable and viable by tackling undesirable externalities such as employee misbehaviour and inadequate infrastructure. IT services may theoretically be outsourced across all geographies but the quality of local political hospitality matters in determining whether the outsourced IT-related businesses stay rooted in particular localities and enrich them as a result.

Thirdly, alterity in Asian techno-modernization may well manifest through the *generation of new socio-economic divides* that go against the conventional expectation that the expansion of the knowledge industry emancipates populations from ignorance and ultimately poverty. The efforts of the World Summit on the Information Society and UNCTAD to promote IT-literacy in the developing world need to be subjected to critical examination (Raboy *et al.*, 2010). The digital divide has been problematized in the official corridors of political power, but the chapters in this volume argue that progress towards a global information society may actually necessitate a new order of dependency that is simultaneously domestic and international. The chapters that explore the vastness of governmental steering in IT projects illustrate this point very clearly. To some extent, the warnings of Johan Galtung against structural imperialism may still be prescient in the present era of globalizing electronic communication. Alterity will likely plague Asian communication for some time, but it serves as a pointed lesson for the rest of the world in the rush to emancipate societies through digital empowerment.

References

Aggarwal, Y. 2012. Moves that rile India's Telcos. *The Business Times* (Singapore), 15 May, p.11.

Atkins, W. 2002. *The Politics of Southeast Asia's New Media*. Richmond: Curzon.

Baark, E. 1997. *Lightning Wires: the Telegraph and China's Technological Modernization, 1860–1890*. Westport: Greenwood Press.

Bach, J. and Stark, D. 2005. Recombinant Technology and New Geographies of Association. In: R. Latham and S. Sassen, eds. 2005. *Digital Formations: IT and New Architectures in the Global Realm*. Princeton: Princeton University Press, pp.37–53.

BBC. 2013. China's 'state-sponsored hackers renew attacks on US'. *BBC News – Technology*. 20 May 2013. Available at <http://www.bbc.co.uk/news/technology-22594140>. [Accessed 24 July 2013.]

Beal, T. 2003. The State of Internet Use in Asia. In: K.C. Ho, R. Kluver and K.C.C. Yang, eds. 2003. *Asia.com: Asia Encounters the Internet*. London: RoutledgeCurzon, pp.27–43.

Bergin, A.; Osman, S.B.; Ungerer, C.; and Yasin, N.A.M. 2009. *Countering Internet Radicalisation in Southeast Asia. An RSIS-ASPI Report*. Canberra: Australian Strategic Policy Institute. Available at: <http://www.rsis.edu.sg/short%20reports/Countering_Internet_radicalisation.pdf>. [Accessed 10 November 2011.]

Castells, M. 1989. *The Informational City: Information Technology, Economic Restructuring, and the Urban-Regional Process*. Cambridge: Basil Blackwell.

Castells, M. 2001. *The Internet Galaxy: Reflections on the Internet, Business, and Society*. Oxford: Oxford University Press.

Castells, M.; Fernández-Ardèvol, M.; Qiu, J.L.; Sey, A. 2007. *Mobile Communication And Society: A Global Perspective*. A project of the Annenberg Research Network on international communication. Cambridge: MIT Press.

Cowhey, P.F. 1994. Public and Private Cooperation in International Informatics. In: E.M. Noam, S. Komatsuzaki and D.A. Conn, eds. 1994. *Telecommunications in the Pacific Basin*. New York: Oxford University Press, pp. 45–69.

Cuthbert, M.L. and Hoover, S.M. 1991. Video beachheads: communication, culture, and policy in the Eastern Caribbean. In: G. Sussman and J. Lent, eds. 1991. *Transnational Communications: Wiring the Third World.* London: Sage, pp.263–278.

Doron, A. and Jeffrey, R., 2013. *The Great Indian Phone Book: How the Cheap Cell Phone Changes Business, Politics, and Daily Life*. Cambridge: Harvard University Press.

Finkle, J., 2014. Beijing to Bar Symantec, Kaspersky Anti-Virus in Procurement: Report. *Reuters.com*, available at http://www.reuters.com/assets/print?aid=USKBN0G30QH20140803 (Accessed 4 August 2014).

Goodman, D.E. 2011. Trying to Stir Up a Popular Protest in China, From a Bedroom in Manhattan. *The New York Times*, 28 April.

Gore, A. 1994. Vice President Al Gore. Information Superhighways Speech. International Telecommunication Union, Monday 21 March 1994. Available at: http://vlib.iue.it/history/Internet/algorespeech.html. [Accessed 27 June 2011.]

Habermas, J. 1991. *The Structural Transformation of the Public Sphere: An Inquiry into a Category of Bourgeois Society*. Cambridge: MIT press.

Hermanns, H. 2007. Culture and Online Politics in East Asia. *Political Science in Asia* 2(2), pp.115–138.

Ho, K.C.; Kluver, R.; and Yang, K.C.C. 2003. Asia Encounters the Internet. In: K.C. Ho; R. Kluver; and K.C.C. Yang, eds. 2003. *Asia.com: Asia Encounters the Internet*. London: RoutledgeCurzon, pp.263–278.

Huang, Y. 2013. In China, most Politics is Local. *International Herald Tribune* 30 January.

IHT. 2003. Chinese Government Granted Access to Windows Code. *International Herald Tribune* 1–2 March.

Johnson, C. 1982. *MITI and the Japanese Miracle: The Growth of Industrial Policy, 1925–1975*. Stanford: Stanford University Press.

Jones, S.G. 1997. The Internet and its Social Landscape. In: S.G. Jones, ed. 1997. *Virtual Culture: Identity and Communication in Cybersociety*. Thousand Oaks: Sage, pp.7–35.

Krishna, S. and Madon, S., eds. 2003. *The Digital Challenge: Information Technology in the Development Context*. Aldershot: Ashgate.

Latham, R. and Sassen, S. 2005. Digital Formations: Constructing an Object of Study. In: R. Latham and S. Sassen, eds. 2005. *Digital Formations: IT and New Architectures in the Global Realm*. Princeton: Princeton University Press, pp.1–34.

Lee, P.S.N. ed., 1997. *Telecommunications and Development in China*. Cresskill: Hampton Press.

McCargo, D. 2003. *Media and Politics in Pacific Asia*. London: Routledge.

MacKinnon, R. 2005. China's Internet: www.(censored). *International Herald Tribune* 9–10 July.

Miard, F. 2012. Call for Power? Mobile Phones as Facilitators of Political Activism. In: Sean S. Costigan and Jake Perry, eds, 2012. *Cyberspaces and Global Affairs*. Farnham: Ashgate Publishing, pp.119–144.

Milikan, M.F. 1967. The Most Fundamental Technological Change. In: D. Lerner and W. Schramm, eds, 1967. *Communication and Change in the Developing Countries*. Honolulu: East West Center Press, pp.3–4.

Noam, Eli M. 1994. The Three Stages of Network Evolution. In: E.M. Noam, S. Komatsuzaki and D.A. Conn, eds. 1994. *Telecommunications in the Pacific Basin*. New York: Oxford University Press, pp.17–31.

Raboy, M.; Landry, N. and Shtern, J. 2010. *Digital Solidarities, Communication Policy and Multi-stakeholder Global Governance: the Legacy of the World Summit on the Information Society*. New York: Peter Lang Publishing.

Richardson, M. 1998. Economics and Politics Curb Asian Press Freedom. *International Herald Tribune* 6 November.

Rodan, G. 2004. *Transparency and Authoritarian Rule in Southeast Asia: Singapore and Malaysia*. London: Routledge.

Schramm, W. 1967. Communication and Change. In: D. Lerner and W. Schramm, eds, 1967. *Communication and Change in the Developing Countries*. Honolulu: East West Center Press, pp.5–34.

Sen, K. and Lee, T., eds. 2007. *Political Regimes and the Media in East Asia: Continuities, Contradictions and Change*. New York: Routledge.

Sethi, V. 2006. *Communication Services in India 1947–2007*. New Delhi: New Century Publications.

Sussman, G. and Lent, J. 1991. Preface. In: G. Sussman and J. Lent, eds. 1991. *Transnational Communications: Wiring the Third World*. London: Sage, pp.ix–xv.

Talisayon, V.M. 1991. *Preparing ASEAN for the Information Century a Comparative Study of Policies and Programs on Computers in Science and Mathematics Education*. Manila: University of the Philippines Press.

Taplin, R. and Wakui, M. 2006. Introduction. In: R. Taplin and M. Wakui, eds. 2006. *Japanese Telecommunications: Market and Policy in Transition*. Abingdon: Routledge, pp. 1–14.

Toffler, A. 1970. *Future Shock*. New York: Random House.

Ure, J. 2008. Nationalism, Regionalism, Globalism and ICTs. In: Jeju Peace Institute and East Asia Foundation, eds. 2008. *Peace and Prosperity in Northeast Asia – Exploring the European Experience Volume One*. Jeju: JPI Press, pp.323–328.

Wacker, G. 2003. The Internet and Censorship in China. In: C. Hughes and G. Wacker eds. 2003. *China and the Internet: Politics of the Digital Leap Forward*. London: Routledge, pp.58–82.

Webster, F. 1995. *Theories of the Information Society*. London: Routledge.

Wong, E. 2013. China's Push for Drones Fuelled by US Secrets. *International Herald Tribune*, 23 Sep. pp.1,4.

PART I
Social Politics of IT

Chapter 1
National Contexts and the Negotiation of Islamic Internet Identity by Southeast Asian Undergraduate Students

Nasya Bahfen

Introduction

The phenomenon of blogs by Muslims in Singapore, the publication of information and news for the consumption of Muslim audiences in Jakarta, the online calls for *reformasi* amongst Muslims in Kuala Lumpur and the proliferation of website forums run by Muslims in Melbourne and Sydney are examples of how members of Islamic communities use Internet technology in the negotiation of their religious identity and alterity. The embracing of the Internet in Southeast Asia and Australia by these Islamic communities reflects both the fluid nature of religious identity as an ongoing process (Baumann and Gingrich, 2004; Peek, 2005) and the dependence of alterity on relationships with both other human beings and technology (Latour and Venn, 2002). Alterity can be seen in the effects of offline political, social and cultural processes on their online communication, through the construction of imagined Muslim communities and in the output of news and information received by Muslim audiences online.

This chapter outlines some of the author's research into Internet usage by Muslim tertiary students in Australia, Indonesia, Malaysia and Singapore. It looks at whether such usage reflects or is reliant on offline political processes – specifically, whether the exploration of Islamic identity and community among these Muslim students varies because of the religious and media environments evident in each country, including:

1. the nature of the state,
2. the politico-legal position of Islam and its adherents,
3. the political economy of the Internet, and
4. the nature of Islam as a national social movement.

On the one hand, these factors reflect national cultures that frame the boundaries of meanings available in identity formation, negotiation and transformation. On the other hand the Internet allows a transnational flow of perspectives and interpretations that facilitates the articulation of a wider Islamic identity (or range of identities) that goes over and beyond the nation-state. The broad finding of this research is that while the nature of Internet technology use in South East Asia does not share the overtly democratizing or empowering characteristics noted in its use in the Arab Spring (Al-Momani, 2011; Chokoshvili, 2011) the Internet plays a role in facilitating the construction of a shared sense of Muslim identity within nation states, and across some of the borders of these nation-states, helping the young Muslim students who use it in the knowledge and practice of their faith. Moreover, the relation of the State to Islam as a social reality, and the State's relation to the Internet as a communication environment, interact to produce a highly politicized context for the exploration and constitution of Islamic community, for young Muslims in this region. These themes emerged after taking into account the questions about Islam that have increased since the September 11 attacks in the United States of America, as well as the significant amount of news coverage devoted to people and incidents related to Islam.

Identity and Southeast Asia's Online Public Sphere

Working definitions of identity stress its fluidity and multidimensional nature, speaking of identity as the defining of a person or group of people based on social subjectivity (Baumann and Gingrich, 2004) and taking into account factors such as group affiliation, sense of self, and social status whether perceived or real (Peek, 2005). Lim (2004) believes that through the formation of alternative social projects, Internet use can be linked to communication and construction of identity, such as in the case of Indonesia where technology played a documented role in a change in that country's power relations. Religion and its relationship to identity is framed differently according to whether a specific religious community is part of a dominant or minority population: the role of religion plays a larger part in the formation of group identity in instances where that group is comprised of migrants or minorities (Zine, 2008; Ng, 2002). It is through constant communication and relationships with others (both other human beings, and an 'other' in the form of technology) that it becomes difficult to define identity on an individual basis – a meaning to which Latour and Venn (2002) ascribe notions of alteration or alterity.

The development of technology and the use of online media has made possible the negotiation of religious identity through an active online public sphere, in which discussion takes place about issues of faith, practice, and interfaith relationships. For instance, for Jewish communities the Internet has provided an opportunity to address the middle east conflict with Arab youth (Yablon, 2007). Lerner (2008) found communities of Orthodox and Haredi Jews use of the Internet spanned religious, communal, personal, and educational purposes including the maintaining of web sites for theological and social information, and that the online presence of these communities reflected the breadth of Jewish religious diversity. The negotiated use of the Internet has also been observed among female members of ultra-Orthodox Jews for whom the medium is officially frowned upon as a carrier of secular values (Livio and Weinblatt, 2007).

The intersection of Islam and the Internet has given rise to a global e-*ummah* – a phrase referencing the 'global village' (McLuhan and Fiore, 1967) used (not exclusively) by McLuhan to describe a future where the main barriers to human communication – the severities of time and distance – could be altered, and the word '*ummah*' referring to followers of the Prophet Muhammad (i.e., Muslim communities). For religious minorities such as British Muslims, the Internet quickly became an important communication tool for the expression of Islamic identity (Bunt, 1999). Members of young Muslim minorities in Western, non-Muslim countries such as the United States use the Internet to engage in the formation of Islamic community and identity on the basis of visibility, individual choice, transnationalism and social ethics (Schmidt, 2004). Young people in both Muslim majority countries and members of Muslim diasporas are adept at Internet communication and use, and mediate their religious identity and practice online, in the process of obtaining both spiritual and material aims (Echchaibi, 2009).

It has often been suggested that the Internet is a manifestation of McLuhan's predictions (Van der Laan, 2009; Hodge, 2003) in that it enables people to talk within international arenas, businesses to reach markets across geographical boundaries, and movements to expand above national or local frameworks. Perhaps most importantly, it demonstrates a process of alterity by allowing entire societies to begin a process of redefinition and engagement, through new modes of communication – thus fulfilling McLuhan's assertion that society was evolving from the timely and methodical linear projection of culture by books and newspapers of the print media era, to a world where the impact of fragmented and instantaneous output of electronic media could be received, literally, at the click of a button; and consolidating Anderson's concept of imagined communities (Anderson, 1991) where a 'nation' is imagined by the users of media because of the impossibility of experiencing it in real time and space.

Studies on societal perceptions of religious communities through the media have focused on newspapers (for example, Ahmad, 2006; and Leth, 2005) or television (for example, Cañas, 2008; Miladi, 2008; Banaji and Al-Ghabban, 2006; Buhle, 2006; and Stratton, 2005), or comparative content and textual analyses of media coverage of Islam or Muslims – for example, Martin and Phelan (2002)'s research on the coverage of Islam by five US based TV networks (CNN, ABC, CBS, NBC and FOX). The research that has looked at the portrayal and self-representation of Muslims online has focused on Islamic communities outside of Asia, such as Europe and the United States (Echchaibi, 2009; Schmidt, 2004; Bunt, 1999). By contrast this chapter focuses on the alterity present in comparing the use of online communication among Muslim students in Southeast Asia, against the backdrop of the relative offline social and political positions that Islam holds in each national situation.

National Contexts

Each of the four countries or societies studied has a unique set of circumstances with regards to the size of its Muslim population, the levels of freedom in which its media operates, and the information technology and infrastructure available to its citizens.

Australia is the home of a slowly consolidating Muslim culture that is the result of a nascent Islamic community comprised of both émigré Muslims and converts. Its members engage in the practice of their faith online to build networks, form and maintain relationships, and spread and consume news and views in an alternative Islamo-public sphere. Australia can be said to operate under a libertarian media environment under which freedom of speech is seen as a vital feature of a functioning democracy, and the media according to this system is seen as a marketplace of ideas in which anything can be published or broadcast for supply to media consumers (Sani, 2005). With first world infrastructure and information technologies available to this Islamic population, the Internet is also used to support the working, educational and social aspirations of particularly younger Australian Muslims – a trend that is observable in Australian society as a whole (Madden and Savage, 2000).

Indonesia is the country with the largest Muslim population in the world, but its modern history is one of overwhelmingly pluralistic national identity encompassing multiple faith histories. Throughout its modern history political and social upheaval combined to alter its media policies and the environment its media (including the Internet) operated in. The collapse of the New Order regime which dominated the Indonesian political landscape for 30 years resulted in a slew of new publications and broadcasting outlets, while surviving older ones were able to enjoy a new environment of media freedom (Eng, 1998). Internet and email played a role in Indonesia's media revolution, proving to be a turning point for the different ethnic and religious groups who became the users of the new medium. The freer post-Suharto media environment also saw the explosion of political tabloids, some of which had an Islamic orientation and explored the relationships between '*reformasi*' (the reform movement) and Islam (Tornquist, 2000). Internet practice in Indonesia is marked by its use as a form of alternative media through its contribution to Indonesia's public sphere, but there are gender and economic dimensions with its use given that the country was the hardest hit by the Asian financial crisis of 1997–98 and took the longest to recover. While the cost of home Internet access is prohibitive to most Indonesian families, public Internet kiosks ('warnet'), universities, wireless hotspots at malls, and workplaces all provide access to users who are predominantly members of the young urbanized population. The digital divide and lack of infrastructure prevents rural Muslim and poorer Indonesians from being able to access the Internet (Hill and Sen, 2002). Indonesia's Islam is pluralistic, and the theological interpretations of various groups establish online presences.

Like Indonesia, Malaysia has a majority Muslim population and minorities of other faith groups. But Malaysia is economically more advanced, with policymakers explicit in declaring entry to the first world as one of the country's development goals (Mahathir, 1999; Barlow, 1997). Malaysian Internet usage reflects an online manifestation of the country's diverse racial composition, and the promotion and support of the Internet from government levels for a computer-literate society. Malaysia's population appears to have embraced the government's push for technology-driven development, with large numbers of Malaysians taking up Internet access of whom the overwhelming majority are young people below the age of 30 (Hashim and Yusof, 1999). However, Malaysian media operates in a restricted environment, and the use of the Internet by political activists and opposition parties signal it as a source of alternative media (Gan, 2002). Blogs and websites are actively used as a source of independent, non-government-sanctioned news about opposition party policies and critical of the ruling party (Holmes and Grieco, 2001). At the same time, young Malaysians use the Internet for business and social purposes (for example specific social network sites. The Malaysian government therefore finds itself juggling two different but critically important goals: the need for technology-led economic development and the importance of a vibrant, flourishing and free Malaysian Internet environment.

Singapore is perhaps the most 'wired' country out of the four studied; economically stable and advanced, its information technology infrastructure is used by its citizens and supported by its government (Kalathil, 2003). Its citizens enjoy high rates of education, home ownership and employment, in addition to an affluent standard of living. However, Singapore's media environment is tightly controlled and offers little space for genuine debate, allowing the Internet to fulfill the role of maintenance of a public sphere (George, 2003). The Internet gave Singaporean underground activism an outlet for the publication of views considered too subversive for the mainstream newspapers and broadcasters. The Singaporean government has attempted to control the publishing opportunities the Internet offered (Wang, 1999), for example through including the Internet in regulatory mechanisms for traditional media. Although Muslims in Singapore comprise the biggest minority (and a politically strategic one) at 16 per cent of the country's population, socioeconomically Singapore's Muslim minority are lacking in representation at the professional level. This disparity has implications for the future of the Malay Muslim community in Singapore, often described as becoming an underclass (Lai, 2003).

Data Sources and Methodology

With Internet usage dominated predominantly by young people in all four countries studied, the material used as the basis for the research also reflected a youth bias. An online survey involving respondents from Australia and Southeast Asia was used as the source of data for this chapter. The respondents were Muslim tertiary students recruited through campus Muslim student organizations. It was proposed that four offline political and social parameters constrained and directed Internet use by these young Muslim students (the nature of the state, the position of Islam and Muslims, the political economy of the Internet, and the nature of Islam as a national social movement). The research methods adopted seek to test out whether these parameters are determinant in the way suggested, and how variations country by country affect the way in which the Internet is used.

Surveys administered online have much appeal to social science researchers. Sourcing respondents via email postings and requesting responses through an Internet survey results in faster turnaround time; permits easier facilitation of international respondents; allows instantaneous recording of data; negates the chance of respondents being affected by interviewer bias; and offers the ease of self-administration of the survey. Online surveys are appealing because of 'the power of self-administration and interactivity on the one hand, and the advantages of speed and massive reductions in cost over interviewer-administered surveys on the other' (Couper, Kapteyn, Schonlau and Winter, 2007). Granello and Wheaton (2004) cite a faster response time, lower cost, and ease of data entry as some of the advantages of engaging survey respondents online. However, an online survey's main limitation is that the method contains inherent difficulties in obtaining a representative sample. In addition, the possibility of low response rates comprises a second limitation with this research methodology. The online survey is therefore a double-edged sword: it offers advantages and links to the topic of Muslim Internet users, but it has limitations.

The survey respondents represented a very specific sub-community of Muslims in Australia and the three Southeast Asian countries that were the focus of the research: those who identified as 'Muslim' with no reference to whether they were Shi'a or Sunni, and who were members of Muslim student organizations at universities in the countries studied. Although Muslims comprise of two main sects (and several schools of thought within each) in practice, university Muslim student organizations will not tend to identify as, for example, a 'Hanbali Sunni Muslim Student Society'. Therefore in this survey the category of 'Muslim' is treated as all-inclusive, in a targeted sample size that was used for several reasons. Young people and students are at the front line where early adaptation of new technology is concerned (Clark, Frith, and Demi, 2004; Jones, 2002) and this holds true in the countries whose Islamic populations are the focus of the research – Australia (Kennedy, Judd, Churchward, Gray, and Krause, 2008), Indonesia (Lim, 2004; Suryani, 2007), Malaysia (Bahfen, 2008) and Singapore (Cheong, 2008). In addition, the Islamic communities in two of those countries (Australia and Singapore) are minority populations. As Islam grows in popularity in predominantly non-Muslim majority nation-states (Abbas, 2007; Haniff, 2003; Smith, 2002) there have been calls for more detailed understanding of both Muslim student groups in minority contexts (as the next generation of Muslims in their respective countries) and how their experiences as students play a role in the formation of their religious identity (Peek, 2005).

Because survey respondents were drawn from Muslim tertiary student populations, such a method would rule out trying to extrapolate any meaning from the survey results to the Australian or southeast Asian Muslim community as a whole. Rather than being representative, the research used a sample that demonstrated the characteristic of volunteer sampling: instead of seeking a random group representative of the Muslim populace in Australia and southeast Asia as a whole, the research aimed to target a specific group of Muslims: those at university using the Internet. Miller (in Babbie, 2001) notes that some groups are ideally suited to Internet survey. For example, visitors to specific websites or the members of certain email lists could be targeted according to how relevant the survey's questions are to that group. The research also used the characteristics of quota sampling in that the group of Muslims the research sought for the completion of the survey (i.e. Internet users) could also be described as a quota sample, gleaned from a variety of sources. Responses were solicited via postings submitted to a Muslim student association (MSA) mailing list; these postings were made to MSAs in the four countries concerned. Similarly non-student community mailing lists requesting responses from Muslim students provided further input. Following these two initial steps, a clear pattern emerged from the data. The greater part of respondents described their location as being from Australia or Singapore, with a much smaller proportion of respondents coming from Malaysia or Indonesia. Unfortunately, the number of respondents from Malaysia and Indonesia remained low, reflecting lower Internet access rates in those countries compared to Australia (Willis and Tranter, 2006) or Singapore (Cheong, 2008). However, the total number of responses was 129 – a similar figure to targeted sample studies on related topics, such as the work of Suryani (2007) on Indonesian student Internet technology use, and Peek (2005) on the development of religious identity among Muslim students in the United States.

The online survey was divided into five sections. It began with basic demographic questions asking such things as the respondent's age, location and gender; followed by an exploration of where and how the survey respondent used the Internet, including information requested about access, the frequency with which the respondent uses the Internet and whether Internet usage is conducted as a primary or secondary activity. Questions were then asked specifically about the use of email and webpages and questions relating to the content and purpose of the web presence of the respondent (if he or she has one). The survey then asked why the respondent used the Internet. For each reason selected, the respondent was then asked to gauge how often he or she used the Internet for that particular purpose. The reasons listed were related to Islamic practice online: seeking clarification on matters of Islamic law, finding information related to the Muslim community or finding news from an Islamic perspective. Finally, the survey asked the respondent how he or she felt overall about the Internet and its potential for the Muslim community.

Findings

From the responses of Muslim students in Australia, Indonesia, Malaysia and Singapore to an online survey it appears that:

Offline policies on Internet freedom do not appear to affect the level of free expression and explorations of religious identity online. For example Malaysia and Singapore have a more conservative approach to Internet freedom than Indonesia and Australia, yet the Muslim students in all four countries who responded to the online survey say they use the Internet to thrash out various viewpoints regarding Islamic teachings and practice; and to defend Islam through online discussions (see Figure 1.1, 'Using the Internet to defend Islam'). Australian Muslims used the Internet as a source of alternative viewpoints among the members of their communities, discussing issues related to Islamic faith and practice online.

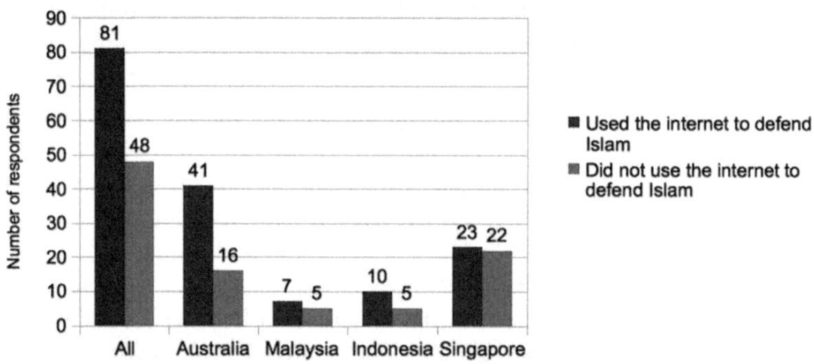

Figure 1.1 Using the Internet to defend Islam

The level of religious freedom given offline to Muslim communities, and in particular the public expression of symbolic aspects of Islamic identity do have an effect on the reasons for Internet usage by the Muslim students surveyed. The results of the online survey responses suggested that the Internet represents a source of practical information for Muslim students living in non-established minority groups, and that their use of the Internet was more practical than that of Muslims living in countries where Islam was the faith of the majority of the population (where practical information such as prayer times or the location of mosques) could be found offline (see Figure 1.2, 'Do you use the Internet to find information on the Muslim community?'). The results of the online survey also suggested that Muslim students in all four countries actively build networks using the Internet, and this activity is more pronounced in countries where Muslims are a minority. The idea of the global Muslim community being maintained through email and websites was invoked in comments by Muslim students about an email forward sent in the aftermath of the 9–11 attacks, depicting a 'Taliban dating agency'. The students agreed the email was insulting to Muslim women in general (not just those of Afghan descent) and mocked Islam. They envisioned email as a way of building links between Muslim women beyond national borders.

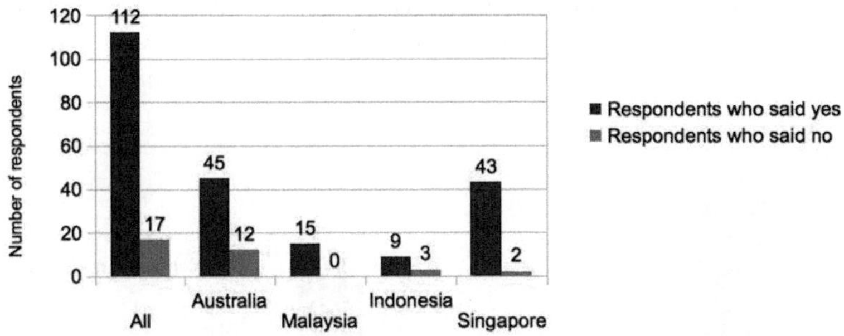

Figure 1.2 Do you use the Internet to find information on the Muslim community?

Islam's political strength within each country studied is not clearly demonstrated by the diversity of opinions and outlets available to members of the 'ummah' or Muslim community. The online survey results appear to suggest that irrespective of whether Muslims constitute a majority or minority in the country concerned, the Internet is used as a means to discuss alternative sources of news related to the Muslim world (see Figure 1.3, 'Finding news from an Islamic perspective'). This is complemented by the content analysis, in which it is argued that postings to Australian online sites or email lists such as the MuslimVillage forum and the Islam-info and Australian Muslim Media mailing lists demonstrates how the Australian Muslim community online uses the Internet to disseminate opinions about the news distributed by mainstream traditional media outlets. This practice provides the Australian Muslim minority population with a form of rebuttal against the ways in which the mainstream media portrays Islam and Muslims, which are seen as hostile and marginalizing.

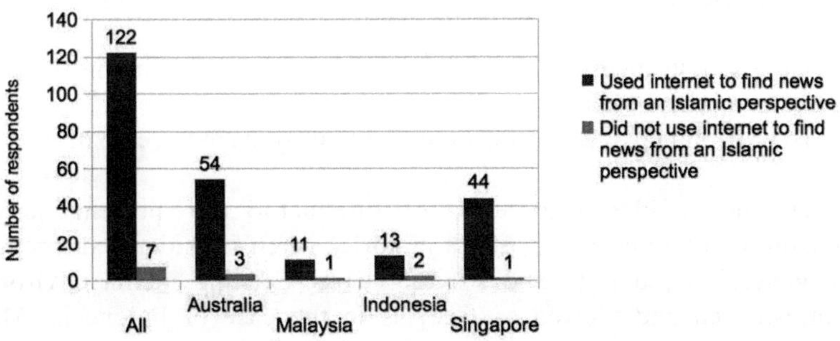

Figure 1.3 Finding news from an Islamic perspective

The offline economic position and social class of the Muslim student users surveyed affects their Internet access and use. The availability or affordability of Internet services in the four countries studied reflecting the specific characteristics of the digital divide in each society. The online survey responses alluded to differences existing in the detail of Internet usage (for example, in whether the source of Internet access was from home or work, and in the frequency of accessing the Internet – see Figure 1.4, 'Respondents who use the Internet daily').

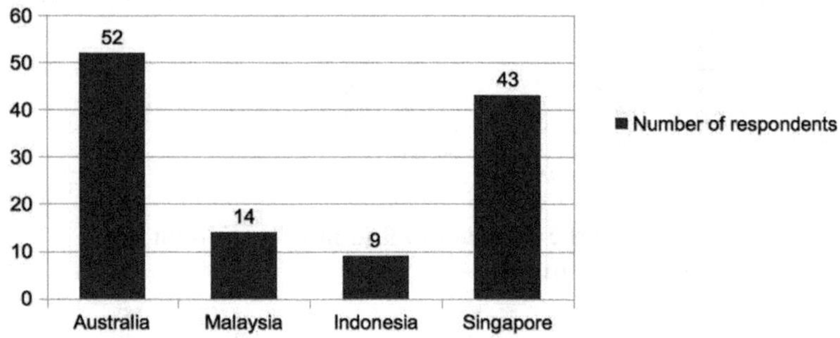

Figure 1.4 Respondents who use the Internet daily

Discussion

It is clear that online communication among this group of Muslim students from Southeast Asia is affected by offline politics. For example, for most of the Muslim tertiary students surveyed for this project, the Internet plays the role of an alternative source of media, irrespective of the size of the Muslim community in their home countries of Australia, Malaysia and Singapore. Two off-line political factors served to moderate and mediate the communication online of these Muslim students in Southeast Asia. The Muslim students surveyed say they turn to the Internet as an alternative news source, where any one of two factors are present:

- The existing media environment is tightly controlled, as in the case of Singapore and Malaysia,
- The Muslim population constitutes a minority, as in the case of Australia.

However, where neither of these two off-line factors were present (i.e. where the Muslim community comprised a majority when considered in proportion to the general population, and where the pre-existing media environment was unrestricted and viewed as free) as in the case of Indonesia, Muslim tertiary students surveyed say they did not primarily turn to the Internet as an alternative news source. Indonesia in general has been cited as a case where a technologically transformative identity has reflected the alterity of the offline political presence, and where identity has shifted through the changing dynamics of power and resistance (Lim, 2004).

While Muslims constitute the majority of the population in Malaysia, the Malaysian Muslim students say they turn to the Internet to find news because of a key off line factor – the non-Internet media environment already being heavily restricted, prior to the widespread adaptation of information communication technologies (Bahfen, 2008). This suggests that in the Malaysian context, web forums and email lists serve to fulfill the media needs of Muslims where the offline output of newspapers, radio stations and television networks are diluted or tightly controlled. When Muslims are a minority, it appears that the Internet acts as a form of alternative news for Muslim tertiary students surveyed from Australia and Singapore, and acts as a place where opinions can be shared through Islamic community-specific discourse, which is not situated within the coverage of offline media output, and where news that is relevant to the Muslim diaspora community can be accessed and disseminated. The size of the Muslim community and the strength of Islam in the given society also impacts in some way on whether the Internet is used for practical purposes. Where a community of Muslims is a minority (as in the case of Australia) the Muslim tertiary students surveyed believe that the Internet is a practical source of information such as halal restaurant locations, or Friday prayer times – information that in countries where Muslims are a majority can be found offline, through personal networks and non-Internet media.

The impact of off-line factors reflects the practical consequences of Internet usage, rather than exerting a disproportionate influence on the use of Internet communication by these students. For example, existing observations about whether the off line media environment is restricted or not serve to increase or decrease the likelihood of the Internet being used as 'alternative' news and information). Whether the Muslim population is a majority or a minority compared to the population at large similarly affects the ability of the Muslim students surveyed to obtain the information they needed via off-line means. The contest here lies not in online communities or off-line socio-political formations but in the inclination of the Muslim student user, given practical considerations. For example, one study of Singapore Muslim Internet users found that instead of linking the use of the technology to institutionalized Islam, members of the country's Islamic communities went online to discuss matters related to their individual practice of the faith (Ho, Lee and Hameed, 2008). How a Muslim student finds out about this week's religious classes and activities (through email and websites, or through speaking to friends and contacts offline, or through reading off-line publications or the noticeboard at the local mosque) may well depend on how established and large the Muslim community in his or country is, and the means of communication both online and offline in which that community engages.

In terms of the wider governance of IT-connected societies and governments, the students' responses suggest that the state's attitudes to religious freedom and expression of Islamic identity and Muslim viewpoints collectively appear to affect the formation of Islamic identity and community online (this can be seen in the use of the Internet by opposition groups in Malaysia, and Malay Muslim dissidents in Singapore). A possible area for further research is to examine the reactions of Muslim students to any regulatory attempts to clamp down on, or restrict, the use and freedom of online communication, such as the deeply unpopular Internet filter proposed by the Australian government which has received widespread condemnation among the population in general (Moses, 2008). National policies on communications infrastructure play a part in determining the amount of time and purposes to which Internet use is put. The Internet appears to be used by Muslim students to find out about, and connect with, other Muslims in their country or region, building an Islamic cyber-community, irrespective of the size of the Muslim population in relation to the population as a whole. The differences in practice amongst Muslims are manifest online, where certain websites or email lists will contain cyber-congregations of Muslims who are followers of a particular theological or political inclination. Given that the Internet is a way to forge networks between Muslims in the process of creating communities of shared thoughts and belief, and the use of the Internet to form networks among Muslims is particularly prevalent in students who are members of minority Islamic populations such as Australia's or Singapore's Muslim community (although the practice also exists among Muslim students who are members of a religious majority, such as in Indonesia and Malaysia), any off-line moves to control Internet use will impact on the online communication patterns of Muslim students.

Conclusion

Information technology has gone some way to redefining the identity of the Southeast Asian Muslim social and political entity. The Internet plays a key role in facilitating the construction of a shared sense of Muslim identity within nation states, and across some of the borders of these nation-states (reflective of Islam's border-less ethos). The argument that this chapter proposed is that alterity can be observed through variances in Internet use by Muslim communities, which can be attributed to offline factors such as differences in systems of governance, the position of Islam and the size of the Muslim population, economic development (leading to digital divide and access issues), and the structure and freedom of media industries in the nation-state. Young Muslim students, caught between modernity and tradition, go online to find Muslim counselling and advice and to find out about Islamic communities offline, located within and external to their countries of origin. The usage of the Internet to seek alternative news and viewpoints is indicative of a paradigm shift amongst Muslims from absorbing news that has been collected and reported by non-Muslim sources, to the selection and channelling of specific and desired information from both Muslim and non-Muslim publications that may be geographically dispersed from the user's physical location. Despite the influence of offline political and social constructs the use of the Internet by Muslim students cannot be categorized as purely political, purely religious, or purely social. Muslims use the Internet for all three purposes – as an online support mechanism for off-line political campaigning; as a discussion and information source for religious knowledge seeking online and its utilization and dissemination offline; and as a complement to offline socializing and textual interaction amongst Muslims and with non-Muslims.

This chapter hypothesized that government policies on Internet freedom will either facilitate or inhibit free expression and exploration of identity. It also hypothesized that policies on religious freedom and in particular the public expression of symbolic aspects of Islamic identity will contribute to the priority accorded different Internet content questions, for example political rights, questions of moral or ethical guidance and personal relationships (to some extent paralleling a common hierarchy of economic, political and social rights). The chapter argued that the political strength of Islam within a society would play a part in Internet expression, and would be demonstrated by the diversity of opinions and outlets available to members of the *ummah*. It also hypothesized that social class and economic position of users would affect their access to and use of the Internet, reflecting the specific characteristics of the digital divide in each society.

The Internet plays the role of information provider to Muslims in Australia and the neighbouring countries of Indonesia, Malaysia and Singapore. The multiplicity of information available online has allowed Muslims to engage in constructive discourse within the bounds of *adab* (Islamic etiquette) about theological issues – for example *aqidah* (belief) and *fiqh* (jurisprudence) – as well news and current events. The Internet is a vital source of information on practical day-to-day matters to which Muslims must attend as believers in Islam, for instance in finding out mosque locations in unfamiliar cities, or looking for halal restaurants to eat in. The Internet also contains a plethora of additional resources from which Muslims can seek information relating to the Qur'an and hadith, although there may be skepticism about the use of the Internet as an information source on *Shariah*. The role played by the Internet in the daily life of Muslim students in Southeast Asia cannot be underestimated but the story of Muslims and their practice of Islam on the Internet is one that is still being written.

References

Abbas, D.T. (2007). 'Muslim minorities in Britain: integration, multiculturalism and radicalism in the post-7/7 period'. *Journal of Intercultural Studies*, *28*(3): 287–300.

Ahmad, F. (2006). 'British Muslim perceptions and opinions on news coverage of September 11'. *Journal of Ethnic and Migration Studies, 32*(6): 961–982.

Al-Momani, M. (2011). 'The Arab Youth Quake: Implications on Democratization and Stability'. *Middle East Law and Governance*, *3*(1–2): 1–2.

Anderson, B. (1991). *Imagined Communities*. London: Verso Books.

Bahfen, N. (2008). 'Modems, Malaysia and Modernity: Characteristics and Policy Challenges in Internet-led Development'. In: *Internationalizing Internet Studies: Beyond Anglophone Paradigms*. G. Goggin and M. McLelland (eds.) New York: Routledge.

Banaji, S. and Al-Ghabban, A. (2006). 'Neutrality comes from inside us: British-Asian and Indian perspectives on television news after 11 September'. *Journal of Ethnic and Migration Studies, 32*(6):1005–1026.

Barlow, H.S. (1997). 'Malaysia – Swettenham's legacy'. *Asian Affairs, 28*(3): 325–334.

Baumann, G. and Gingrich, A. (Eds.). (2004). *Grammars of Identity/Alterity: A Structural Approach* (Vol. 3). Oxford: Berghahn Books.

Buhle, P. (2006). *Jews in American Popular Culture*. Westport: Praeger.

Bunt, G.R. (1999). 'islam@britain.net: "British Muslim" identities in cyberspace'. *Islam and Christian-Muslim Relations, 10*(3): 353–362.

Cheong, P.H. (2008). 'The young and techless? Investigating Internet use and problem-solving behaviors of young adults in Singapore'. *New Media and Society, 10*(5): 771–791.

Chokoshvili, D. (2011). *The Role of the Internet in Democratic Transition: Case Study of the Arab Spring* (Doctoral dissertation, Central European University).

Clark, D.J., Frith, K.H., and Demi, A.S. (2004). 'The physical, behavioral, and psychosocial consequences of Internet use in college students'. *Computers Informatics Nursing, 22*(3): 153–161.

Couper, M.P., Kapteyn, A., Schonlau, M., and Winter, J. (2007). 'Noncoverage and nonresponse in an Internet survey'. *Social Science Research, 36*(1): 131–148.

Echchaibi, N. (2009). 'Hyper-Islamism? Mediating Islam from the halal website to the Islamic talk show'. *Journal of Arab and Muslim Media Research, 1*(3): 199–214.

Eng, P. (1998). 'A new kind of cyberwar'. *Columbia Journalism Review, 37*(3): 20–22.

Gan, S. (2002). 'Virtual democracy in Malaysia'. *Nieman Reports, 56*(2): 65–67.

George, C. (2003). 'The Internet and the narrow tailoring dilemma for Asian democracies'. *Communication Review, 6*(3): 247–268.

Granello, D.H. and Wheaton, J.E. (2004). 'On-line data collection: strategies for research'. *Journal of Counseling and Development, 82*(4): 387–393.

Haniff, G.M. (2003). 'The Muslim community in America: A brief profile'. *Journal of Muslim Minority Affairs, 23*(2): 303–311.

Hashim, R. and Yusof, A. (1999). Internet in Malaysia. *Informatik Forum*, Wien, Austria.

Hill, D.T. and Sen, K. (2002). 'Netizens in combat: conflict on the Internet in Indonesia'. *Asian Studies Review, 26*(2): 165–189.

Ho, S.S., Lee, W., and Hameed, S.S. (2008). 'Muslim surfers on the Internet: Using the theory of planned behaviour to examine the factors influencing engagement in online religious activities'. *New Media and Society, 10*(1): 93–113.

Hodge, B. (2003). 'How the medium is the message in the unconscious of "America Online"'. *Visual Communication, 2*(3): 341–353.

Holmes, L. and Grieco, M. (2001). 'The Internet, email, and the Malaysian political crisis: the power of transparency'. *Asia Pacific Business Review, 8*(2): 59–72.

Jones, S. (2002). 'The Internet Goes to College: How Students Are Living in the Future with Today's Technology'. Pew Internet and American Life Project, 15 September 2002.

Kalathil, S. (2003). 'Dot com for dictators'. *Foreign Policy,* March–April (135): 42–45.

Kennedy, G.E., Judd, T.S., Churchward, A., Gray, K., and Krause, K. (2008). 'First year students' experiences with technology: Are they really digital natives'. *Australasian Journal of Educational Technology, 24*(1): 108–122.

Lai, A.E. (2003). 'Introduction'. In: *Beyond rituals and riots: ethnic relations and social cohesion at a time of uncertainty.* A.E. Lai (ed.) Singapore: Eastern University Press.

Latour, B. and Venn, C. (2002). 'Morality and Technology The End of the Means'. *Theory, Culture and Society, 19*(5–6): 247–260.

Lerner, Heidi G. (2009). 'Internet resources for researching orthodox Judaism'. *Journal of Religious and Theological Information, 7*(3): 161–169.

Leth, G. (2005). The construction of indifference: the Swedish Press and the 'Reichskristallnacht'. Conference Papers – International Communication Association, 1–24.

Lim, M. (2004). 'Informational terrains of identity and political power: the Internet in Indonesia'. *Indonesian Journal of Social and Cultural Anthropology, 27*(73): 1–11.

Livio, O. and Weinblatt, K.T. (2007). 'Discursive legitimation of a controversial technology: ultra-orthodox Jewish women in Israel and the Internet'. *Communication Review, 10*(1): 29–56.

McLuhan, M. and Fiore, Q. (1967). *The Medium is the Mass Age, an Inventory of Effects*. New York: Bantam Books.

Madden, G. and Savage, S.J. (2000). 'R&D spillovers, information technology and telecommunications, and productivity in ASIA and the OECD'. *Information Economics and Policy, 12*(4): 367–392.

Mahathir, M. (1999). 'Malaysia on track for 2020 vision'. *Perdana Leadership Foundation,* Accessed July 2008, from http://www.perdana.org.my/antarctica/?newsid=5287.

Martin, P. and Phelan, S. (2002). 'Representing Islam in the wake of September 11: a comparison of US television and CNN online messageboard discourses'. *Prometheus 20*(3): 263–269.

Miladi, N. (2008). 'Mediating wars and conflicts: North African TV audiences in the UK and the changing security landscape'. *Journal of Arab and Muslim Media Research 1*(3): 245–257.

Moses, A. (2008). 'Net censorship plan backlash'. *Sydney Morning Herald* 11 November 2008.

Ng, K.H. (2002). 'Seeking the Christian tutelage: Agency and culture in Chinese immigrants' conversion to Christianity'. *Sociology of Religion, 63*(2): 195–214.
Peek, L. (2005). 'Becoming Muslim: The development of a religious identity'. *Sociology of Religion, 66*(3): 215–242.
Sani, M.A.M. (2005). 'Media freedom in Malaysia'. *Journal of Contemporary Asia, 35*(3): 341–367.
Schmidt, G. (2004). 'Islamic identity formation among young Muslims: the case of Denmark, Sweden and the United States'. *Journal of Muslim Minority Affairs, 24*(1): 31–45.
Smith, J.I. (2002). *Muslim Minorities in the West: Visible and Invisible*. Walnut Creel: Altamira Press.
Stratton, J. (2005). 'Buffy the Vampire Slayer: what being Jewish has to do with it'. *Television and New Media, 6*(2): 176–199.
Tornquist, O. (2000). 'Dynamics of Indonesian democratisation'. *Third World Quarterly, 21*(3): 383–424.
Van der Laan, J.M. (2009). 'How the Internet shapes religious life, or the medium is itself the message'. *Bulletin of Science Technology and Society, 29*(4): 272–277.
Wang, G. (1999). 'Regulating network communication in Asia: a different balancing act?' *Telecommunications Policy, 23*(3/4): 277–287.
Willis, S. and Tranter, B. (2006). 'Beyond the "digital divide": Internet diffusion and inequality in Australia'. *Journal of sociology, 42*(1): 43–59.
Yablon, Y.B. (2007). 'Feeling close from a distance: peace encounters via Internet technology', *New Directions for Youth Development, 2007*(116): 99–107.
Zine, J. (2008). 'Muslim youth in Canadian schools: Education and the politics of religious identity'. *Anthropology and Education Quarterly, 32*(4): 399–423.

Chapter 2
Migrants, Mobiles and Money: Alterity and the Confluence of Three Transnational Flows

Fernando Paragas

Since 1974, when the government started the official deployment of Filipinos in overseas destinations, migrant work has become a fixture in contemporary Philippine landscape. In 2012, according to the Philippine Overseas Employment Administration (POEA), 1.8 million Filipinos were deployed abroad, of whom nearly half a million were new hires.

Migrant workers have traditionally been at the periphery of global capitalism since their labor is cheaper than for capital or information to move across borders. From the purview of Philippine policy, the export of labor was also supposed to be only a short-term measure to address rising unemployment and currency flow deficits. Indeed, there was stigma attached to migrant labor because it reflected the government's inefficacy in finding work for its citizens and because most of its workers were engaged in predominantly semi-skilled and skilled work. Accordingly, there was little in terms of social support, labor rights, and industry services for those employed in migrant work. However, the increasing complexity and profitability of migrant employment in the last two decades has resulted in a new government rhetoric which has espoused migrant workers as the country's modern-day heroes. Greater consciousness about the travails of migrant workers, particularly in light of high-profile cases of abuse and distress, has led to international policies that protect and promote migrant workers' rights.

Both rhetoric and policy have helped improve migrant workers' positioning in Philippine society. Beyond this macro-level, top-down impetus, however, migrant workers' actions, through formal participation in organizations or informally through their patterns of behavior, have arguably resulted in an alterity both of themselves and the government and industries which have sought to support them, primarily because of their significant contributions to Philippine business and economics. This chapter investigates this alterity in migrant work through the intersections of labor flows, communication flows through mobile telephony, and monetary flows through remittances. These flows are important because as the demographics of the migrant workforce have changed, so have the communication technologies they use to communicate with their partners and the means with which they send money from host to home countries. Moreover, inasmuch as most migrant workers go abroad to improve their family's economic status, such engagement involves the discussion of how income remittances are sent, received, spent, and saved.

Thus, through the use of various technologies, the workers and their communication partners maintain and nurture their relationships and seek to mitigate the social costs of being distanced from each other. Indeed, in the last 35 years, migrant workers have shifted the preferred medium for their transnational exchange of messages from postal mail to fixed telephony to mobile communications. The latest shift towards mobile telephony is particularly important because it facilitates constant contact across territories. Moreover, whereas before mobile phones only served as a communication medium for this fiscal discourse, new mobile phone financial services for remittances are transforming mobile phones as media for money as well.

Research Questions

Chong and Yahya write in the introduction that "alterity in the cases of diasporic communication and the roles of the developmental state in fostering communication modernization may well reveal the *centrality of authoritarian politics in determining the extent of embrace of electronic media* within transnational and national contexts" (p. 25). Indeed, the Philippine state in its efforts to modernize the country's telecom industry has prioritized the landline infrastructure, without much success (Paragas, 2012; Sussman, 1991). Instead, the public in general and migrant workers in particular, have instead opted to use mobile phones, rendering the landline network largely underutilized. This shift towards mobile telephony is particularly important because it facilitates micro-coordination (Ling and Yttri, 2003) across territories. This research thus explores how new services for cross-country remittances, from the purview of migrant workers, imbue mobile telephony among migrant workers with the possibility of a new dimension of alterity:

How are mobile phones located in the everyday lives of migrant workers? How are financial issues discussed over the mobile phone? What do they think about remitting money over the mobile phone?

By answering these questions, the research is able to examine how migrant workers use the mobile phone to negotiate their role as their family's earner and manager of income now that requests for money can now be made and answered through a text or a phone call. It is also able to explore the extent to which the intersections among the flows of labor, communication, and finances as mediated by mobile telephony have resulted in alterities in their migrant work. In particular, the chapter argues that alterity is strong, nuanced, or weak depending upon the profundity and universality of changes and implications from these intersections on issues such as daily interactions, financial dynamics, gender roles, and the social uses and conceptions of technology.

Methodology

This research uses in-depth interviewing given its focus on how people use mobile phones. It is the appropriate technique for data collection because, as Jensen (2002) writes,

> in-depth interviewing, with its affinities to conversations, may well be suited to tap social agents' perspective on the media, since spoken language remains a primary and familiar mode of social interaction, and one that people habitually relate to the technological media. (p. 240)

In-depth interviewing also solicited greater detail and a higher level of disclosure among the informants than other methods could. Moreover, since the intersection between mobile phones and financial services is an emergent topic, there is limited literature on which to ground a quantitative study.

Interviews were conducted by senior undergraduate students in the Communication Research program at the University of the Philippines. Interviews began with a uniform stating that introduced the topic, ensured informants' anonymity, and sought their informed consent. Accordingly, all names in this article are pseudonyms. Interviews followed a semi-structured interview guide with a demographic profile sheet and the following sections: life and work abroad and in the Philippines, remittance process to the Philippines, the role of mobile phones in migrant life, migrant work and financial issues. The interviews were conducted in a combination of Filipino and English. The verbatim data were coded into matrices to facilitate thematic coding. The quotations here are translations by the author.

Interviews were conducted online, using instant messaging. Because all informants were current overseas workers who were living abroad, it would have been expensive to interview them over the telephone since each interview lasted around an hour. The use of instant messaging also allowed for the automatic archiving of conversations. There was initially some concern about the use of online interviewing since Internet use among migrant workers was skewed towards higher-income professionals. However, because remittance services over mobile phones are new, their early adopters, in line with the Theory of Diffusion of Innovations (Rogers, 2005), are more likely to be using technologies which are more advanced than their colleagues do. Indeed, caregivers and domestic workers, who less likely used the Internet for their transnational communication, were among the interviewees.

A total of 30 informants were interviewed for this study. They were purposefully selected using maximum variation sampling. This ensured a diversity of informants according to sex, age, marital status, host country, work, and income—the six variables which significantly differentiate the different demographic groupings of OFWs (overseas Filipino workers) (Paragas, 2009).

Table 2.1 Profile of informants

Pseudonym	Gender	Age	Marital Status	Host Country	Work	Income
Alex	Male	27	Married	Qatar	Accountant	750
Andres	Male	30	Married	USA	Caregiver	3,000
Angela	Female	55	Married	Italy	Domestic Worker	2,250
Anne	Female	26	Single	KSA	Medical Technologist	750
Claire	Female	26	Single	Japan	Process Engineer	1,000
Danny	Male	33	Married	Japan	Plant Engineer	1,800
Dina	Female	40	Married	Kuwait	Domestic Worker	1,750
Edna	Female	25	Single	Japan	Process Engineer	1,500
Ellen	Female	53	Married	Japan	Factory Worker	750
Francis	Male	41	Married	USA	Telecom Engineer	5,000
Gabriel	Male	36	Married	Germany	Second Deck Officer	5,000
George	Male	39	Married	Singapore	Electrician	2,750
Gina	Female	23	Single	UAE	Salesclerk	1,250
Jane	Female	40	Single	Japan	Electrical Engineer	1,750
Jasmine	Female	26	Single	Singapore	System Analyst	1,750
Joel	Male	45	Married	KSA	Inventory Officer	750
John	Male	49	Married	S Korea	Researcher	1,250
Leo	Male	33	Married	UAE	Finance Manager	2,250
Lourdes	Female	30	Single	USA	Teacher	3,500
Luisa	Female	29	Single	Belgium	Domestic Worker	1,250
Mark	Male	26	Married	Qatar	Auditor	1,250
Michelle	Female	26	Single	Italy	Nanny	500
Mila	Female	38	Married	Italy	Domestic Worker	1,250
Nick	Male	26	Single	Singapore	Finance Associate	1,750
Norma	Female	43	Married	Malaysia	Domestic Worker	1,250

Pseudonym	Gender	Age	Marital Status	Host Country	Work	Income
Oliver	Male	23	Single	Japan	Equipment Engineer	1,250
Pearl	Female	56	Married	Japan	Domestic Worker	2,800
Rudy	Male	29	Single	KSA	Clerk	750
Sheila	Female	27	Single	UAE	Nurse	1,750
Victoria	Female	28	Married	Hong Kong	Domestic Worker	1,750

With the emergence of mobile Internet and the popularity of social media, Facebook pages were also studied to test whether the proposed alterity continuum remains applicable to the evolving nature of mediated content and its exchange among migrant workers. Keywords such as "OFW," "overseas Filipino workers," and "migrant workers" were used to search for these online pages. Most popular pages were then studied as cases, together with their websites, if any.

Results And Discussion

Strong alterity: Migrant work and mobile phones

The 1989 National Telecommunication Development Plan (NTDP) focused on strengthening the landline network to address the backlog of one million unmet applications for a telephone line (Paragas, 2012; Sussman, 1991). However, by the time the landline infrastructure was built, mobile telephony had been introduced in the country and its use made accessible by pre-paid subscription schemes. Thus, contrary to governmental intent, mobile phones instead became the main medium for telephony and the Philippines became identified as the texting capital of the world. By 2001, mobile telephony had been considered such an integral part of Philippine society such that it was seen to have played a pivotal role in the ouster of the Philippine president (Paragas, 2005b; Pertierra, 2005; Pertierra, Ugarte, Pingol, Hernandez, and Dacanay, 2002).

Migrant workers were among the early adopters of mobile telephony in the late 90s since they could afford its usage fees and they found it as a viable instrument to keep in touch across borders (Pertierra, 2007; Paragas, 2005b). Mobile phones became the latest in a series of communication technologies which migrant workers have used to maintain and nurture relationships that have been rendered transnational by overseas employment (Tyner and Kuhlke, 2004). Migrant workers have shifted from letters and pictures sent by post (CIIR, 2003) to telephone calls (Benitez, 2006; Mahler, 2001; Panagakos and Horst, 2006; Parreñas, 2002) which Vertovec (2004) called the "social glue of globalization" (p. 219). Mobile phones have become the central medium for transnational communication because of their universality in both home and host countries, as studies in Jamaica (Horst and Miller, 2005; Horst, 2006) and El Salvador (Benitez, 2006) have shown. In host countries, meanwhile, mobile phone ownership and use patterns, unlike those for computer-based means of online communication, are not skewed towards higher income professionals (Paragas, 2009).

OFWs have not been able to optimize the Internet in their cross-border communications because of 1) infrastructural constraints in the landline network in the Philippines which the NTDP has only belatedly tackled and 2) poor personal access to and limited skills in devices required to access the wired Internet. The introduction of Internet-enabled smart phones addressed both issues and, as a result, has expanded the utility of online communications among migrant workers.

That mobile phones provide all sectors of the increasingly diverse migrant worker pool with equivalent communication access is important particularly for those who labor in private places as domestic workers and caregivers (Lan, 2003). Heretofore, these workers, especially those who have become victims of abuse and distress, have had little means to connect with individuals and organizations that can possibly help them. Workers who live with their co-workers and employers are also afforded a venue for private conversations, something which they did not have before when they could only use public phones or the company telephone.

Studies on mobile telephony can inform this choice of mobile phones for transnational communication. Through the perpetual contact (Katz and Aakhus, 2002) that mobile phones provide their users, migrant workers, for instance, are better able to micro-coordinate (Ling and Yttri, 2003) or hyper-coordinate (Campbell and Russo, 2003) the activities of their communication partners in the Philippines. This then leads to a sense of co-presence (Arminen, 2009) in which migrant workers who are absent in the Philippines are able to remain virtually involved in daily affairs there. Conversely, their families and friends there develop a sense of "ambient virtual co-presence" in which people have "an ongoing background awareness of others" (Ito and Okabe, 2005, p. 264 in Panagakos and Horst, 2006, p. 112). Pertierra (2005) referred to this as an "absent presence" in their original home communities" (p. 26).

Mobile phones were central in the transnational communications of almost all of the informants. The portability of mobile phones was in itself an alterity from the form of previous communication technologies and which also resulted in an alterity in the way migrant workers communicate between home and host societies. Rudy, a clerk in Saudi Arabia, said "I prefer cell phones because the old way is difficult. Nowadays it is faster. I do not call often. But I call if there's a birthday or when there's an occasion in the family." Alex, an accountant in Qatar, said "I keep in touch with them through mobile phone because it is the fastest way compared to snail mail. With mobile phones you are just one click away from your loved ones, as they say." Indeed, other informants noted how they shifted from landlines to mobile phones as they saw greater convenience with the newer technology.

Norma, a domestic worker in Malaysia, said "I contact my family through the cell phone because it is the most convenient. You can bring it anywhere." The handiness of the mobile was crucial for Gabriel, a Second Deck Officer, whose work was based in Germany but which required him to travel around the world. He said, "I use the cell phone when I am roaming because I can use SMS or make voice calls. Since I am often in the US and Hong Kong, I have bought SIM cards to use in my cell phone for both places to save money." This portability and the sense of connection which it brought, was important for Sheila: "I use the cell phone to keep in touch with my family and friends because I can carry it with me most of the time. It makes me connected to all sorts of information." Gina, meanwhile, contrasted the portability of mobile phones with another communication technology: "Roaming through the cell phone is the easiest because if you don't have a laptop you cannot chat from there. And you cannot be staying too long at computer shops."

Mobile phones have multiple uses, but the informants primarily used them for calling and texting. John, a researcher in Korea, said "I call because text messaging is cumbersome, especially if the message is long. For calls, you can easily cover many issues in a short time span although it is more expensive. There reverse is true for SMS." Three other informants also echoed the interplay between the price and the convenience of either texting or calling. Nick, a Finance Associate in Singapore, said, "We talk over the cell—calls if it is more urgent because they are more expensive; text is cheaper but sometimes they don't receive it or their reply is not as timely." Similarly, Danny, a Plant Engineer in Japan, said "I use text when I just want to check how they are but I call immediately when the topic is urgent and important." For Mark, meanwhile, the interplay is between the ease of making a call and the difficulties that attend texting: "Of course it is easier to call; my fingers get some rest. All of the things I want to talk about I can discuss in detail over a call. With text sometimes it gets cut and the person who receives it cannot understand it."

Beyond the alterity in form, the mobile phone also resulted in an alterity in migrant work relationships. Luisa, a domestic worker in Belgium, said she would call her mom and other relatives often because she "wants to know if they are ok and what is happening to them every time. I can hear that everybody is ok." The mobile phone was also an instrument through which affection is expressed daily. Norma, who had two children who were 12 years old and 20 years old respectively, said "I text them when I am free from work so I can let them feel that I remember them every moment and for them to know how important the cell phone is in our life." Mila, who worked in Italy, echoed this sentiment, "I call everyday even if only briefly, if only to kiss them. I miss kissing them. So even if only through the phone it is already ok." Three informants also alluded to this loneliness of a migrant workers' life who works away from the Philippines, and the ability of mobile phones to mitigate it. Joel, an Inventory Officer in Saudi Arabia, said "I send text messages because it is also easy. But if I really miss them and I want to hear their voice, I call them. But when I call and I am unable to reach them, and when what I need to say is really important, I text it so they can read it." Dina, meanwhile, said "I call when I want to speak to a particular person, to hear their voice."

In discussing their choice of medium to connect to their family members in the Philippines, the informants invariably underscored price concerns. Though many of them said phone calls were expensive, the informants said they were ultimately worth the cost, as Angela said, "While I think calling is better and used for urgent matters, it is really more expensive than texting. Still, I prefer calling." Joel echoed this, "Even if you say the Internet is cheaper and allows you to talk longer, the mobile phone is still better because you get to talk to each other." Spending on calls is an important concern given that the pursuit of money is at the center of migrant work.

Smart phones have reinforced the strong alterity of mobile phones in the migrant worker experience as they remove the dichotomy between the Internet and mobile phones, particularly in terms of cost and access concerns. Messaging apps such as Skype, Viber and Whatsapp when used with free Wi-Fi can enable cross-border communications without the recurring costs of a regular texting and voice calls. Bundled data plans which are required where there is no free Wi-Fi connections entail significantly lower costs when one compares the transmission of one bit of data (Allain, 2011).

The emergence of OFW pages in social media indicates the increasing importance of the Internet as a communication platform for migrant workers. In Facebook, for instance, the Pinoy OFW (2014) page has over one hundred thousand users, more than double its subscribers a year before. Moreover, over 2,000 of its users are active. Other pages such as Overseas Filipino Workers (2014) and OFW Masaya Kasama [Happy Together] (2014) respectively have 50,000 and 38,000 subscribers. Though membership is not limited to active OFWs, these pages enable those who have a stake in migrant work to share posts on politics, economics, social and phatic issues.

Nuanced alterity: Mobile-mediated micro-coordination of money

Aside from their regular communication, remittances are the other primary link between OFWs and their family and relatives in the Philippines. Remittances are important because it is the pursuit of higher income, even at the risk of downward social mobility, that drives migrant employment (Parreñas, 2001; Tacoli, 1999; Tyner, 2004). In 2008, overseas workers remitted US$22.8 billion to the Philippines, an amount which is approximately equal to eight per cent the country's gross domestic product (Chipongian, 2014). Their economic contributions have impelled governments and organizations in the Philippines and elsewhere to recognize migrant workers as the country's modern-day heroes and various organizations to capitalize on their monies (Horst, 2005; Paragas, 2006).

Indeed, studies have argued that these transnational remittances have resulted in various alterities. Specifically, studies have argued how remittances allow women "to produce, appropriate and distribute surplus labour in innovative ways" (Gibson, Law and McKay, 2001, p. 365), how they "progressively rework gender relations, support education and the acquisition of professional skills and facilitate local community development" (Vertovec, 2001, p. 575), or how they enable "the stimulation of change within a variety of sociocultural institutions" (Vertovec, 2004b, p. 985). Other studies, however, indicated that far from these utopian assertions, remittances do not result in a significant alterity of migrant workers' lives. At the grassroots level, for instance, Tacoli (1999) noted that her respondents, both males and females, had little say on the use of their remittances. After all, remittances were used primarily for basic needs (Anderson, 2001; Vertovec, 2004b), with the rest going to housing and healthcare (Sampson, 2003; Vertovec, 2004b), the education of children or siblings (Krinks, 2002; Sampson, 2003; Tacoli, 1999; Vertovec, 2004b), and the repayment of debts incurred before or during the recruitment process (Krinks, 2002).

Accordingly, the interviews in this study the extent to which alterity has transpired because of the migrant workers' use of mobile phones to micro-coordinate (Ling and Yttri, 2003) their remittances. Micro-coordination transpires when the remittance is attended by an extensive correspondence, by voice calls and/or text messages, on how the money it to be spent. It is differentiated from simply remitting the money with minimal instructions on how it is to be budgeted.

According to the informants, their main conversation partners were also usually the caretakers of their remittances. These partners were generally within the immediate family: spouses, children, parents, and siblings. In this context, therefore, there was no alterity. However, on the other hand, the alterity transpired insofar as the spouse who was left behind did not automatically assume the role of financial manager in the Philippines. In the case of four of the married female migrant workers, finances within the nuclear family became an affair of the extended family. Pearl, a mother of four, said it was her sister who would receive her remittances but she would provide her with specific instructions over the phone. Norma, who had two children, said her mother "usually takes care of the finances of the children because she is with my children all the time and my husband is also working." Norma would call her family and tell them "to prioritize those bills which need to be paid such as the utilities and the tuition fees. Only after there are leftover funds could they buy other things." Such instructions, she said, were important because it was her way for her children to realize the difficulties she faces at work and for them to become responsible with her remittances.

Angela, who had four children, and Ellen, who had three children, both discussed their remittances with their eldest sons. Angela said she would call her family "with specific instructions and ask them to keep the receipt. In case I have questions then they will need to send it to me. I think I have a healthy control, because I do give them instructions and they follow them." Ellen ultimately decided to entrust the finances to his son because her husband did not know how to budget their money. Her efforts to instruct her family on what to do with the remittances also became a sore point before his son became her fund manager at home. She said her family "did not want to hear me questioning where exactly the money went and how much exactly was being spent for particular expenses." She added that "we often argued over the phone since after I would call them to tell them that I would be sending money soon, the next call I would receive would be a surprise telling me that the money was not enough and that I had to send more." Though Dina did not have problems with her husband's handling of her money, she echoed Ellen's frustration about the apparent inadequacy of her remittances despite her efforts at micro-managing their budget.

One unmarried female informant also said she micro-coordinated her remittance. Gina said she entrusted her father with her remittance but she would still call him with specific instructions because she wanted to manage her money. While her remittance was not big, she said "it is like a sign of respect for me that they report to me how the money is spent and how much has been deposited in the bank."

For other informants, the Internet, together with the mobile phone has resulted in an alterity about financial discussions. Sheila, who was single, said she and her father, who was their family treasurer, would always put everything in writing. She said this was their way "to discipline ourselves, to adhere to specific payment schemes." Sheila added that her family in the Philippines would even scan receipts and send these as email attachments to her. Similarly, Alex, who had two young boys, used emails to discuss finances. He said, "Financial matter is always discussed in a hierarchy of emails. In these emails, I have some specific instructions on which should be taken into priority. This is because without instructions and a system on financial issues, we will never move from our current position." Like Sheila, Alex used email attachments for financial matters. In his case, he and his wife would exchange Excel spreadsheets of the computation of their finances.

Informants also used a mix of media for their discussions. Jane said she would give instructions and a breakdown of how her remittance was to be spent through email, text, and chat. Michelle said she and her partner kept financial discussions simple. She said, "If it's something that needs to be paid for, then I send the money and she goes and pays for it, and just keeps the receipts for me and sends me an update via chat, SMS or phone call. I am kept informed by my partner."

Half of the informants did not micro-coordinate their remittances as said they did not give explicit instructions on finances. This indicated the extent to which alterity due to the use of communication technology relates with other values such as trust. Two unmarried female respondents said they remitted money to their parents with little instructions. Lourdes said, "I let them handle the money because I trust them so much. So much part of our communication is about the remittance but it is not a big deal because I am now the breadwinner." Luisa said she would send money to her mother because it was she "who took care of the problems there and so it is easy for her to manage it." While they talked about money over the phone, she did not say her family was doing a fiscal report to her because she already knew where the money would go and "they can decide without telling me because they know that they are doing."

Gabriel, Danny, and Leo, John, all married men, said their wives handled their finances, not unlike when they were working in the Philippines. For example, John said, "my wife runs the finances in the family even if I am home … I am not that concerned because I trust my wife. After remitting the money, I have no control over it anymore. And I can say that my family is spending my remittances wisely and judiciously." Like Luisa, George said that while he and his wife talked about financial matters, this was not tantamount to a report. "I do not need to be strict because they really just spend on the basics. We talk about it through the phone, rarely through instant messaging," he explained. Similarly, Mark would call her wife with no particular instructions except to say that the kids come first and to settle all monthly expenses.

A married woman, Victoria, said her husband managed her remittances for their family, which included their two young children. Like her male counterparts, she said she gave no instructions. But, unlike them, she seemed to be wistful about it. She said, "I give no specific instructions, and perhaps this is my mistake. It seems as if it is they who tell me what to do. And then all I do is to send more money."

Two informants said they did not discuss their remittance in depth so text messages were enough to talk about it. Anne said, "For me, money is money. You cannot bring it if you're dead. So if you have it, share it with your loved ones." Joel, meanwhile, said he and his wife, who handled their money, would usually talk about their family over the Internet and it was rare that they touched on their finances. Instead, his wife would simply text him a basic summary of expenses.

Social media have made public the heretofore personal discussion of remittances and related financial concerns. The Pinoy OFW Facebook page regularly posts topics on investments, financial scams, career development, and scholarships. Four of its ten most popular posts were related to loan schemes for livelihood and housing as well as contributions to the national social security and housing programs for privately employed individuals. Moreover, the main Pinoy OFW website, http://www.pinoy-ofw.com, provides additional information these topics. Its section on money remittance posts the prevailing currency exchange rates, provides advice on saving and investing money, and compares and contrasts different remittance processes. These articles do get shared in Facebook and Twitter, though they hardly generate comments from users.

Activist groups such as Migrante International have tried to move the online discussion of remittances to the public sphere by holding the Zero Remittance Day on 19 September 2013 (Ellao, 2013), the anniversary of the omnibus policy for migrant workers. The movement asked OFWs not to send money to the Philippines on that day to highlight the economic contributions of migrant workers and to protest of alleged misuse of the Priority Development Assistance Fund that is allocated to members of the legislature (Diaz, 2013). Though the movement received much coverage and commentary in the media, it did not generate significant support beyond Hong Kong, where OFWs have a history of staging protests. A subsequent rally in Manila on 22 September did not get the same traction as earlier indignation rallies against government corruption.

Weak alterity: The mobile phone as remittance medium

Overseas workers abroad can now remit money to the Philippines using their mobile phone. To avail themselves of the service, customers go to an outlet accredited by the mobile phone company to remit their money to a mobile phone number in the Philippines from various parts of the world. (The service is now available in key cities in Australia, Austria, Brunei, Canada, Greece, Hong Kong, Ireland, Italy, Japan, Korea, Malaysia, New Zealand, Palau, Qatar, Saudi Arabia, Spain, Singapore, Switzerland, Taiwan, United Arab Emirates, United Kingdom, and the United States.) Recipients then get a transaction confirmation through a text message which they can then present to accredited outlets for their money. It must be qualified that this is not purely a mobile phone transaction. First time users have to accomplish a registration form to use the service. Moreover, because there is no system that links bank accounts to mobile phones for this remittance facility, participating parties have to go physically to an accredited outlet to send and get their money. The remitted cash can also not be directly used to pay for other goods and services from the mobile phone itself.

This system is an expansion of a popular system in which mobile phone users can exchange load credits through texting. For example, users with extra credit can send their credit to other phones, especially those of pre-paid users whose credit balance is running low. Thus, money as a material object is disembodied in the purchase of phone credit and rendered transmittable to others. Money which heretofore was exchanged for a single subscription, or the operation of a single unit, can now help sustain many other units. Together with images and sounds, money has become embedded in mobile phones, ready for transmission. (Note: For Globe Telecommunications' Share-a-load, pre-paid users can remit up to PhP300.00 (US$6.00), and post-paid users can remit up to PhP500.00 (US$10.00). For Smart Communications' *Pasaload* [Pass-a-load], users can remit up to PhP300.00 (US$6.00). Each transaction has an average charge of PhP2.00 (US$ 0.04).)

Before the introduction of these services, communication and remittances have had an indirect link as the two dominant flows for transnational families. On one hand, they are facilitated by different technologies. On the other hand, however, they are engaged in reflexivity: remittances fund the costs entailed in international calls while such calls serve to discuss remittances. Recent innovations in technology, however, have merged these flows into the mobile phone, providing a new layer of the alterity potential of mobile telephony.

The remittance of money via the mobile phone presents opportunities and pitfalls for migrant workers. By merging remittances and communication, the new system affords them with a unified system to exchange money and messages, enabling them to send money and talk about how to spend it almost simultaneously.

This greater control of their money can perhaps lead to more productive uses of remittances as conceptualized in literature. Conversely, however, the constancy of mobile communication and the expediency with which money may be remitted over the phone may open migrant workers to greater and more frequent requests for remittances.

Studies in Finland show that age and gender significantly differentiate adoption of m-banking, with younger customers and men more likely to use it (Laukkanen and Pasanen, 2008). Moreover, younger people who earn well in good jobs do not see as much risk in m-banking as other people do (Laukkanen, Sinkkonen, Laukkanen, and Kivijarvi, 2008). Younger people also felt more secure with the use of personal identification numbers in accessing their m-banking accounts (Laukkanen, Sinkkonen, Kivijarvi, and Laukkanen, 2008). The issue of security is particularly important in the adoption of m-banking, together with issues of costs and perceived complexity (Laukkanen and Pasanen, 2008). The positive attributes of m-banking, meanwhile, include its location-free nature and the immediacy and convenience in its performance (Laukkanen and Pasanen, 2008; Laukkanen and Lauronen, 2005).

The availability of remittance services over the mobile phone means the two dominant transnational flows (messages and money) in the migrant work experience can now transpire across mobile phones through a load crediting system. However, almost all of the informants were either not keen or knowledgeable about the service, indicating perhaps a limit to the possible alterity in the use of mobile phones for financial transactions. Even the convergence of the Internet and mobile phones in smart phones has done little to promote the use of direct mobile remittances. Instead, growth is projected only in mobile banking (Lowe, 2013), in which the mobile phone is an instrumental rather than an intrinsic part of the remittance process.

All the informants remitted their money through either wire transfer or bank-to-bank transfer. They found these systems credible, safe, and stable, unlike newer remittance services such as those via the mobile phone, as Mark, Joel, Victoria, and John said. In particular, John noted that "I have heard and read about it but I am not curious about using it. I am more confident using bank remittance where my wife can receive the amount I am sending within minutes after remitting." Mark echoed this, "I heard that before but I never tried because I have a bank account which is very safe." Joel qualified, "Perhaps the time will come I might have to send money through the mobile phone but I am not that positive about it. It is not that I don't trust it. It is just that I already have my standard practices with bank-to-bank transfer." Victoria said the service "has just been introduced and it is not that credible yet. Also, unlike Western Union, it does not have many outlets." Ellen, meanwhile, preferred and trusted door-to-door courier service as it had not failed her at all.

The trepidation over the new technology is also rooted on the informants' strong sense of caution. Andres said he was afraid of being duped because he said there were a lot of people who would try to fool others. "It is better to be cautious," he said. Luisa and Dina had heard of the service, but felt quite uncomfortable about how it was administered. Dina explained, "I have not used it at all because I may only be tricked by it." Claire, meanwhile, said "I don't want to risk my money. It might go to waste. It is a good innovation but I guess not as reliable and safe compared to a bank."

The informants also expressed fears about the possible failure of technology. Lourdes said that she also did not trust online banking where she would simply call the bank to transfer money as she felt this was not safe. "It is just that I would rather deal with safe measures," she said. Oliver, meanwhile, knew how mobile remittances worked but feared the system could be hacked or erroneously sent to someone else." This sentiment was echoed by George, "I have not tried it because I don't need it. It does not seem to have security features. If it is only through text, nobody can prove you have sent the money."

That the current service still required customers to go to banks also defeated the itinerant feature of mobile phones. Gabriel said he was not interested in the service because it required the opening of an account with the telecom company, which would then only duplicate his bank account. Nick and Gina, meanwhile, said there was no need for the service because customers still needed to go to a bank to withdraw the money then to bring the money to the mobile phone company's outlet. Alex noted these duplications as well as the possibility of hidden deductions by the participating banks. However, he qualified that it might be a good service for "people in a very tight schedule and always on the run. In the urgency of the remittance, this is feasible."

Some informants such as Francis, Jane, Rudy, Norma, Danny, and Michelle said they only had a vague idea about the service and would need more information about it. Francis said, "it seems like a good idea but they need to explain it thoroughly first." Danny said, "I don't know the pros and cons of the procedures. Only when it is as well tested as online banking would I consider using it." Michelle had a similar reply, "I would think unless we can perfect the system of being able to send simple text messages and ensure that the recipients get them, and then this may be something that would need to be explored a bit further before I actually get around to using it."

There is reason for concerns about mobile phone remittance systems. Pinoy-OFW (2011), for instance, recommends using mobile phones for remittances, but its links for the two biggest service providers, Smart Communications' *Padala* [Remit] http://www1.smart.com.ph/money/ and Globe's *Gcash* http://www.globe.com.ph/gcash/, did not work. The websites of either provider works well and provides comprehensive overviews of the nature and processes of mobile remittances. However, the transitory nature of links can undo the perceived stability of such services. Moreover, either service is not present in social media. In Facebook, for instance, the keywords Globe Gcash results in a page where Globe Sucks serves as the profile image. Of the several Smart Padala pages in Facebook, meanwhile, none was the official page from Smart Communications.

Only a couple of informants were favorable to the idea of mobile remittances. Pearl said the idea appealed to her because "you have to wait for banking hours to send money. With mobile phones you can easily send money." Leo said his business in the Philippines was actually engaged in mobile remittances and vouched that the service was credible and charged lower service fees compared to wire and bank transfer services.

Conclusion and Implications

The nuances in alterity discussed in this paper indicate how migrant workers work within, or seek to challenge, existing structures. These nuances then inform the ability and the motivation of migrant workers to effect changes in their lives and their community which transcend their roles in their family and at work.

Starting in 1989 with the deregulation of the Philippine telecom industry (Paragas, 2012; Sussman, 1991), migrant workers were presented with two options for mediated communication: landline telephony in which the government had invested heavily or mobile telephony which the industry had started to provide and prioritize. Migrant workers opted for the latter and it was their patronage of the industry which helped diffuse mobile telephony among Filipinos in the Philippines or abroad. Because the industry leveraged on mobile telephony by providing pre-paid payment schemes and lower subscription rates which made services affordable to the public, any alterity that could be imputed from mobile telephony was a product not of the state, but of the industry and the public. The collective patterns of use by migrant workers of mobile phones have since resulted in the continuing launch of products and services by telecom companies which seek to cater to the specific needs of migrant workers and their family members. This development then shows how migrant workers can render themselves visible as an audience for business and industry. One must remember, however, that appropriation that leads to alterity is primarily driven by migrant workers as two remittance-centered cases in this study shows. Not because OFW social media communities have emerged online means they can easily be harnessed by activist groups for pro-social initiatives. Moreover, mobile remittance systems that cater specifically for migrant workers do not readily have a ready consumer base if they are not able to compete on an equal footing with current providers of similar services.

The mobile phone in itself represents an alterity in the array of communication technologies of migrant workers. Previous ways of communicating across borders such as letters and cassette tapes sent via postal mail resulted in asynchronous communication and reinforced the temporal and spatial distance between the host and home countries of migrant workers. Access to and the use of landline phones, which could facilitate synchronous communication, were inconvenient for most migrant workers who lived in spaces shared with other workers or their employers. Moreover, because of the inefficiencies in the Philippine telecom industry, the country did not have a viable landline system until the late 1990s, during which time mobile phones were already being introduced. Mobile phones thus became the main mode of mediated interpersonal communication (Benitez, 2006; Levitt and Schiller, 2004; Panagakos and Horst, 2006) as they afforded transnational perpetual contact (Katz and Aakhus, 2002). Likewise, mobile phones as a handy and personal device which accompanied people everywhere provided migrant workers the privacy and immediacy which landline phones did not.

Interestingly, by enabling this temporal synchronicity, mobile phones helped realize an alterity towards an approximation of life before the spatial separation between migrant workers and their family. In other words, the alterity was, it could be argued, a technologically-enabled co-presence (Arminen, 2009) or "absent presence" (Pertierra, 2005) which was impossible among migrant workers before given the communication platforms at their disposal prior to their adoption of the mobile phone. This co-presence, or the idea that someone was virtually present even if he were physically absent, helped mitigate the loneliness that attended the separated living arrangements of migrant workers and their family. However, because migrant workers primarily used voice calls and text messages, the possible alterity from mobile phones' many other features—such as the exchange of multi-media messages and the use of video calls which could facilitate visual co-presence—was not fully realized. Smart phones, as the convergence of the Internet and mobile phones, can perhaps enrich the practice of co-presence as they are less bound by the infrastructural, cost, and skills concerns that have heretofore prevented migrant workers from fully utilizing mobile phones.

Remittances, which realized migrant workers' goal to earn a higher income abroad and to improve the socio-economic status of their family in the Philippines (Parreñas, 2001; Tacoli, 1999; Tyner, 2004), were another way in which migrant workers nurtured co-presence in the home country. Tacoli (1999) wrote migrant workers had little say in the use of remittances because of traditionally-ingrained norms in which parents provided for their children. Moreover, migrant workers who were single or who were wives deferred to their father or their husband as the family's main provider even if they were essentially the family's breadwinners. However, even if workers wanted to exercise greater control over the remittances then, it was not practical in the absence of avenues for constant communication. Remittances during the time Tacoli wrote her paper were transmitted across borders much more expediently compared to messages.

The intersection of migrant work and mobile telephony indeed showed significant repercussions on family communication. Did this intersection, however, facilitate subsequent changes in familial dynamics, particularly with respect to family finances? The answer to this question was two-pronged. On the one hand, because of mobile phones, migrant workers were able to discuss how their remittances were to be spent. Even if the migrant workers knew their monthly expenses were basic (Anderson, 2001; Sampson, 2003 Vertovec, 2004b) and recurring, they still provided instructions on which items to prioritize as an assertion of their role as breadwinner and as indication of respect for them. On the other hand, even with mobile phones, others did not detail how their remittances were spent, neither for lack of interest nor control. Indeed, for this group, their deep sense of trust on the people they chose to handle the remittances superseded the opportunity to discuss finances over the mobile phone. The continuum of experiences here indicates the limitations in the transformative potential of mobile telephony with respect to the finances. Talk over mobile phones simply reinforced patterns of behavior among migrant workers as greater coordination did not automatically involve a more nuanced discussion of the use of money and the shared responsibility of how to handle finances. However, smart phones may change the nature and intensity of such discussions as they allow access to online content about remittances and finances. This information can trigger conversations about savings and investments, topics transcend recurring expenses.

The changing profile of the migrant workforce, which now comprise a majority of women, was seen as a foundation for the reworking of gender roles (Gibson, Law and McKay, 2001) and relations (Vertovec, 2001) in Philippine society where traditionally men served as breadwinners and women served as the managers of domesticity in the family. The changes in gender roles were particularly true for the married female migrant workers who found themselves with the dual roles in nurturing the emotional welfare of the family, which they performed through the mobile phone, while assuming the additional role of earning the family's main keep.

Contrary to expectations that women's role in the family would change as they became migrant workers or as wives assumed the role of the head of the family once their husbands are deployed abroad, findings indicated that little alterity in gender dynamics for three reasons. Firstly, female migrant workers felt some resentment against their attempts to control their money or they felt quite helpless implementing this control. Secondly, the husbands of the female migrant workers generally did not assume domestic obligations. Instead, it was the other women or the older children in the family who served as the receiver of migrant workers' communications and remittances. Thirdly, married male migrant workers maintained their customary role as main breadwinner and their wives continued to be the custodians of the household. The minute difference as regards male workers was the desire among some to compensate for their absence by expressing their emotions towards their family more vividly over the mobile phone.

Finally, the facility to remit over mobile phones was a merger between the two dominant transnational flows of messages and money in the migrant work experience. It also extended the possible alterity in migrant workers' finances as these related to mobile phones. However, the migrant workers' numerous apprehensions about it indicated trepidation over technological innovation (Laukkanen, Sinkkonen, Kivijarvi, and Laukkanen, 2008); even one that was introduced in a medium which was as deeply integrated as the mobile phone was in the migrant workers' lives. The competent performance of wire and bank transfer gave migrant workers limited reasons to try alternatives in remitting their money. Moreover, caution took precedence over adoption in the light of limited understanding, worries over technological failure, and the undue duplication of standard practices. Finally, the currently physical nature of mobile phone remittances defeated the location-free benefits of m-banking (Laukkanen and Pasanen, 2008; Laukkanen and Lauronen, 2005). Given the study's findings that mobile telephony emerged from the interaction between industry and the public, the enrichment of alterity from the mobile phone's value-added services would thus emanate from the congruence between what the public appropriates and what the industry provides. Mobile phone companies need to partner with established banks, make transactions location-free, and target men and younger customers (Laukkanen and Pasanen, 2008) if remittances via mobile phones were to get widespread support from migrant workers. This can help dispel notions about the seemingly transitory nature of online services.

In conclusion, alterity at the intersection of migrant labor, mobile communication, and remittances showed the normative tendencies of migrant workers. Alterity was strongest where it was most basic—emphatic communication which maintains familial relations. It was also strongest when there was impetus to find an alternative, as it was with the preference of mobile over landline telephony or other media. Conversely, it was weakest when current practices were seen as reliable and credible and precluded the need to find an alternative. This was the case with the use and potential of mobile phones as remittance media.

Where the intersection sought to transgress the status quo and the issues became more complex, the possibility of alterity became weaker. Micro-coordination of daily life in particular did not significantly dwell on remittances, which was surprising since money was the key driver behind migrant work. Instead, migrant workers maintained their old patterns of behavior, particularly when gender relations came into play. Thus, mobile telephony redefined the medium and perpetuity of normative communication among migrant workers but has not had as much impact on how finances could be discussed and gendered family roles could be transgressed. However, the emergence of smart phones holds some promise as they enable online information and services to mediate in the traditional dyadic flow of migrant worker communication.

References

Allain, R., 2011. How much does your data cost? *Wired,* [online] 21 June. Available at: <http://www.wired.com/wiredscience/2011/06/how-much-does-your-data-cost/> [Accessed 23 March 2014].

Anderson, B., 2001. Different roots in common ground: transnationalism and migrant domestic workers in London. *Journal of Ethic and Migration Studies, 27*(4), pp.673–683.

Arminen, I., 2009. New reasons for mobile communication: Intensification of time-space geography in the mobile era. In: R. Ling and S. Campbell, eds. 2009. *The Reconstruction of Space and Time through Mobile Communication Practice*. Piscataway, NJ: Transaction Publishers. pp.89–108.

Benitez, J., 2006. Transnational dimensions of the digital divide among Salvadoran immigrants in the Washington DC metropolitan area. *Global Networks 6*(2), pp.181–199.

Catholic Institute for International Relations, 1987. *The labour trade: Filipino migrant workers around the world.* Nottingham: Russell Press Ltd.

Chipongian, L., 2014. 2013 remittances reach $22.8 billion. *Manila Bulletin,* [online] 18 February. Available at: <http://www.mb.com.ph/2013-remittances-reach-22–8-billion/> [Accessed 23 March 2014].

Donner, J., 2007. The rules of beeping: Exchanging messages via intentional "missed calls" on mobile phones. *Journal of Computer-Mediated Communication, 13*(1), pp.1–22.

Ellao, J.A., 2013. Migrants' group amplifies Zero Remittance Day with march to Mendiola. *Bulatlat,* [online] 22 September. Available at: <http://bulatlat.com/main/2013/09/22/migrants-group-amplifies-zero-remittance-day-with-march-to-mendiola/> [Accessed 23 March 2014].

Gibson, K., Law, L., McKay, D., 2001. Filipina Contract Migrants, Economic Activism and Class Transformations. *International Feminist Journal of Politics, 3*(3), pp.365–386.

Globe Gcash, 2012. Globe Gcash [Facebook]. 22 August. Available at <https://www.facebook.com/gcash.globe> [Accessed 23 March 2014].

Horst, H., 2006. The blessings and burdens of communication: cell phones in Jamaican transnational social fields. *Global Networks. 6*(2), pp.143–159.

Jensen, K.B., 2002. The qualitative research process. In: K.B. Jensen, ed. 2002. *A Handbook of Media and Communication Research.* London: Routledge. pp.235–253.

Katz, J. and Aakhus, M., 2002. *Perpetual contact: Mobile communication, private talk, public performance.* Cambridge: Cambridge University Press.

Krinks, P., 2002. *The Economy of the Philippines: Elites, inequalities and economic restructuring.* New York: Routledge.

Lan, P., 2003. Among Women: Migrant Domestics and Their Taiwanese Employees Across Generations. In: B. Ehrenreich and A.R. Hochschild, eds. *Global Woman: Nannies, Maids, and Sex Workers in the New Economy.* New York: Metropolitan Books. pp.169–189.

Laukkanen, T. and Lauronen, J., 2005. Consumer value creation in mobile banking services. *International Journal of Mobile Communication, 3*(4), pp.325–338.

Laukkanen, T. and Pasanen, M., 2008. Mobile banking innovators and early adopters: How they differ from other online users? *Journal of Financial Services Marketing, 13*(2), pp.86–94.

Laukkanen, T., Sinkkonen, S., Kivijarvi, M., and Laukkanen, P., 2008. Innovation resistance among mature consumers. *Journal of Consumer Marketing. 24*(7), pp.419–427.

Laukkanen, T., Sinkkonen, S., Laukkanen, P., and Kivijarvi, M., 2008. Segmenting bank customers by resistance to mobile banking. *International Journal of Mobile Communication, 6*(3), pp.309–320.

Levitt, P. and Schiller, N., 2004. Conceptualizing simultaneity: A transnational social field perspective on society. *International Migration Review, 38*(3), pp.1002–1039.

Ling, R. and Yttri, B., 2002. Hyper-coordination via mobile phones in Norway. In: J. Katz and M. Aakhus, eds. *Perpetual contact: Mobile communication, private talk, public performance.* Cambridge: Cambridge University Press. pp, 139–169.

Lowe, A. (2013). OFW remittances via online, mobile banking growing. *Rappler,* [online] 28 March. Available at: <http://www.rappler.com/business/24859-moneygram-ofw-remittance-via-online,-mobile-banking-growing> [Accessed 23 March 2014].

Macheroni, G., 2007. Global Nomads' Network and Mobile Sociality: Exploring new media uses on the move. *Information, Communication and Society, 10*(4), pp.527–546.

Overseas Filipino Workers, 2014. Overseas Filipino Workers Group [Facebook]. 23 March. Available at < https://www.facebook.com/ofw.page> [Accessed 23 March 2014].

Panagakos, A. and Horst, H., 2006. Return to Cyberia: technology and the social worlds of transnational migrants. *Global Networks. 6*(2), pp.109–124.

Paragas, F., 1999. *Distant Voices, Proximate Purses*. Unpublished manuscript, Newsweek-Asian Federation of Advertising Associations.

Paragas, F., 2005a. A Case Study on the Continuum of Landline and Mobile Phone Services in the Philippines. In: S.D. Kim, ed. *When Mobile Came: The Cultural and Social Impact of Mobile Communication.* Seoul, Korea: Communication Books. pp.178–197.

Paragas, F., 2005b. Migrant Mobiles: Cellular Telephony, Transnational Spaces, and the Filipino Diaspora. In: N. Kristof, ed. *The Global and the Local in Mobile Communication: Places, Images, People, Connections*. Vienna: Passagen-Verlag. pp.241–249.

Paragas, F., 2009. Migrant Workers, Mobile Phones, and Temporal and Spatial Simultaneity. In: R. Ling and S. Campbell, eds. *The Reconstruction of Space and Time through Mobile Communication Practice*. Piscataway, NJ: Transaction Publishers. pp.39–66.

Paragas, F., 2012. Systems framework to telecommunication policy: the Philippine experience, 1989–2009. *Info, 14*(2), pp.57–71.

Parrenas, R., 2001a. *Servants of globalization: Women, Migration and Domestic Work.* Stanford, CA: Stanford University Press.

Parrenas, R., 2001b. Mothering from a distance: Emotions, gender, and inter-generational relations in Filipino transnational families. *Feminist Studies, 27*(2), pp.361–390.

Parrenas, R., 2002. Human sacrifices. *Women's Review of Books, 19*(5), pp.16.

Pertierra, R., 2005. Mobile phones, identity and discursive intimacy. *Human Technology. 1*(1), pp.23–44.

Pertierra, R., 2007. *The Social Construction and Usage of Communication Technologies*. Quezon City: University of the Philippines Press.

Pertierra, R., Ugarte, E., Pingol, A., Hernandez, J., and Dancanay, N., 2002. *Txt-ing Selves.* Manila, Philippines: De la Salle University Press.

Philippine Overseas Employment Administration (POEA), 2012. *2008–2012 Overseas Worker Statistics.* [online] Available through: POEA Website <http://www.poea.gov.ph/stats/2012_stats.pdf>. [Accessed 23 March 2014].

Pinoy-OFW, 2011. 7 Money Remittance, Money Transfer Tips for OFWs. *Pinoy-OFW,* [online] 16 September. Available at: <http://www.pinoy-ofw.com/news/10937-money-remittance-money-transfer-tips.html> [Accessed 23 March 2014].

Pinoy-OFW, 2014. Pinoy OFW Group [Facebook]. 23 March. Available at <https://www.facebook.com/OverseasFilipinoWorkers> [Accessed 23 March 2014].

Rogers, E., 1995. *Diffusion of Innovations*. New York: Free Press.

Sampson, H., 2003. Transnational drifters or hyperspace dwellers: an exploration of the lives of Filipino seafarers abroad and ashore. *Ethnic and Racial Studies, 26*(2), pp.253–277.

Sussman, G., 1991. The Transnationalization of Philippine Telecommunications: Postcolonial Continuities. In: G. Sussman and J. Lent, eds. *Transnational Communications: Wiring the Third World.* London: Sage Publications Ltd. pp.125–149.

Tacoli, C., 1999. International migration and the restructuring of gender asymmetries: Continuity and change among Filipino labor migrants in Rome. *International Migration Review, 33*(3), pp.658–682.

Tung, C., 2000. The cost of caring: The social reproductive labor of Filipina live-in home health caregivers. *Frontiers: A Journal of Women Studies, 21*(1/2), pp.61–82.

Tyner, J., 2004. The Philippines: The Dilemma of Philippine International Labor Migration. In: M. Toro-Morn and M. Alicea, eds. *Migration and Immigration: A Global View*. Westport, CT and London: Greenwood Press. pp.161–176.

Tyner, J. and Kuhlke, O., 2000. Pan-national identities: representations of the Philippine diaspora on the world wide web. *Asian Pacific Viewpoint, 41*(3), pp.231–252.

Vertovec, S., 2001. Transnationalism and identity. *Journal of Ethnic and Migration Studies, 27*(4), pp.573–582.

Vertovec, S., 2004a. *Global networks, 4*(2), pp.219–224.

Vertovec, S., 2004b. Migrant Transnationalism and Modes of Transformation. *International Migration Review, 38*(3), pp.970–1001.

Chapter 3
Blogging Singapore: Control and Excess between Offline and Online Worlds

Kwoh-Jack Tan[1]

Al Gore's vision of the Information Society – as articulated in the editors' introduction, a global community of economic progress and democratic politics – is also a vision of globalizing society and international relations. His belief, though, is indicative of a monocultural "one-world" perspective that underpins much of the West's notions of global relations. As has been argued, thinking about "the international" has failed to engage with the non-Western world – two-thirds of the rest of the world – "except as an appendage to the body of thought developed in relation to the First World" (Darby, 2008, p. 95). One urgent corrective in envisioning a more truly globalizing society must be to recognize and work through alterity, where re-thinking the international takes its bearings from practices in the non-West, in this instance, Asia.

This chapter is an attempt to show, through alterity and the case of Singapore, that Gore's international visions may take a while yet to be fulfilled. Even though IT has enabled hitherto suppressed or marginal voices in Singapore to be articulated and heard, resulting in the apparent formation of a more progressive online Singaporean world that connects to global norms of greater openness as well as various forms of cyberactivism, the extent of IT being harnessed as a democratizing tool has overall been limited (Soon and Kluver, p. 246). The ruling People's Action Party has also assiduously attempted to curtail this online world, by delegitimizing it as an unreliable, "dangerous" Other, and by drawing on a wide-ranging array of subtle and heavy-handed controls, accentuating a kind of ambivalence that characterizes the Internet in Singapore (Lee and Kan, 2009). Nonetheless, its dominance over offline spaces has not automatically translated into a similarly robust control over online spaces – the process of contestation and re-contestation remains an ongoing, dynamic and complex one. However, I will argue that overwhelmingly, even those sharing the norms, beliefs and practices of Internet culture, and who are "anti-government", are also deeply embedded in a uniquely Singaporean "culture of excess" (Yao, 2007, pp. 27–8, 44). This refers to an all-consuming anxiety, grounded in the ruling party's particular telling of "the Singapore Story", that both paralyzes and serves as a spur to action in

1 I thank Alan Chong for his encouragements and comments on this chapter, and various research assistants without whom this chapter would not have been written.

order to avert national collapse – a kind of excess which underpins its impulses to control. Consequently, the Singaporean experience suggests that IT does not necessarily lead to political liberalization – in fact quite the opposite: through its repeated attempts to rein in the Internet, the ruling party has managed to reinforce the argument that authoritarian controls function as necessary requirements for the country's continued economic progress (George, 2012).

The spread of Internet usage in Asia has prompted academic and media commentators to presage how authoritarian and semi-authoritarian regimes face a trade-off between connectivity and control. Governments have sought to harness the Internet as a key infrastructure to build an important future engine of economic growth and, thus, buttress their performance legitimacy. Indeed, the economic benefits to be had from having a relatively free flow of IT-enabled communications is a major reason why the Singapore government has desisted from outrightly controlling it, despite its soft-authoritarian inclinations. To foster a conducive environment for their development strategies, relatively freer flows of information have been tolerated. At the same time, there has been an increased concern about maintaining control over socio-political expression, organization and mobilization that could potentially be unleashed via this relatively new medium. Ho *et al.* have posed the question about how attempts to assert state control might set up a "clash between the international culture of the Internet and the values of nations and peoples of Asia" (Ho *et al.*, 2003, pp. 8–9). While Castells has observed that the Internet owed its genesis, in part, to a "culture of freedom" and how "principles of openness" and a "spirit of freedom" (Castells, 2001, pp. 17, 29, 33) continue to be defining cultural characteristics, he has also noted that:

> The Internet is not an instrument of freedom, nor is it the weapon of one-sided domination. The Singapore experience is a case in point. Guided by a strong, capable government, Singapore has fully embraced technological modernization as a development tool. At the same time, it is widely considered to be one of the most sophisticated authoritarian systems in history. Attempting to steer a narrow path between these two policies, the government of Singapore has tried to expand the use of the Internet among its citizens, while retaining political control over this use by censoring Internet Service Providers. And yet … even in Singapore, civil society has been able to use the Internet to broaden its space of freedom, to articulate the defence of human rights, and to propose alternative views in the political debate. (Castells, 2001, p. 164)

Indeed, Singapore continues to exhibit this dialectical struggle between control and resistance, though it is limited to the Internet medium (Penfold, 2003, pp. 90–2). Trocki has argued how, post-independence, the ruling People's Action Party (PAP) has successfully cultivated a "culture of control" (Trocki, 2006), through legal-political means as well as through its policies on education, national military service, the economy, housing and the family. To a large extent, this has been possible due to the PAP government's overall success in delivering prosperity and bringing Singapore, in Lee Kuan Yew's famous phrase, "from Third World to First" (Lee, 2000). But as shall be elaborated in this chapter, this culture of control has also been fundamentally enabled by the PAP's habitual generation of narratives of crises and invocation of Singapore's "traumatic" founding beginnings: the 1964 race riots, separation from Malaysia in 1965, Singapore's multi-ethnic polity and its vulnerable position in the region and the world. As Heng and Devan (1992) argue, by constantly invoking Singapore's founding moments of fragility and trauma, not only does the state ratify and reinforce its originating purpose, its access to wide-ranging instruments of control in the name of the national interest is continually augmented.

This culture of control and crises narratives effectively encapsulates the traditional mass media. The mass circulation newspapers, for instance, begun with libertarian impulses, ironically begun during British colonial rule, and which the Singapore's anti-colonial nationalist elites led by Lee Kuan Yew exploited to great effect. But the mass media gradually came under authoritarian licensing and censorship controls by the post-independence PAP leadership, most notably the Newspaper and Printing Presses Act (NPPA) that came into effect in 1974, a few decades before the advent of mass-use Internet. Under the NPPA, newspapers are required to apply for annual permits and issue management shares to government nominees, thereby allowing the government to intervene over editorial direction and senior editorial appointments. It also enables the government to restrict the circulation of foreign publications. And recognizing radio and TV's capacity to reach a broader audience, and more powerfully so compared to the newspapers, these media remained state-owned, and strictly controlled by the Broadcasting Act right from the start. The ability of the Singapore government to regulate these traditional media can also be attributed to the fact that despite their broad reach, the production of content remains limited, and thus susceptible to governmental control. In contrast, the Internet on top of its sheer compounded connectivity and interactivity, is a "generative" technology, liberally conferring just about anyone with Internet access the role of a content provider (Zittrain, 2008). This makes the Internet, if it is to be harnessed towards economic development in an irreversible information age almost impossible to control, apart from intensifying surveillance and/or creating a great firewall of information blockade. Nevertheless, as George (2010) has argued, the Singapore's policy of "light touch" Internet regulation is not one of static control, but one that recognizes the near-impossibility of regulating the Internet on the one hand, and one that seeks dynamic equilibrium with the PAP constantly seeking to retain a dominant position. Furthermore, a proliferation of Internet usage also makes the citizenry more amenable to surveillance, and thus, the prevention of effective popular dissent.

Taken together, these more entrenched offline modes of state control and socialization produce that alterity of a more liberal Internet culture, at the same time as they embed (or have already embedded) Netizens within this characteristically Singaporean culture of excess. Early encounters between the cultures of control and the Internet, such as the closures of the Sintercom and

Fateha websites, have reproduced and, arguably strengthened the culture of excess. However, local denizens of cyberspace have learnt lessons from these early encounters as well as from further afield. Just as the authorities gingerly attempt to exert control in this brave new world, so too Singaporean bloggers have responded in varied ways; sometimes eliding control and excess, sometimes turning the government's logic and narratives back upon them. Noting how racial issues have been made out by the government to be especially "sensitive" issues with dire national repercussions, bloggers are beginning to notice that the more unabashed remarks about race in Singapore have been articulated by the PAP leadership itself. In response to the recent arrest of online cartoonist Leslie Chew under charges of sedition for playing up (or rather, drawing out) racial issues, the popular blog Temasek Review Emeritus writes with characteristic, almost reckless temerity: "How about Lee Kuan Yew's repeated racist statements, speeches and hate writings … insulting the Malay Muslims consistently and continuously? Why no sedition charges to date or even a reprimand?" (TR Emeritus, 2013).

In this chapter, selected encounters between the authorities and the Singaporean socio-political blogosphere, such as Martyn See, mrbrown, *The Online Citizen*, and the charging of bloggers for sedition are examined. Drawing on de Certeau (1984), whose emphasis on the struggles between the dimensions of place and time fit well with how control and resistance have played out over the struggles in the attempt to extend offline authority over the online world, these instances are explained as cases of *strategies* of control in contention with *tactics* which leveraged on the nature of the Internet to resist control. For de Certeau, a strategy represents the exercise of a power relationship by a subject through its delimitation of a space which it defines as its own and from which it uses as a base in conducting relations with targets and threats. The principle effects of a strategy are, first, a "mastery of place over time" where the delimited space allows the accretion of authority and advantage for use in future expansion – such as by amending legislation to extend offline authority into the online world. Second, a "mastery of places through sight" where all within the defined space can be objectified via observation and measurement – for example, by the monitoring of online activity and exercising requirements to present oneself for heightened official scrutiny via registration. And third, by constituting itself through "the power of knowledge … to provide oneself with one's own place … inaugurated through the constitution of their 'own' areas" (de Certeau, p. 36) seen by attempts to define some offline spaces as more legitimate and credible than others as well as to impose such differentiated readings on offline as opposed to online worlds. In contrast, a tactic is "an art of the weak" which has no place of its own and plays on its "absence of a proper locus", utilizing surprise, hit-and-run, poaching and guile to confound the attempts of strategies to fix them in place, objectify them and render them as knowable, readable and predictable (de Certeau, p. 37). The chapter then concludes by drawing parallels with experiences elsewhere in East Asia.

Control and Excess

> Since men live upon the land and not upon the sea, great issues between nations at war have always been decided – except in the rarest cases – either by what your army can do against your enemy's territory and national life or else by the fear of what the fleet makes it possible for your army to do. (Corbett, 1988, p. 16)

Since people live physically in the real world and not in the Internet, online encounters between the cultures of control, excess and resistance are necessarily grounded in prior and ongoing real world events and experiences. In a similar vein, Lyon reminds us that the "supposedly virtual aspects of the Internet" are not separate "from bodily life in geographical places … Rather, the Internet is superimposed upon and integrated with already existing forms of communication" (Lyon 2003, pp. 68–9). The culture of control has its origins in real life Singapore where it conditions the online experience not just through its ability to deliver real life consequences unto online behaviour but, more fundamentally, in the way it has already left its mark on IT users, in varying degrees, even before their first online foray.

The origins of the culture of control in Singapore have been traced to the coming to power of the PAP and its success in imposing its particular brand of discipline and order on Singaporean society which saw many pre-existing elements from colonial and pre-colonial society systematically co-opted, cut down to size, deliberately neglected or utterly erased, particularly during the period from 1964–74 (Trocki, 2006, p. 5). The totality of the party-state's control was achieved not only through legal instruments, such as the Internal Security Act and Public Order (Preservation) Act, but also radiated from policies administering public housing, urban redevelopment, organized labour, conscription, the birth rate and so on. In a similar vein, Rodan's assessment is that authoritarian political control has been intimately linked with social and economic transformation through "a consolidation and extension of state economic assets and social jurisdiction". Furthermore, he sees these dynamics as having reinforced each other historically, noting how "the increasing affluence of many Singaporeans has gone hand in hand with a growing dependence on the state, producing vulnerability to both cooption and political discipline" (Rodan, 1998, pp. 66–7).

Control was needed to produce order and social stability which were, in turn, required to consolidate Singaporean national identity centred on the inter-linked principles of meritocracy and multiracialism (Trocki, 2006, p. 138). Challenges to specific policies (such as the dismantling of Chinese medium schools) were, more often than not, securitized (Buzan and Wæver, 2003, pp. 23, 71–6) by the party-state as challenges to those key principles of Singaporean national identity and, thus, an existential threat to Singapore itself. The smoothness of such transitions is very much lubricated by the naturalizing discourse of "the Singapore Story" – a reference to the first volume of founding father Lee Kuan Yew's autobiography (1998) – "the story tells of tumultuous struggle where brave and practical men – less frequently women – fought against incredible odds and brought the modern nation into being". "The Singapore Story" is repeatedly "experienced as trauma driving the unbearable need to retell the past sufferings and, of course, their remedies". From this, a "culture of excess" is called into being "that would ceaselessly [alert] people to real and imaginary dangers and to find means to prevent them" (Yao, 2007, pp. 30, 32).

While the Internet is a relative open space, especially in comparison with offline spaces, bloggers do not start from a clean slate; they have been immersed in controlled Singaporean society and the narratives of "the Singapore Story". Suffused experiences and imaginings of control and excess, the themes of national anxiety are manifested in the day-to-day practices of IT users; blogging that might impinge on multiracialism (seditious comments disparaging races or religions) or meritocracy (scurrilous allegations of nepotism at the highest levels) are studiously avoided; even where the Out of Bounds markers are not transgressed, pseudonymity, just in case, is not an uncommon *modus operandi*. To paraphrase Marx, IT users do not make history in the Singaporean blogosphere under circumstances of their own choosing, but under circumstances existing already, given and transmitted from the past and from the cultures of control and excess.

Early Encounters

A prominent example from the past is the "Singapore Internet Community" (Sintercom) website. Founded in 1994, it was an independent website with a team of editors, led by Tan Chong Kee – then a PhD student in the Asian Languages Department of Stanford University, who "fell in love with the idea of building a Web site where Singaporeans all over the world can meet and discuss things which concern them – A Web home away from home" (Sintercom, "Our Philosophy", undated). The site hosted discussions on food in its "Makan" section, socio-political commentary in its "Speakers' Platform" section and published letters that had been rejected for publication in the forum page of the main English-language Singapore national daily (and government-linked) newspaper, *The Straits Times*, in its "Not the ST Forum" section. Then Tan received a letter, dated 5 July 2001, from the Singapore Broadcasting Authority (SBA) to register Sintercom as a political website under the SBA (Class Licence) Notification (Sintercom, 2001). When the regulation had been first promulgated, Sintercom issued an open letter decrying it and was not required to register (Sintercom, 1996). It is not known what brought about the subsequent change in the regulator's stance but, worried that he was being put "in a situation where I could be hauled into court anytime" (Sintercom, 2001) and feeling "too tired" (Ellis, 2001) to carry on, Tan closed down the website on 20 August 2001.

With the telling and retelling of the Sintercom story, the website's rise and fall has become a key traumatic event in the academic discourse on Singapore's socio-political websites. Lee has described it as the "first and highly public invocation [of Clause 4 of the SBA's Class Licence Notification] … to deal with the 'political nuisance' of civil society caused by Sintercom" (Lee, T., 2005, p. 82). Johal noted Tan's discomfort with "the ambiguity of the drift net legislation" and lamented that an opportunity was missed to seek judicial review to "nail down" the boundaries of the legislation (Johal, 2004, p. 6). Penfold has cited this as an example of how "self-censorship may flourish even where specific restrictions look less stringent" (Penfold, 2003, p. 91). In contrast, Cherian George has pointed out that, during the same period, the Think Centre was also asked to register its website under the same regulation. It complied and did not suffer any adverse consequences thereafter. George's pithy assessment was: "Arguably, Sintercom overreacted" (George, 2007). What is so striking is how it reflected the attitude of an email from SBA to Tan, dated 20 July 2001:

> Registration is a simple administrative procedure. It only needs content providers to give SBA the particulars of the website and those who are responsible for the editorial content. This is as straight forward as the filling of a form. There is no cause for Sintercom to *over react* over such a simple request. (Sintercom, 2001, emphasis added)

Tan responded by inviting the SBA to vet past Sintercom material, so as to reduce the ambiguity of what was permissible and what was not, citing Section 4(4) of the SBA Internet Code of Practice: "A licensee who is in doubt as to whether any content would be considered prohibited may refer such content to the Authority for its decision" (MDA, 1997 – the Media Development Authority is the successor Authority to the SBA). However the SBA's reply, dated 7 August 2001, declined to take up Tan's request and merely reiterated how the burden of responsibility lay with him. It is not implausible that it was this impersonal, and probably non-malicious, demonstration of the flexible exercise of the discretionary powers of the regulatory authority in the inflexible pursuit of its goal – rather than the initial registration order itself – was the last straw that confirmed Tan's fears about what could happen in a worst case scenario now that a strategy of bureaucratic surveillance (Dandeker, 1990, pp. 37–8) was being applied to Sintercom. If Tan's decision to close down Sintercom was indeed an over-reaction, he had nonetheless reacted very much in accordance with the practices of a culture of excess – he was alert to a threat, possibly real or possibly imagined, and had sought to pre-empt the possible consequences that might have emanated from it.

Not longer afterwards, in July 2002, the police initiated an investigation on Zulkifar Mohamad Shariff, editor of Fateha.com, for alleged criminal defamation in three articles on his website that questioned the suitability of Yaacob Ibrahim, the Minister-in-charge of Muslim Affairs, for his portfolio. He also criticized the appointment of Ho Ching as Executive Director of Temasek Holdings in another post. Earlier that year, Fateha had already courted controversy when it campaigned against the Ministry of Education's prohibition of the *tudung* (female Muslim headscarf) in its schools. Zulkifar eventually fled to Australia before the police formally pressed charges (George, 2005, p. 18, Lee, 2005, p, 90). The Fateha case reinforced how the red lines around the two key tenets of multiculturalism and meritocracy were hair triggers for setting off official anxiety and corresponding actions to ward off the possible dangers of communalism and loss of faith in authority.

Singapore Rebel

A challenge to authority and control was put in motion when on 12 January 2005, Martyn See Tong Ming submitted *Singapore Rebel*, a 26 minute film he had made about controversial opposition figure Chee Soon Juan, to the Singapore International Film Festival (SIFF). In mid-March, he withdrew it from the SIFF after being advised that the Ministry of Communications and the Arts (MICA) had deemed it to be in violation of the Film Act's prohibition on partisan political videos. A police investigation ensued, during the course of which he was repeatedly interviewed and had to surrender his video camera and all existing copies of his film. In early August 2006, See was issued with a "stern warning" and the case was closed.

See was not the first to run afoul of the Films Act. Almost three years before the *Singapore Rebel* saga, four lecturers from Ngee Ann Polytechnic's Department of Film and Media Studies had to submit written apologies and withdrew *A Vision of Persistence*, a 15 minute film about J.B. Jeyaratnam, another controversial opposition figure, from the SIFF (AFP, 2002). The significance of See's case, for this article, is while he ostentibly subjected himself to strategies of control by submitting his films for classification as required and cooperating fully with the police investigation, at the same time he was also employing tactics of resistance. He used video-hosting sites, initially Google Video and then YouTube, which were outside of Singaporean jurisdiction and much too popular to completely block, to circumvent the bans on his films; he had used the transnational breadth of the Internet to operationalize a tactic of *sanctuary*, placing his films beyond the reach of a Singapore-based strategy of control.

The ban itself also possibly played into a tactic of *amplification*, where other voices join in and fuels a virtuous/vicious (depending on your point of view) cycle as awareness spreads and more voices join in. Firstly, the film's proscription by the authorities made it newsworthy. Secondly, this action lent it a certain street credibility, rebellious glamour, or even sympathy given the "David vs Goliath" inequality of the clash. Arguably more people, piqued by curiosity and being able to satisfy that curiosity by accessing the video-hosting websites, saw *Singapore Rebel* as a direct result of the ban than if it had been allowed to be screened at the SIFF. The paradox that this tactic played on, in this case, is that in order to exercise a strategy of control via proscription, the object to be subjected to control must be named. This ironically used the official voice to create much more awareness of the proscribed object than its makers could have ever been able to muster on their own.

In the past, control could be maintained as, once proscribed, the offending object effectively ceased to exist. But this was, as described above, bypassed by the tactic of sanctuary.

See also worked hard to sustain interest via his blog (singaporerebel.blogspot.com) with regular updates where he meticulously recorded his journey; generating some sympathy for his predicament in particular and greater awareness about Singapore's censorship of films in general. Word had also spread about *Singapore Rebel* via wire service reports and other websites such as the then-popular Tomorrow.sg aggregator (13 November 2005) and was discussed by prominent long time socio-political bloggers such as Steven McDermott of *Singabloodypore* and Gilbert Koh of the now defunct *Singapore Legal Mumbo Jumbo Demystified.* In an interview with Lee Kuan Yew, *TIME Asia* (5 December 2005) asked the Minister Mentor about the ban on *Singapore Rebel* to which MM Lee opined: "Well, if you had asked me, I would have said, to hell with it. But the censor, the enforcer, he will continue until he is told the law has changed. And it will change …" On 11 September 2009, the ban on *Singapore Rebel* was lifted and given an M18 rating under the Films Act which had been amended in March that year. In the meantime, See had gone on to make more films. *Zahari's 17 Years,* about a former ISA detainee, has remained banned since April 2007 while *Speakers Cornered* was passed by the censors and rated NC16 in April 2008. In 2010, See submitted a video recording of a speech by former political detainee Dr Lim Hock Siew. It was gazetted as a prohibited film, and the MDA directed that he "surrender all copies of the film in his possession and to take down all digital copies of the film that he had uploaded onto the Internet" (MDA, 2010); See duly complied. Yet, in a seeming oversight, *Zahari's 17 Years* remains available online.

mrbrown Comes to Town

Lee Kin Mun, also known by his online moniker of mrbrown, has been tickling the funnybones of Singaporeans since releasing *Singapore National Education* (SNE) Part 1 online on 24 September 1997. Released weekly, and later intermittently, SNE finally concluded, with its 108th instalment, on 25 July 2005. Each SNE Part consisted of 20 to 30 one-liners; each making a wry observation about current affairs in Singapore over the past week, often criticizing unpopular policies such as Electronic Road Pricing. SNE was hosted on various sites, including Sintercom, as well as newsgroups like soc.culture.singapore and soc.culture.singapore.moderated and was also circulated via email.

Although the PAP's fearsome reputation for not looking fondly upon political dissent is not undeserved, the party-state itself has acknowledged that some jocular grumbling and rude humour about it and its policies exist on the ground. In April 2002, newly elected PAP Members of Parliament had attributed "coffeeshop criticisms of officialdom" to "the government's failure to listen to the people" (Yao, 2007, p. 136). Much of these "coffeeshop criticisms" were verbose, boastful, exaggerated, highly colloquial and often expressed as jokes are usually referred to less decorously as "talking cock"; they were a reminder, both to Parliament and the "cock talkers" themselves, that "the State is not always the hegemonic centre of things, at least not at the hawker centre" and that "the pleasure of 'talking cock' can still be socially engaging and subversive" (Yao, 2007, pp. 136, 137).

Despite the lived experience and rich tradition on the ground, political satire in Singapore's media has been relatively rare. Jack Neo's mainstream movies, such as *I Not Stupid* (2002), are the exception to the rule where the PAP state's nanny tendencies, the education system, the foreign talent programme as well as aspects of the Ugly Singaporean were roundly subjected to an almost didactic pillorying onscreen – often, it must be said, to audiences' delight (Yao, 2007, pp. 141–58). A similar delight helped to drive SNE's popularity and establish mrbrown as a prominent voice of socio-political satire alongside others such as the TalkingCock.com team led by Colin Goh or the Singapore Donkey blog (though the latter two have been markedly less active since late 2009). The Internet certainly facilitated this phenomenon; it was a virtual underground coffeeshop writ large where audiences could come, enjoy and go as they pleased and without being physically observed.

The case of mrbrown is interesting for the discussion of the alterity of online and offline politics in Singapore due to the way, in the run up to and just after the General Election of 2006, he transgressed the boundaries of both worlds with his "Tur Kwa" podcast and *Today* newspaper article.

Parliament was dissolved on 20 April 2006, with Nomination Day a week later and the General Election was held on 6 May (Government of Singapore, 2006). Earlier in the month, Senior Minister of State for Information, Communications and the Arts Balaji Sadasivan had spelt out, in reply to a parliamentary question, that, under the Parlimentary Elections Act (Amended) (2001), podcasting and videocasting with political content by individual bloggers were not allowed during the period of election campaigning. Reprising a now familiar strategy of control via bureaucratic surveillance, he "added that individual bloggers can discuss politics, but have to register with the Media Development Agency if they persistently promote political views" (Channel News Asia, 2006a). The announcement was greeted with dismay and anger by the opposition and some bloggers who felt that it would "have a chilling effect on free speech" (*The Straits Times*, 5 April 2006). Far from being chilled, mrbrown started a podcast series on 25 April 2006 which commented on political events but replaced real life details with different names and setting them in a non-Singaporean context such as Greek mythology. And in a cheeky reference to Sadasivan's pronouncements, he called it "the persistently non-political podcast".

The sixth instalment of the podcast series achieved cult status, becoming popularly known as the "Bah chor mee" (minced meat noodles) or "Tur kwa" (pork liver) podcast, when the 2 minute and 58 second long audio clip parodied the then-ongoing war of words between the leading lights of the ruling PAP and the Workers' Party's James Gomez. The incident started when Gomez claimed, on 26 April 2006, that he had not received his minority candidate certificate, a requirement for his team to contest the Aljunied Group Representation Constituency, from the Elections Department. Gomez claimed that he had applied for it two days before but the Elections Department did not have any record of such an application (CNA, 2006b). The Elections Department then produced closed circuit television footage to prove that Gomez had put the form back into his bag instead of submitting it (CNA, 2006c) and he admitted that this presented an accurate picture a few days later, attributing his mistake to his busy schedule (CNA, 2006e). Gomez was then repeatedly attacked by senior PAP figures, such as Deputy Prime Minister Wong Kan Seng and Foreign Minister George Yeo (the leading PAP MP in Aljunied GRC), who claimed that the incident raised serious questions about Gomez's character and called on the Workers' Party to drop him as a candidate – which it refused to (CNA, 2006f, g, h). The Elections Department lodged a police complaint against Gomez for allegedly threatening its officials over the missing form but the case was eventually closed with a "stern warning" for him (CNA, 2006i, j).

At the height of the furore, on 1 May 2006, mrbrown's podcast was released and rapidly became a hit among Singaporeans. In the podcast, a character named Jeff Lopez queues for his lunch at the hawker centre's *bah chor mee* stall. When the stallholder, called the *Bah Chor Mee* Man, serves him his noodles, Lopez is unhappy that the portion includes *tur kwa* (pork liver) and chides the *Bah Chor Mee* Man for including it despite his earlier request not to. Whereupon a "Did Too, Did Not" type exchange ensues before the *Bah Chor Mee* Man shows Lopez a CCTV recording that proves his version of events was the correct one. Lopez apologizes and tries to pay for the noodles but is hectored by the *Bah Chor Mee* man who demands that he explain why he claimed to have said that he had requested *tur kwa* not to be included in his noodles. When Lopez apologizes again, the Bah Chor Mee Man then also demands that he explain why he is apologizing: "Sorry also must explain". These were inclusions which echoed the phrasing of Gomez's public apology and George Yeo's dismissal of it (CNA, 2006d). The podcast then fades out as the two continue to argue, seemingly without end in sight (Lee, 2006a). While it is doubtful that the podcast itself had any influence on the election results or even with respect to the substantive resolution of the original dispute between the PAP and Gomez, the timeliness, pithiness and wit of the podcast had employed a tactic of humour to reframe the entire issue from high politics and electoral drama to merely that of a petty squabble. The Lopez/Gomez character was not portrayed in an entirely favourable light but the *Bah Chor Mee* Man/PAP composite character came across far worse, brimming with all the neuroses of a culture of excess and being a "sore winner" of the argument (George, 2006).

If the authorities had heard the podcast and were none too amused by it, there was no direct sign of displeasure or retribution other than a jocular passing reference to it in the Prime Minister's National Day Rally which mrbrown parodied with his "harmless podcast" (Lee, 2006d). However, mrbrown was soon to be at the receiving end of an official rebuke, from K Bhavani, Press Secretary to the Minister for Information, Communication and the Arts, for his *Today* newspaper column article, "S'poreans are fed, up with progress!" (Lee, 2006b). In the aftermath, *Today* discontinued mrbrown's column (Lee, 2006c). While the earlier examples of strategies of control with respect to Sintercom, Fateha and, to a lesser extent, Singapore Rebel emphasized how the authorities attempted to extend offline methods of control to online forms of social life and behaviour, Bhavani's letter presaged an alternative strategy of control that relied on the delineation of different standards of control over offline and online news reporting and commentary: "mr brown is entitled to his views. *But opinions which are widely circulated in a regular column in a serious newspaper should meet higher standards.* Instead of a diatribe mr brown should offer constructive criticism and alternatives" (Bhavani, 2006 – emphasis added). She went on to explicitly circumscribe the scope of offline journalistic endeavour: "It is not the role of journalists or newspapers in Singapore to champion issues, or campaign for or against the Government. If a columnist presents himself as a non-political observer, while exploiting his access to the mass media to undermine the Government's standing with the electorate, then he is no longer a constructive critic, but a partisan player in politics".

This implied that online "citizen journalism" and commentary would not be subject to the stringent control and surveillance applied to the traditional mainstream media, except when breaches of the norms of multiculturalism and meritocracy occurred. But it also suggested that the authorities had granted themselves a licence to ignore online speech – being just part of the online chatter, like "coffeeshop criticisms" and therefore of lower standards, the reasoning goes, the authorities may refuse to dignify it with any response at all. This was the case even for relatively high profile figures like author Catherine Lim who had previously been at the receiving end of strong rebuttals after having two offline articles discussing the "great affective divide" between State and society published in *The Straits Times*; she confessed to being "disappointed" after there was no response to an open letter to the Prime Minister that she had posted on her blog (Lim, 2007).

The Online Citizen and Al Jazeera

The crystallization of the "Bhavani doctrine", as some netizens chose to call it, took place just as the trend of "citizen journalism", independent of the government-linked mainstream media, began to gather momentum. This trend manifested in the appearance of websites, not unlike Sintercom but built on more contemporary software such as WordPress. The two most prominent examples are *The Online Citizen* (TOC) and the *Wayang Party*; the latter was re-constituted with the new identity of the *Temasek Review* (and then *Temasek Review Emeritus*). At the time of writing, it was embroiled in a dispute with the government-linked sovereign wealth fund Temasek Holdings which had requested the website to change its name to avoid any association with its operations.

The mission of these citizen journalism sites was to provide news and commentary, a alternative discourse to the print media of Singapore Press Holdings and the visual media of Mediacorp Singapore, on a regular basis. TOC was explicit about this: "TOC began in December 2006 with a simple aim in mind: telling the stories about Singapore and Singaporeans that weren't being told in the mainstream press". In direct contradiction of Bhavani's separation of news reporting from opinion or advocacy, TOC aims "to redefine news, through the merger of opinions and reporting – forever blurring the lines between editorial and news. The quasi opinions and veiled 'viewpoints' of the mainstream media will be routinely exposed and questioned by *The Online Citizen*; so that in the end, we will have a better and more inclusive Singapore" (TOC, undated).

This neo-Sintercom model has the advantage of creating a focal point in contrast to the scattered and disjointed individual blogs as well as pooling resources, such as time, money, leads, sources, photographs and so on that a blog run by a lone individual lacks. More ambitiously, it sought to move beyond an emphasis, largely out of necessity, of the secondary commentary on news produced by others and to produce original news stories of its own. It could be reasoned that however much bloggers could point out mistakes, apply critical insight and sophisticated deconstruction was applied to the news produced by the "nation-building press", it was still a reactive mode of resistance and that the mainstream media still set the agenda of what was to be discussed. The power of the tactic of contradiction when injecting new and previously unknown information into the overall discourse was demonstrated, sporadically, in the course of the 2006 General Election campaign – a memorable example was gay activist Alex Au's publication, on his Yawning Bread blog, of photographs he had taken which showed a huge crowd attending a Workers' Party election rally in Hougang (Au, 2006a). Similar coverage by the local mainstream media was belated – a similar photograph of the same event was belatedly published four days later and prompted speculation that their hand had been forced by the buzz created online (Au, 2006b).

TOC managed to create a buzz of its own with its week-long feature on the issue of homelessness in Singapore. From April 2010, its correspondents reported on how groups of people who claimed that their Housing Development Board flats had been repossessed had been raided and moved elsewhere by the authorities (TOC, 2010a). They later met with and interviewed a couple who were camping at the beach side, claiming to have nowhere else to go (TOC, 2010b). Given that the provision of public housing for over 90 per cent of the population is one of the party-state's most proud and worthy achievements, this disturbed the dominant discourse of a government had claimed to have largely eliminated homelessness, a problem that still plagued developed countries. Later, the couple were featured in a two minute clip produced and aired by Al Jazeera English which had established a presence in Singapore since December 2007.

The issue having clearly crossed the Bhavani line, the Minister for Community Development, Youth and Sports Vivian Balakrishnan attacked Al Jazeera for failing to ascertain the faces and simply taking the couple's story at face value. Balakrishnan went on to complain that: “Even worse, some irresponsible websites had gone on to fuel these falsehoods by circulating this widely on the Internet” (*Today*, 2010). TOC claimed credit as one of those “irresponsible websites” (TOC, 2010c) even though the Minister did not credit them with breaking the story, only of spreading Al Jazeera’s story. Nonetheless TOC probably felt that credit was due based on the not implausible assumption, given the sequence of events, that an international media channel had picked up a similar theme that it had focused on and had interviewed what appeared to be the very same couple. This case could be repeated in the future, if more foreign media companies take up Singapore’s push to become a regional and global media hub, as there could be more avenues for local bloggers to amplify the contradictions that they will presumably uncover.

“Racist”, “Seditious” Bloggers

Perhaps this culture of excess is most pointedly displayed in 2005, when the state arrested three bloggers in 2005 for making expletive-laden racist comments on the Internet against the Malay-Muslim community and charged them under the Sedition Act (Reuters, 2005).

The first two instances related to a letter written to *The Straits Times* about whether or not taxi cabs should be allowed to carry uncaged pets, in view of Islam deeming the saliva of dogs to be unclean. Participating in an Internet forum for dog lovers on this topic, Nicholas Lim according to the Deputy Public Prosecutor, used highly insulting words and “preached intolerance” of Islam and the Malay community (*The Straits Times*, 2005). As a result Lim was given a “nominal” jail term of one day and fined a maximum of $5,000. The second blogger Benjamin Koh similarly spewed vulgarities at the Muslim Malay community, derided and mocked their practices and beliefs. As *The Straits Times* reported, one comment compared Islam to Satanism, while others were “so extreme they cannot be printed”. Senior District Judge Richard Magnus in his ruling, observed that Koh’s online postings were “particularly vile”, and he was subsequently convicted of two charges under the Sedition Act and jailed for one month (*The Straits Times* 2005). Soon after, a 17 year old Singaporean student pleaded guilty to sedition with his blog post entitled “The Second Holocaust” advocating genocide against the Malays (CNA, 2005).

This was the first time the sedition laws – inherited from British colonial rule – were invoked since Singapore’s independence 40 years ago. The sedition laws were used by the British administrators to curtail freedom of speech, especially that of the press, so as to exert political control over the colony. Under Singapore’s Sedition Act, it is seditious to promote feelings of ill-will and hostility between different races or classes of the population. The use of such laws to restrain speech on race and/or religion is unique in Singapore, and conveys the government’s objection to types of racial and religious speech that it deems harmful (Neo, 2011). Charging the three bloggers under the sedition act is a new phenomenon and a “broad-ranging state proscription” of freedom of speech – largely motivated by the state's fixation with ensuring peaceful interaction among the various ethnic and religious groups in Singapore (Neo, 2011, p. 253).

In imposing the sentence, the judge referred to the present fears of terrorism, as well as the 1964 race riots, which now form a common Singaporean trope of national crisis to be averted. The 1964 race riots, which had been largely attributed to political and media incitations of preexisting unhappiness between the Chinese and Malay racial groups in Singapore, and which was one reason for Singapore's separation from the Federation of Malaysia in 1965, thereby impelling Singapore into sudden and uncertain statehood. In recalling the riots, Magnus called for "especial sensitivity of racial and religious issues in our multi-cultural society" (*The Straits Times*, 2005), The reference to terrorism also articulates a fear that vilification of the Malay-Muslims will feed the Islamic fundamentalist movement allegedly active in the region and Singapore – most notable the Jemaah Islamayah group, of whom 11 members were been detained without trial. The fear is also that the risks of Islamic terrorism have heightened racial suspicions against the Malay-Muslim community, and of racial sensitivities all round. Magnus added: "Young Singaporeans, like the accused persons before this court, may have short memories that race and religion are sensitive issues. They must realise that callous and reckless remarks on racial or religious subjects have the potential to cause social disorder, in whatever medium or forum they are expressed". The irony is that by repeatedly invoking that historical episode – and a contested one at that – the episode that is well past and perhaps forgotten, returns as a constant reminder, and render such recurrences a potentiality. Extrapolating to the nation-at-large, he asserted that it is every Singaporean's responsibility to respect other races and religions – the "only appropriate social behavior, independent of any legal duty, of every Singapore citizen and resident" (*The Straits Times*, 2005). The bloggers' imprisonment under the Sedition Act was meant as a "sentence of deterrence", to draw a "red line on the ground", as their comments threatened not only a racial group but the "very fabric of Singapore society" (Reuters, 2005). Arguably, this presumes individual actions will have deleterious effects on a national scale, and demonstrates how such excessive fears result in impunity measures by the state.

The online community's reactions have been mixed. Those who support the judgement express the need to consider Singapore's racial composition and the sensitivities involved, along with the attendant anxieties that these issues can potentially escalate into national crises. At the same time, these perspectives also reveal the extent to which the state has been effective in embedding the citizenry in this culture of excess. As Henry Tan, a law academic, writes in his blog:

> We may be the free citizens of the Internet in theory but in reality, we are still very much the citizens of the country that issued our passports. And in the context of Singapore, while we are still undergoing the slow process of development and integration of social freedoms, we have to remember that we are located physically in a region where religious tolerance is absolutely key – something that the blogsphere does not concern itself about, the boundaries of national

> countries. … I suspect that very soon the educational institutions in Singapore will review their curriculum on the basis of our national harmony – racial tolerance by understanding the differences of our races and religion. (Tan, 2005)

Those who disagreed with the judgement felt that this would set back Singapore's desire for a more open society, while some others questioned the use of the Sedition Act. They also questioned whether or not racial issues are really that sensitive to begin with. Blogger Tedbasser, for instance, believes that these developments are counterproductive to Singapore's recent attempts to shed its "nanny state image":

> If Singapore were to embrace more and more of democracy, then the country has to accept the influx of both positive and negative aspects of it. At the same time, it has to start giving people more credit to be able to think and discern for themselves. The Sedition Act and the enforcement of such, thus, seems to be a direct contradiction to the "open and consultative" image that the government has been portraying. In short, the very presence of the Sedition Act undermines any hope for the people that they will be heard. Furthermore, the presence of such an Act only seeks to encourage the much-talked-about "climate of fear" that promotes political apathy; and also restricts mental development, and very possibly, even impedes innovation or creativity. … If we aren't given the chance to think for ourselves now, then when? (Tedbasser, 2005)

Yet even Tedbasser's disagreements with the court rulings stem fundamentally from that culture of excess: that Singapore "walks on a tightrope of sensitive relations", surrounded by two prominent Muslim-majority countries, and containing a large Muslim minority internally. Racial riots in Singapore may even lead to "similar violence between the protestants and catholics in Belfast", and, mirroring Magnus's comments, even increasing Singapore's risks of terrorist threats from Muslim extremists (Tedbasser, 2005).

Whether or not commentators online agree with the rulings, the use of punitive state laws on Internet postings have had an overall chilling effect on Internet discourse. One goes as far as to wonder if "we will get locked up if we blog about PAP" (SingaporeMacross, 2005). Unaware of where the "out-of-bounds markers" are – deliberately ill-defined markers of acceptable critique that governs Singapore society – bloggers will most likely be "extremely careful" from now on, not knowing whether one is "breaking some rules again …" (pseudo-marc, 2008). To the extent that the freedom of the Internet and its stridency have been a due to its relative anonymity, this episode has also shown that online identities can – and will – be traced by the state. In the words of forum participant Poolman: "Now then I know, or now we know, so dun play play … Someone is watching!" (SgForums, 2005). This episode has revealed the extent of the state's reach, ability and intent to rein in offenders from behind the veil of Internet anonymity, that the Internet is not out of bounds from offline strictures. In all, this reflects the state's culture of excesses as well as the embeddedness of the Singapore citizenry within such a culture.

Conclusion

Although Singapore has often been thought of as *sui generis* given its small size, Castells (2001) has looked at it as a signal case – that it is neither an instrument of freedom nor a weapon of one-sided domination. At the time of writing, the Singapore government has just passed – unilaterally – new licensing rules for online news sites. Under the new ruling, which were announced on 28 May 2013 and came into effect just three days later on 1 June, websites that regularly report an average of at least one article per week on Singapore's news and current affairs over a period of two months, and have at least 50,000 unique visitors from Singapore each month over a period of two months, will need to apply for individual licences have to be renewed every year. They must also put up a performance bond of $50,000, similar to that required for niche TV broadcasters. They are also expected to remove content that is in breach of MDA standards within 24 hours, once notified to do so. This material could cover content that is against the public interest, public security, or national harmony (*The Straits Times*, 2013).

Although the Minister for Communications and Information Dr Yaacob Ibrahim has repeatedly insisted that the government has not shifted away from its "light touch" regulation, and that he expects websites to continue operating as before, the online community has trenchantly contradicted the minister's claims. Former Nominated Member of Parliament and regular online commentator Siew Kum Hong has noted that the new rulings constitute a "significant retreat" from the "light touch" approach – in addition to being the first country in the world to regulate socio-political blogs in the same way as it regulates political parties, it is now "probably the first and only democratic country in the world" to require gazetted websites to put up monetary bonds (Siew, 2013). Furthermore, contrary to the government's stand that this new ruling seeks to align online websites with the regulation of offline news providers, Siew has pointed out that there is no requirement for the traditional print media to recall content within 24 hours. In other words, select Internet sites are now subject to discriminatory treatment. It remains to be seen whether or not this new ruling will remain firmly in place, or if concessions would be made to placate an increasingly concerned citizenry, who held a protest gathering called "#FreeMyInternet" on 8 June 2013, where more than two thousand activists turned up. At present, the MDA has agreed to "tweak" the original wording of the licensing rules, but has stated that the "key thrusts of will not be changed" (Tan, 2013). Yet, as it is, the new legislative structures have already claimed their first casualty: former *The Straits Times* associate editor Bertha Henson had decided to shut down her newly set up online socio-political website, Breakfast Network (BN), after being asked by the MDA to register under the Broadcasting (Class Licence) rules (*Today*, 2013). According to MDA, this was to prevent foreign influence on Singapore politics through its local media platforms. Henson decided not to register as she found the official forms unduly "onerous", and its stipulations vague. As such, the MDA ordered BN to cease its online services, including its Facebook and Twitter perations. As Henson lamented:

"The demand to register or else – has created a wrinkle in our barely-formed plans to become a sustainable and progessional outfit" (Yahoo News, 2013). The whole episode had been, to this veteran Singapore journalist, a "farcical" one (*Today*, 2013). In the light of this outcome, it is evident that further liberalization and maturity of Singapore's online political sphere will remain an uphill task, including encouraging he others to join in such start-ups as well as in creating a sustainable community of such websites.

The Singaporean expressions of control, excess and resistance between the off- and online worlds remain a dynamic one, perhaps more so with the rise of the Internet and the Singapore economy's dependence on a free flow of information networks. But what is abundantly clear is that for certain, Gore's vision of a global democratic society due to the liberating forces of the Internet may take a while yet to be realized in Singapore – and perhaps for those other developing countries that are seeking to emulate Singapore's models of governance.

The Singapore case could tell us much about the interaction between the Internet and the offline socio-political world outside of the West. From the cases explored above, one can draw a parallel between the cases of *Singapore Rebel* and Malaysiakini.com with respect to the tactic of amplification. Just as how the ban provided the initial spark of news interest which was then fed by Martyn See's chronicling of the police investigation, James Chin has observed how Malaysian "Ministers have referred to [MalaysiaKini.com] unfavourably, giving it free publicity in the process … Government criticism of the site often backfired, since every time a minister or senior official attacked MK.com or other anti-establishment websites, traffic to the site immediately went up as people became curious about the content of the websites" (Chin, 2003, pp. 136–7).

The tactic of humour, explored in the discussion of mrbrown, is also one that has been used by netizens elsewhere in East Asia. For example, a music video entitled *The Song of Grass Mud Horse* (*Cao ni ma zi ge*) emerged in 2009 in reaction to a Chinese Internet censorship campaign that targeted websites hosting pornography and other forms of "spiritual pollution". The video showed plush toys representing mythical animal who sang a short, catchy and cheerful song about their idyllic lives. However, numerous words in the song are phonetically identical to profanities – for example, Grass Mud Horse can be understood as "Fuck your mother". The double meaning of the lyrics, juxtaposed with the cute visual imagery, threw down the gauntlet at the censors; they could proscribe the video as "smut" but this would also make them look humourless (Can't you take a joke?), petty (Even this must be censored?) and, paradoxically, dirty-minded (*You* think it's obscene, *I* think it's just a cute animal song).

Humour has also been employed in specific cases of perceived injustice such as the "My Dad is Li Gang" (*Woba shi Li Gang*) meme that started after Li Qiming, the son of the influential deputy head of the Public Security Bureau of Baoding's Beishi district, allegedly knocked down and killed Chen Xiaofeng while driving; he shouted the above-mentioned words as he sped away from the site of the accident on 10 October 2010. The meme used the utterance as an absurd catchphrase and was applied to parodies of classical texts, poetry, proverbs, pop songs, commercial jingles; the driving combination of indignation and humour made it so popular online that, demonstrating the synergies between tactics of humour and amplification, the meme was reported by Chinese mainstream media ten days later (see, for example, SZTV News, 21 October 2010), leading to Li Qiming's arrest and a grovelling apology by Li Gang on national television (*Financial Times*, 2010b).

The artist, Ai Weiwei, an avid blogger and Twitter user, whose team made and uploaded a video interview with the deceased's father in the Li Gang incident, has also valorized the tactic of humour. In an interview with the *Financial Times* (2010a), he said: "Humour is a necessary ingredient when you're living under an authoritarian society. I'm in a battle against any system that tries to limit our imagination. Only with this humour and art do we have a superior advantage, and we will win every time". However, Ai's case also demonstrates the costs when the tactic falls foul of a strategy of calibrated coercion; he was placed under house arrest after refusing to call off a planned party serving ten thousand river crabs (*hexie*) to protest against the forced demolition of his art studio in Shanghai – also a dig at President Hu Jintao's vision of a harmonious society (*hexie shehui*) and, incidentally, also a creature that appeared in *The Song of Grass Mud Horse*.

The literature on the Internet in China also offers parallels with respect to the tactic of contradiction. Li, Xing and Kluver (2003) had examined how Internet chatroom had forced the Chinese media to respond to news culled from foreign wire services and other outlets during the spy plane crisis. They argued that while "the Internet might not directly undermine authoritarian regimes, it certainly introduces information that forces authoritarian governments to respond to and account for more outside sources, thus increasing the transparency and professionalism of the Chinese sources themselves" (Ho, *et al.*, 2003, p. 13).

The Internet will remain another arena of contestation in the future of East Asia's polities as the authorities and IT users learn from the past and from across national boundaries in a dynamic process of attempting to appropriate the technologies of the Internet in pursuit of their own varied purposes. This might be further analysed as the emerging dialectics of Internet-assisted democratization in East Asia. It is slow, messy and suffers frequent reversals. If Singapore's experience is any indication, the effects of Internet-assisted activism will be long-term and subtle (George, 2010). The spaces and terrain of online spaces are being transformed by strategies of control which employ technological fixes, encroaching legislation, entrenched socio-political norms of what is "credible" and "legitimate" and the converse. At the same time, the tactics of resistance will also continue to use the possibilities of the Internet's ever-changing and ever-changeable milieu to adapt, to surprise and to delight.

References

Agence France Presse, 2002. Documentary on Jeya withdrawn from film festival, 4 January. Available at: http://www.singapore-window.org/sw02/020104af.htm [Accessed 3 March 2013].

Au, A., 2006a, On Houang field. Yawning Bread, [blog] 1 May. Available at: http://www.yawningbread.org/arch_2006/yax-581.htm [Accessed 3 March 2013].

Au, A., 2006b, Flat-footed and worse. Yawning Bread, [blog] May. Available at: http://www.yawningbread.org/arch_2006/yax-591.htm [Accessed 1 June 2013].

Bhavani, K., 2006. Distorting the truth, mr brown? *Today*, 3 July. Available at: http://www.mrbrown.com/blog/2006/07/letter_from_mic.html [Accessed 20 February 2013].

Buzan, B. and Wæver, O., 2003. *Regions and Powers: the structure of international security.* Cambridge: Cambridge University Press.

Castells, M., 2001. *The Internet Galaxy: reflections on the Internet, business, and society*, Oxford: Oxford University Press.

Channel News Asia, 2006a. Podcasting is not allowed during elections, 3 April.

—— 2006b, Elections dept Says WP candidate did not apply for minority certificate, 26 April.

—— 2006c, Elections dept confirms WP's James Gomez did not submit minority form, 27 April.

—— 2006d, Apology by WP's James Gomez does not properly address issue: George Yeo, 30 April.

—— 2006e, WP's Gomez admits he did not submit form to elections dept, 30 April.

—— 2006f, gomez stage-managed elections department episode: DPM Wong, 2 May.

—— 2006g, FM George Yeo says WP can drop gomez after polling day, 3 May.

—— 2006h, WP says it will not drop Gomez from Aljunied GRC, 3 May.

—— 2006i, Police say no arrest so far over election department's complaint, 8 May.

—— 2006j, WP's Gomez let off with stern warning in run-in with elections dept, 12 May.

Channelnewsasia.com, 2005. Third racist blogger sentenced to 24 months supervised probation, 23 November. [Online] Available at: http://forums.vr-zone.com/chit-chatting/44764-third-racist-blogger-sentenced-24-months-supervised-probation.html [Accessed 5 July 2013].

Chin, J., 2003. Malaysiakini.com and its impact on journalism and politics in Malaysia. In: K.C. Ho, R. Kluver and K.C.C. Yang, eds., *Asia.com: Asia encounters the Internet.* London: RoutledgeCurzon, pp. 129–42.

Corbett, J. S., 1988. *Some Principles of Maritime Strategy*. Annapolis: United States Naval Institute.

Dandeker, C., 1990. *Surveillance, Power and Modernity: bureaucracy and discipline from 1700 to the Present Day.* Cambridge: Polity Press.

Darby, P., A disabling discipline?, 2008. In: Reus-Smit, C. and Snidal, S., eds., *Oxford Handbook of International Relations*. Oxford; New York: Oxford University Press.

de Certeau, M., 1984. *The Practice of Everyday Life*. Berkeley: University of California Press.

Ellis, E., 2001, Tech talk: Sintercom no more, *TIME Asia*, [Online] 21 August. Available at: http://www.time.com/time/business/article/0,8599,171971,00.html [Accessed 22 January 2013].

Financial Times, 2010a. A cultural revolutionary. 13 November.

Financial Times, 2010b. The big screening. 18 November.

George, C., 2005. Calibrated coercion and the maintenance of hegemony in Singapore. *Asia Research Institute Working Paper*, No. 48, Singapore: National University of Singapore.

George, C., 2006. Singapore elections: two positive signs. *Air-Conditioned Nation* blog, [blog] 7 May, Available at: http://cherian.blogspot.com/2006/05/singapore-elections-two-positive-signs.html [Accessed 24 February 2013].

George, C., 2007. Looking for patterns in 10 years of "light touch" regulation. 23 August, Available at: http://journalism.sg/2007/08/23/looking-for-patterns-in-10-years-of-light-touch-regulation/ [Accessed 24 February 2013].

George, C., 2010. Control-Shift: the Internet and political change in Singapore. In: Chong, T., ed., *Management of Success: Singapore reassessed*. Singapore: Institute of Southeast Asian Studies, p. 258.

George, C., 2012. *Freedom from the Press: journalism and state power in Singapore*. Singapore: National University of Singapore Press.

Government of Singapore, 2006. General Election 2006. 20 April, Available at: http://www.elections.gov.sg/pressrelease/20060420b.pdf [Accessed 24 February 2013].

Heng, G. and J. Devan, 1991. State fatherhood: the politics of nationalism, sexuality, and race in Singapore. In: A. Parker, M. Russo, D. Sommer and P. Yaeger, eds., *Nationalisms and Sexualities*. New York: Routledge.

Ho, K.C., R. Kluver and Kenneth C.C. Yang, 2003. Asia encounters the Internet. In: K.C. Ho, R. Kluver and K.C.C. Yang, eds., *Asia.com: Asia encounters the Internet*. London: RoutledgeCurzon, pp. 1–17.

Johal, T., 2004. Controlling the Internet: The use of legislation and its effectiveness in Singapore. Asian Studies Association of Australia, *15th Biennial Conference of the Asian Studies Association of Australia*. Canberra, 29 June–2 July 2004.

Lee, K.M., 2006a. The persistently non-political podcast no. 6. *The mrbrown Show*, 1 May, Available at http://www.mrbrownshow.com/?p=67 [Accessed 14 January 2013].

—— 2006b. S'poreans are fed, up with progress! *Today*, 30 June, Available at: http://www.mrbrown.com/blog/2006/07/today_sporeans_.html [Accessed 14 January 2013].

——2006c. Regarding *Today*. mr brown [Blog], 6 July. Available at: http://www.mrbrown.com/blog/2006/07/regarding_today.html [Accessed 14 January 2013].

—— 2006d. The mr brown show: a harmless podcast. *The mrbrown show*, 22 August, Available at: http://www.mrbrownshow.com/?p=197 [Accessed 14 January 2013].

Lee, K.Y., 2000. *From Third World to First: the Singapore story*: 1965–2000. Singapore: Times Editions.

Lee, T., 2005. Internet Control and Auto-regulation in Singapore. *Surveillance and Society* 3(1), pp. 74–95.

Lee, T. and Kan, C., 2009. Blogospheric pressures in Singpore; Internet discourses and the 2006 general election. *Journal of Media and Cultural Studies*, 23(6), December, pp. 871–86.

Li, X., X., Qin and R. Kluver, 2003. Who is setting the Chinese agenda? The impact of online chatrooms on party presses in China. In: K.C. Ho, R. Kluver and K.C.C. Yang, eds., *Asia.com: Asia encounters the Internet.* London: RoutledgeCurzon, pp. 143–158.

Lim, C., 2007. No Official Reply to My Open Letter. 9 December, Available at: http://catherinelim.sg/2007/12/19/no-official-reply-to-my-open-letter/ [Accessed 15 January 2013].

Lyon, D., 2003. Cyberspace, surveillance, and social control: The hidden face of the Internet in Asia. In: K.C. Ho, R. Kluver and K.C.C. Yang, eds., *Asia.com: Asia encounters the Internet.* London: RoutledgeCurzon, pp. 67–82.

Media Development Authority, Singapore, 1997. *Internet Code of Practice*. [Online] 1 November. Available at: http://www.mda.gov.sg/Documents/PDF/licences/mobj.981.Internet_Code_of_Practice.pdf [Accessed 31 March 2013].

Media Development Authority, Singapore, 2010. Online videos: When MDA will use classification. *The Straits Times*, 16 December.

Neo, J., 2011. Sedition in Singapore! Free speech and the offence of promoting ill-will and hostility between different racial groups. *Singapore Journal of Legal Studies*, December, pp. 351–72.

Penfold, C., 2003. Global technology meets local environment: State attempts to control Internet content. In: K.C. Ho, R. Kluver and K.C.C. Yang, eds., *Asia.com: Asia encounters the Internet.* London: RoutledgeCurzon,rzon, pp. 83–96.

Pseudo-marc, 2008. Two bloggers charged under seditoin act. [Blog] 3 May, Available at: http://pseudo-marc.blogspot.sg/2008/05/two-bloggers-charged-under-sedition-act.html [Accessed 5 July 2013].

Reuters, 2005. Singapore jails two bloggers for racist Internet posts. 7 October.

Rodan, G., 1998. The Internet and Political Control in Singapore. *Political Science Quarterly* (113)1, Spring, pp. 63–89.

Siew, K.H., 2013. New rules "will make netizens more cynical". *The Straits Times*, 1 June.

SingaporeMacross, 2005. Two bloggers charged for racist remarks, SG Forums. [Online] 13 September. Available at: http://sgforums.com/forums/8/topics/152349?page=5 [Accessed 5 July 2013].

Sintercom, u.d. Our Philosophy. [Online] Available at: http://web.archive.org/web/19981207024219/www.sintercom.org/philosophy.html [Accessed at 12 January 2013].

—— 1996. SBA's Reply to SIntercom's open letter of appeal. 24 September 24, [Online], Available at: http://web.archive.org/web/20010724222743/www.sintercom.org/sba_response.html [Accessed at 12 January 2013].

—— 2001. Sintercom to register with SBA. 17 July, [Online], Available at: http://web.archive.org/web/20010814074535/sintercom.org/sba/index.html [Accessed at 12 January 2013].

Soon, C. and R. Kluver, 2007. The Internet and online political communities in Singapore. *Asian Journal of Communication*, 17(3), pp. 246–65.

The Straits Times, 2005. Racist bloggers jailed, 8 October.

The Straits Times, 2006, Opposition parties slam podcast ban rule. 5 April.

SZTV News, 2010. Netizens' Composition Competition – My Dad is Li Gang (*Wangyou zhaojudasai – Woba shi Li Gang*), 21 October. [Online] Available at: http://www.tudou.com/programs/view/lcm9UZ5Ovjk/ [Accessed at 31 March 2013].

Tan, H. Will jail time end racist blogging? [Blog] Available at http://bytelawyer.blogspot.sg/2005/10/will-jail-time-end-racist-blogging.html_ [Accessed 4 June 2013].

Tan, W., 2013. MDA working with licensed news sites to make new rules "clearer". *Today*, 5 July, p. 2.

Tedbasser, 2005. Public relations concerning "sedition". [Blog] 14 September, Available at: http://tedbasser.livejournal.com/43953.html [Accessed 5 July 2013].

The Online Citizen, u.d. About Us. [Online] Available at: http://theonlinecitizen.com/about/ [Accessed 31 March 2013].

—— 2010a. Raiding the homeless – part two, 3 April. [Online] Available at: http://theonlinecitizen.com/2010/04/raiding-the-homeless-%E2%80%93-part-two/ [Accessed 31 March 2013].

—— 2010b. Do you want us to stay at the beach?, 8 April. [Online] Available at: http://theonlinecitizen.com/2010/04/do-you-want-me-to-stay-at-the-beach/ [Accessed 31 March 2013].

—— 2010c. MCYS Minister slams TOC over homeless issue?, u.d. [Online} Available at: http://theonlinecitizen.com/2010/04/mcys-minister-slams-toc/ [Accessed 31 March 2013].

TIME Asia, 2005. Lee Kuan Yew Reflects, 5 December [Online] Available at: http://www.time.com/time/asia/covers/501051212/lky_intvu5.html [Accessed at 20 February 2013].

Today, 2010. Setting the record straight on the homeless, 28 April [Online] Available at: http://www.todayonline.com/Singapore/EDC100428–0000058/Setting-the-record-straight-on-homelessness [Accessed 20 February 2013].

Today, 2013. Breakfast Network will have to shut down: MDA, 10 December [Online] Available at http://www.todayonline.com/singapore/breakfast-network-will-have-shut-down-mda [Accessed 1 February 2014].

Today, 2013. MDA, Breakfast Network continue to cross swords, 17 December [Online] Available at http://www.todayonline.com/singapore/mda-breakfast-network-continue-cross-swords [Accessed 1 February 2014].

Tomorrow.sg, 2005. Videoclip of the banned "political film" Singapore Rebel by Martyn See, 13 November, [Online] Available at: http://tomorrow.sg/archives/2005/11/12/videoclip_of_the_banned_politica.html [Accessed 20 February 2013].

TR Emeritus, 2013. How come Lee Kuan Yew's book with seditious writings is still selling?. [Blog] Available at: http://www.tremeritus.com/2013/04/25/how-come-lkys-book-with-seditious-writings-is-still-selling/ [Accessed 4 June 2013].

Trocki, C.A., 2006. *Singapore: Wealth, power and the culture of control.* Abingdon: Routledge.

Wong, T., 2013 New MDA licensing scheme for news websites. Singapolitics, [Online] 28 May, Available at: http://www.singapolitics.sg/news/new-mda-licensing-scheme-news-websites [Accessed 5 July 2013].

Yahoo News, 2013. Singapore opinion news site Breakfast Network to shut down, 10 December 2013, Available at: http://sg.news.yahoo.com/blogs/singaporescene/kitchen-closed-161623269.html [Accessed 1 February 2014].

Yao, S., 2007. *Singapore: The State and the culture of excess.* Abingdon: Routledge.

Zittrain, J., 2008. *The Future of the Internet – and how to stop it.* New Haven and London: Yale University Press.

Chapter 4
Grassroots Democratic Movements' Dependency on New Media in Contemporary Malaysia: Prospects and Limitations

Pui Yee Choong

Introduction

The ideal role of media in any democratic society is to highlight important social and political issues that concern the society. It is supposed to be non-partisan and to serve the role of check and balance in a particular state. Yet the role of the mainstream media in Malaysia is far from ideal. In general, the mainstream media in Malaysia toed the government line, if not altogether serving as the government's mouthpiece. Among various reasons, this is chiefly because Malaysia is an illiberal democracy (Case 2005; Bell, Brown, Jayasuriya and Jones 1995; Zakaria 1997). The traditional broadsheets of Malaysia such as *The Star*, *Utusan Malaysia* and the *New Straits Times* are known to avoid highlighting negative issues concerning the ruling coalition, Barisan Nasional (BN). This is because all these mainstream media are either owned or linked to the leaders in the BN coalition and strict censorship is often employed. Aside from official censorship from the editors, journalists are just as cautious in reporting sensitive political stories to avoid facing negative consequences, such as official reprimands, from the authorities (Chin 2003). Thus, these mainstream media largely reflects only the ruling BN coalition's views.

Since the 1960s, the media has been indirectly used as the apparatus of the state. The ruling elites monitored the information in the media to ensure their vested interests are well served and to influence the perceptions of the public (Anuar 2005) as well as to limit the circulation of threatening ideas (Rodan 2005). The role of media is especially important during election time as it can be used as a platform by the ruling elites to campaign. The state control of the media is further evidenced following the 1987 Weeding Operation, or *Operasi Lalang* which resulted in the detention of 106 activists under the Internal Security Act (ISA).[1] Three daily newspapers namely *The*

---

1 The Weeding Operation refers to the detention of 106 Malaysians under the Internal Security Act amidst the mounting racial tensions in 1987. It started with the appointment of around 100 Malay principals to vernacular Chinese schools. The United Chinese School Committees Association of Malaysia staged a gathering to protest against such a move from the government and they were supported by Chinese politicians from both the ruling

Star (an English daily paper), *Sin Chew Jit Poh* (a Chinese daily paper) and *Watan* (a Malay daily paper) questioned the rationale of detaining these activists who were regarded as affronts to the government (Anuar 2005). As a result, the publishing licenses of these papers were revoked. Such action from the authorities is widely believed to silence these supposedly independent voices (Means 1991).

Unsurprisingly, the mainstream media has always been dogged by the image of lacking in independence, and Malaysians have acquiesced to such norms. In the past, not many people from the general public dared to question the state's authority or make negative remarks about the government openly or officially. Even when the general public is vaguely aware of the issues of corruption or cronyism associated with the BN leaders, there is still a shortage of platforms to voice out their discontentment officially. There is also a lack of options to register their discontentment beyond the procedural act of voting during election. The BN has always been perceived as an invincible regime before the 2008 general election as it has enjoyed a two-thirds parliamentary majority conferred by multiple electoral mandates over the decades.

However, the emergence of the new media and its increasing popularity among the general public and politicians in recent times has raised several challenges to the state. Chief among many reasons is the fact that the new media is able to circumvent strict censorship from the state and opens up a more liberal space for the general public to voice their views, to search for information, as well as to compete for influence. In other words, the liberty to connect to a different realm of information is almost limitless. For instance, prior to the 2008 general election, the opposition coalition, *Pakatan Rakyat* (PR), which comprised the People's Justice Party (PKR), Pan Islamic Party (PAS) and Democratic Party (DAP), has galvanized and utilized the new media to vie for influence and have successfully raised many issues to the fore via this platform. Issues such as the corruption and cronyism within the BN coalition, which are rarely highlighted in the mainstream media, were pushed to the fore of the public discourse by the supporters of the opposition parties through blogs. In tandem, alternative news portals also picked up such stories and reported them accordingly. Consequently, citizens who are privileged to consume such information through the new media are offered alternative views of the current affairs of the state and exposed to the less positive side of the BN coalition. With the cumulative effect of new media in providing alternative views, the opposition coalition managed to deny BN its "customary" two third majority votes in the 2008 general election. This election had been termed a media war by former Prime Minister, Abdullah Badawi. The impact was so extensive to the point where he had to acknowledge his coalition had lost the media war even though it was returned as the governing coalition with a reduced majority:

---

coalition as well as opposition parties. However, their demand was subsequently countered by UMNO Youth in a rally. Racial tensions escalated as the issue was couched as an ethnic one and the authorities detained the 106 activists to stop the tensions from escalating.

"We certainly lost the Internet war, the cyber war. It was a serious misjudgment."[2] Since then, the Internet-based movements have been collectively hailed as a player in Malaysian politics[3] and the cyberspace of Malaysia is also named as the new frontier.[4]

Notwithstanding the role of new media, there are other important factors which are equally important in affecting the current social and political dynamics in Malaysia. One factor is the vibrant civil society. The civil society in Malaysia encompasses non-governmental organizations, social movements advocating for human rights, clean and fair elections and other environmental movements. This sphere also includes loosely structured mass based movements such as Islamic and youth movements, non-Islamic religious movements, public intellectuals and professional groups that are actively involved in the debates in the public discourse (Weiss 2009). Generally, most of these movements are perceived to be progressive and even left-leaning. However, there had also been an increase of right wing NGOs in recent years. Some examples are *Perkasa* and *Jati* which are founded to champion Malay rights and the supremacy of Islam. These two movements are infamous for their provocative remarks and extremist tendencies. It is important to note that some, if not all, of these civil society movements also utilized the new media for their causes in various ways to make their voices count for the purpose of the political mobilization of their agendas.

This chapter seeks to investigate how new media is utilized by different movements in Malaysia. This chapter will demonstrate how new media serves the role of alterity for movements and the general public, in particular the left-leaning movements to contest against the discourse of the state. I will investigate the different movements' dependency upon new media to advocate alternative ideas or causes, to magnify certain social and political issues in creative ways and for the purpose of mobilization. This chapter also seeks to discuss the implications and limitations of such trends. The first part of this chapter will broadly sketch the usage and growth of new media in today's Malaysia. Next, the paper will move forward to discuss two specific movements, namely Bersih 2.0 and *Loyar Burok*, as well as some examples of popular web-based satirical video initiatives to illuminate their varying degrees of dependency upon the new media. The reason for selecting these few examples is because all these illustrate different degrees of dependency upon the new media by non-party political movements. The implications for each movement arising from these dependencies are different as well. Lastly, the

---

2 *The Straits Times*. 26 March 2008, "BN's Biggest Mistake: Ignoring the Internet". Available at http://www.straitstimes.com/Free/Story/STIStory_220475.html (Accessed on 30 March 2011).

3 Koh Lay Chin. "Was This the Election Made on the Internet?" in http://bersih.org/?p=1127 (accessed on 12 August 2011).

4 Lee Siew Lian. "Cyberspace is now the New Frontline" in http://bersih.org/?p=1120 (accessed on 12 August 2011).

chapter will delve into the analysis of the implications and limitations of the nexus of new media and grassroots political movements in Malaysia.

Understanding New Media in Contemporary Malaysia

In this chapter, the term new media refers to the "on demand" access of any ordinary citizens to any unregulated content especially the Internet which allows active digital participation. This means anyone who possesses the required digital device such as computer, smartphone or digital tablet to connect to the new media can be a participant in this virtual space. Some examples of the new media includes individual or group webpages, blogs, alternative news portal, social media websites such as Facebook and Twitter and video sharing websites such as YouTube.

In today's Malaysia, the popularity of new media has grown alongside the development of the Malaysian economy, which has afforded access and led to the proliferation of computer usage and advancements in broadband networks across the country (Liow and Afif 2010). The increasing affordability of hand held electronic devices like smart phones or digital tablets have also facilitated the end-users' convenient access to the Internet. As of 2012, there are 17.5 million[5] Internet users in Malaysia out of a population of 29 million people and the number of Internet users is expected to grow to 25 million in 2015.[6] These numbers clearly illustrate the growing usage of new media by ordinary Malaysians. The increasing number of new media users also suggests that the new media medium is increasingly becoming a vital source of information. New media has become crucial to the dissemination of information as well as raising issues that are unreported by the mainstream media to the public. As there is a lack of regulation and censorship in this realm, many alternative news portals had increased in recent times as well. For instance, alternative news portals such as *Malaysiakini*, which started in the 1990s, is now one of the most popular news portals in Malaysia. It is famous for reporting news that are rarely covered by the mainstream media and *Malaysiakini* has enjoyed a steady increase of readership over the years. *Malaysiakini*'s slant is generally pro-democratic, secular and multi-racial in perspectives. It also publishes in Malay, Chinese, Tamil and the English language (Weiss 2013). Hitherto, it has two million regular users and more than 40 million views each month.[7] Its primary credit lies undeniably in its broad coverage of social and political issues in Malaysia, giving readers a better sense of current affairs of the state.

5 Malaysia Social Media Statistics http://blog.malaysia-asia.my/2013/09/malaysia-social-media-statistics.html.

6 2014 Budget: 25 million Internet users by 2015 http://www.nst.com.my/latest/font-color-red-2014-budget-font-25-mill-Internet-users-by-2015–1.384975 (Accessed 18 January 2014).

7 http://www.mdif.org/malaysiakini-malaysia/ (Accessed 20 January 2014).

Apart from *Malaysiakini*, some examples of other popular news portals that had mushroomed in recent years include *The Malaysian Insider, Free Malaysia Today, Malaysia Chronicles* and *The Malay Mail.* Such proliferation of alternative news portals had also affected the sales of the printed media since the alternative news portals are seen to be more willing to highlight sensitive social and political issues. Besides, they are also providing room for readers to interact via the comments column in every article. Therefore, instead of merely providing news, such alternative news portals also encourage exchange of ideas among its readers. As a result, it indirectly encourages participation of the readers in putting in their two cents' worth of opinion. This is in addition to challenging the credibility of the mainstream media by bringing more social and political issues to the fore (Gowing 2009).

Another form of new media that has made its mark in the socio-political scene of Malaysia is the mushrooming of blogs from political leaders, social activists and public intellectuals. For example, many political leaders maintain blogs and use it to share their thoughts on Malaysian socio-political issues by writing short insightful pieces. They would use their blogs to stake their positions, raise issues and even delegitimize their political opponents. The more skilful political bloggers will probably manipulate the readers' sentiments to empathize with their political leanings as well. In addition to that, as the nature of blogging is informal and personal, they can attract followers and cultivate a sense of shared empathy among readers. This is especially so among bloggers who write reflective and personal pieces. Some examples of political leaders who maintain blogs are the former Prime Minister of Malaysia, Tun Mahathir Mohammad, veteran opposition leader Lim Kit Siang, and Anwar Ibrahim. Although the views of bloggers are unofficial, it nonetheless garnered attention and it will indirectly affect the sentiments of their supporters or detractors. However, it is also important to note that not all bloggers comment solely on political issues.

Another popular feature of new media in contemporary Malaysia is the ubiquitous use of social network sites among Malaysians such as *Facebook* and *Twitter*. In 2012, there was an estimated 13.3 million Facebook users[8] and Malaysians were ranked as the fifth highest number of Facebook users in Asia.[9] Given the nature of Facebook as an open and a user-friendly platform, it encouraged active participation and interaction among users. Interestingly, aside from posting snapshots of their day-to-day lives, from what they eat to how they feel, a segment of Malaysian Facebook users utilized this platform to share their political thoughts and repost politicians' views or even to "check in" on some political events and to assert their commitments to certain political parties. It is also important to note that politicians had also utilized this platform to get closer to their constituents by making "friends"

---

8 http://blog.malaysia-asia.my/2013/09/malaysia-social-media-statistics.html (Accessed 20 January 2014).

9 http://www.forbes.com/sites/limyunghui/2012/07/16/facebook-in-asia-growth-deceleration-continues-latest-stats/ (Accessed 20 January 2014).

and updating their latest political activities through this realm. For instance, during the 13th general election in Malaysia, the Facebook page of the opposition coalition and some contesting candidates were also used to update their campaigning activities such as their venue, time and location for their rallies or other publicity events.

Furthermore, such social media platforms had also been used as a platform of publicity for certain civil society groups and social movements. While these civil society movements do retain a website, they will also create a *Facebook* and *Twitter* account to ensure their presence is being felt in the virtual space. By tapping into the social media platform, it also increased the presence of the movement among social media users. Some examples of civil society movements that also utilized social media platforms are Bersih 2.0 (Clean) which advocates for electoral reform, and *Himpunan Hijau* (Green Assembly) which protests against the building of the foreign-owned rare earth refinery in Kuantan. *Twitter* is especially instrumental to these movements during their organized rallies as organizers and participants of the rally can post live updates of the gathering and warn incoming protestors to stay away from areas where the authorities are stationed in strength.

Twitter is equally imperative in the dissemination of information and competition of influence just like any news portal. This micro-blogging platform has been used to stake positions on issues, in addition to providing live updates of a particular event. For instance, two hours into the counting of votes during the 13th general election in Malaysia on 5 May 2013, the opposition leader Anwar Ibrahim claimed that PR has won the election. His irresponsible short statement of not more than 140 words set off confusion and raised false hopes among his supporters and established the precursor to the 5 May rally to protest against the ultimate BN victory. This tweet also hardened the opinion of his supporters in believing that the election in Malaysia was not fair, nor free. It has largely strengthened the hostile sentiments against the BN coalition.

Clearly, one cannot simply dismiss the role of new media in affecting the socio-political dynamics in Malaysia. As explained briefly above, the new media platform has provided an alternative space for the general public to express their views and politicians to vie for influence. It has also accelerated the growth of alternative news portals to contest the credibility of the mainstream media and such trends had since encouraged a more vibrant public sphere. New media has also facilitated the growth of social movements in Malaysia as it allows netizens to participate in the online platforms. Social movements and civil society movements had also utilized this terrain for mobilization and raising contentious issues to the fore of public discourse. With this in mind, the chapter will now devote its attention to discussing the nexus of grassroots movements and new media. We will look at three examples of movements that are dependent on the new media to varying degrees.

Bersih and Bersih 2.0: Mobilizing Through the New Media

Bersih (Clean) started out as the Joint Action Committee for Electoral Reform. It was formed in July 2005 and soon came to be known as Bersih.[10] The objective of Bersih is to push for electoral reform in Malaysia. The first batch of the Bersih committee comprised members from opposition political parties, as well as representatives from the following NGOs: Suara Rakyat Malaysia (Suaram), Women's Development Collective (WDC) and Writers' Alliance for Media Independence (WAMI).[11] In 2007, the opposition coalition engineered a public rally under the auspices of Bersih and campaigned for electoral reform. The publicity and mobilization of participants to the rally was essentially done via the new media in the form of blogs, emails and text messages. This was because it was impossible to publicize the event openly as the organizers might run the risk of being detained under the Internal Security Act (ISA), with the police treating it as a largely an anti-establishment rally. In the end, the rally was held successfully with an unofficial estimation of 50,000 participants,[12] an impressive turnout by Malaysian standards. However, the protestors were ultimately dispersed with chemical-laced water and tear gas cannons.

The 2007 Bersih Rally was indicative of the importance of new media to inform and to literally "give form" to public sentiments. This new media was utilized to disseminate information and to mobilize support. Without this medium, it would have been difficult for Bersih to make good on its promise to organize the rally as the general public was only made aware of the event through text messages, emails, and blogs and not through official mainstream broadsheets. To further encourage the people to take to the streets, stories of corruption were associated with the lack of clean and fair elections in the blogs of activists and opposition politicians, who are after all the main supporters of the Bersih movement. This consequently enlarged the issue of electoral reform in conjunction with other issues to attract more supporters. Inevitably, this garnered the movement more attention if not credibility.

Marking its third anniversary in 2011, Bersih rebranded itself as Bersih 2.0 to shed its partisan shade. It was helmed by former Bar Council president, Ambiga Sreenevasan. Interestingly, during its launch, Ambiga asserted, "We know where to go and make noise. We know how to do it loudly,"[13] suggesting that they were more than ever not averse to taking their cause directly and openly to the streets. Bersih 2.0 has since been monitoring and calling for electoral reforms, making themselves the unofficial "watchdog" of elections. Hitherto, their website,

10 Bersih means Clean in the Malay language.

11 About Bersih, http://bersih.org/?page_id=352 (Accessed on 20 January 2014).

12 http://www.themalaysianinsider.com/malaysia/article/bersih-rally-to-benefit-pakatan-more-than-2007-protest-says-mat-sabu (Accessed 21 January 2014).

13 Reform of face Rallies, Bersih 2.0 warns E.C at http://www.malaysiakini.com/news/147889 (Accessed on 18 April 2014).

containing press statements, commentaries, as well as reports, is the main source of information for their activists. Other sources of information are through their Facebook and Twitter accounts. They also held press conferences prior to and after the general elections. Its visibility and persistence for the cause of electoral reform has garnered itself some credibility among the urban middle class Malaysians.

Four years down the road, Bersih 2.0 organized its second rally on 9 July 2011. Prior to the rally, the Home Minister had announced that no permits would be granted for any rally or gathering on that day. Tensions mounted as Perkasa and UMNO youth wing announced that they would stage counter-rallies should Bersih take to the streets. Closer to the day of the rally, hundreds of Bersih 2.0 supporters in various states of Malaysia were detained by the police on the grounds that they were waging war against the monarch, reviving communism, as well as possessing Bersih T-shirts and Bersih paraphernalia. In the midst of the volatile political climate, the King intervened and urged moderation from all parties involved and granted an audience to Ambiga.

All these events leading to the actual rally were reported by the alternative news portals and had been extensively commented upon by concerned citizens as well as politicians in the social media. The unusually large scale of detention of ordinary citizens who had unabashedly displayed their support for Bersih 2.0 also indicates the state's intense displeasure towards this movement. The series of events leading up to the rally had aided the publicity of the mass participation event and Bersih supporters had interpreted police pre-emption as a form of suppression and intimidation towards the movement. Many postings and updates of these events were also seen on the Bersih Facebook and Twitter accounts. While some showed their support, others criticized its intention to take matters to the street. The point is, regardless of how the public viewed Bersih's rally, it still generated significant attention and discussion both offline and online.

In the end, Bersih 2.0 managed to mobilize tens of thousands of Malaysians onto the streets of Kuala Lumpur. Certainly, it was not all rosy for the protesters as they were dispersed once again by the authorities with chemical-laced water and tear gas cannons. Even then, supporters of the movement alleged that such action from the authorities served as a form of overt intimidation. By framing it in such a way, it will also likely gain the widespread public sympathy Bersih supporters hoped for while simultaneously painting the authorities as behaving in far less democratic fashion. This was an act of deliberate social polarization, and awakening of the conscience, and all performed through sight and sound through social media and alternative news portals.

In addition to that, the diasporic Malaysians who resided in different parts of the world also organized their own Bersih 2.0 gathering[14] to show their solidarity. Some examples of participating cities were Melbourne, Hong Kong, London, Sydney, Canberra and Osaka. These diasporic Malaysians generally got to know

14 http://www.themalaysianinsider.com/malaysia/article/bersih-to-go-global-with-july-9-rally.

about Bersih 2.0 through the new media and hardly through the traditional broadsheets. They contacted Bersih 2.0 in Kuala Lumpur to express interest in coordinating similar gatherings. While this is definitely an unintended effect of Bersih 2.0, it still suggests the power of new media to unite people for a common cause across vast geographical and political distances. Such solidarity can only happen when these diasporic Malaysians are made aware of Bersih 2.0 through the new media. The tweets and videos that were shared by Malaysians all over the world also increased the publicity of Bersih 2.0 and dramatized the importance of free and fair elections.

In addition to that, soon after the rally, ordinary citizens compiled recorded video clips of the events to highlight the excessive use of chemical-laced water by the authorities and the intimidation practised by police officers towards journalists and protestors.[15] These videos captured the police intimidation towards the weaponless protestors as well as the unjust confiscation of the media equipment of journalists. These videos were uploaded onto the video sharing website, YouTube by ordinary citizens. The point made by such recorded evidence is that it is hard to refute the suggestion that the authorities in Malaysia were an illiberal government bent on brutally crushing dissent. As a result, these images will also imbue a sense of deep-seated anger among the ordinary citizens, especially supporters of Bersih 2.0, as they can vividly see, remember and replay the heavy-handedness of the government's response to their movement of conscience.

The Bersih rallies clearly illustrated how anti-establishment and reformist movements in Malaysia depend upon the new media terrain for validation and mobilization (Gamson and Wolfsfeld 1993). The new media in the form of social networks, news portals, and micro-blogs allowed the movement to circumvent state restrictions to get their message across and attract supporters. In the aftermath of the rally, citizens who volunteered to compile and upload videos that cast the authorities in a negative light further enhance the movement's credibility. Additionally, when alternative news portals reported all the events leading up to the second Bersih 2.0 rally in 2011, it also helped publicize the movement as socially relevant. Hence, the role of new media is crucial in accounting for the popularity of Bersih 2.0 as well as its successful mobilization of people out on the streets.

Loyar Burok: More Than a Blog

Another movement that is dependent on the role of new media is *Loyar Burok*. Originally, *Loyar Burok* was merely a blog started by six lawyers. It was used as a platform for advocacy on human rights issues and a focal point for legal opinion

15 http://www.youtube.com/watch?v=vCetbFLceFI and http://www.youtube.com/watch?v=linnq9sZeVc (Accessed 22 January 2014).

through its blog.[16] *Loyar Burok* started to gain popularity during the Perak crisis of 2009. The Perak crisis refers to a complicated constitutional crisis that occurred after three legislators from the PR coalition of the Perak state government defected. At the peak of the crisis, the state government collapsed. As there were lots of legal issues surrounding the Perak crisis, the blog started getting lots of attention during that period as concerned citizens attempted to unravel the issue. Since then, the blog has continued to highlight various contemporary issues including, human rights, constitutional, and religious issues in Malaysia, albeit with a casual tone and comical slant. *Loyar Burok* also allowed other writers to express their thoughts and ideas in the blog. These writers ranged from university students, activists, lawyers and all sorts of middle class professionals.

Subsequently, *Loyar Burok* has grown beyond a blog. A significant highlight of *Loyar Burok* is the establishment of its center on March 2011. This center is named as the Malaysian Center of Constitutionalism and Human Rights (*Pusat Rakyat Loyar Burok*). It aims to be an open space for conducting education initiatives, engagement with the public, and a resource center for advocacy. For instance, one of the off-shoots of *Loyar Burok* is the *Undi Malaysia* (Vote Malaysia) initiative. It is an education movement to engage youths in Malaysia to ask the right questions and make informed decisions. As a result, the lawyers behind *Loyar Burok* conduct workshops to teach the younger generations about their constitutional rights. Apart from that, the center is also open for interested parties to hold seminars, debates and even concerts for free. In essence, this center is meant to be space for different things as long as it contributes to the advocacy of human rights. Hence, *Loyar Burok* is no longer just a blog, but a loosely defined social movement. The strength of *Loyar Burok* lies ultimately in its ability to target the young educated middle class Malaysians who are mostly Internet savvy.

Having said that, it is still important to note that *Loyar Burok's* popularity is still confined to the more educated urban and mostly English speaking Malaysians who enjoy the vast information that the Internet provides. In contrast to *Bersih 2.0, Loyar Burok's* is less visible and popular. It is also limited in the sense that it could not reach a cross-section of Malaysians from different walks of life. One common explanation is that it does not hold large scale rallies and brings its agenda onto the streets. It lacks the spectacle of Bersih 2.0, instead it operates on a more progressive and subtle manner. Even then, the impact of *Loyar Burok* cannot be underestimated as it has the strength to produce cumulative effects among those who benefit from its initiatives.

In sum, *Loyar Burok* has evolved from being merely just a blog that dwells on legalistic issues to a loose group of diverse enthusiastic young adults who are armed with better knowledge to understand the socio-political issues of the day. Its *Undi Malaysia* initiative and activities in the center had also educated the young ones to understand their rights and allow them to learn in a less formal environment.

16 *Loyar Burok*. http://www.loyarburok.com/selected-exhortations/loyarburok-in-the-star-cheeky-take-on-human-rights/ (Accessed 14 January 2014).

The blog has moreover served as a platform for the brightest and sharpest minds to share ideas and engage in healthy debates. Where Bersih 2.0 made its impact loudly on the streets, the impact of *Loyar Burok* is more cumulative and subtle. Nonetheless, what remained new is its offering of a space, be it in the form of the blog or its center, to allow people to be controversial in a safe environment. One must finally recognize that *Loyar Burok* evolved from the Web into an offline presence, and this is the uniqueness of its ripple effects.

Satirical Videos and Short Films

Another vital feature of the new media landscape in Malaysia is the satirical videos and short films that are freely accessible on the Internet through various websites. In contrast to the movements like Bersih 2.0, where there are designated committee members sustaining the cause and keeping the movement alive with conscious intention, satirical videos or short films can be put up by ordinary Malaysians with the intention to just satirize. Although these actions are not necessarily loaded with lofty goals or objectives, people who are engaged in such activities do have a story to tell. One example is PopTeeVee, a web TV network. One significant section in this web TV network is *That Effing Show* which is an online video commentary that satirizes various social and political issues in Malaysia. The program hosts depict contemporary issues in Malaysia with large doses of sarcasm and comical anecdotes. Certain policies in Malaysia are shown up to be neither logical nor constructive with its creative jokes and reenactments of some politicians' speeches, as well as the dramatization of the daily lives of ordinary Malaysians by the program hosts. Sometimes, they even lampoon certain political leaders' insensitive remarks by mimicking them. Furthermore, the languages used by the hosts are predominantly English and Malay, occasionally interspersed with some Chinese and Indian dialects and it is easily relatable to many Malaysians.

Another set of users who have employed the new media platform to highlight contemporary issues through satirical videos is a group identifying themselves as *Nasi Lemak 2020.* The people behind *NasiLemak2020* are not associated to any TV network. The people behind this initiative made satirical videos by using Hong Kong productions such as Stephen Chow movies, and especially drawing upon the famous hit, *Infernal Affairs*, dubbing it with different voices to lampoon Malaysian socio-political issues. They select various short scenes from these movies and situate these scenes in the Malaysian context and reinterpret it by dubbing it with renewed conversations. For instance, in the film, *Infernal Affairs*, there is a scene where the protagonist, a spy, was having a conversation with his superior and the voice of this protagonist is dubbed to be someone who is a Malaysian opposition supporter and he "vowed" on screen to expose the corruption of the BN government; stating that it is impossible to rely on the Malaysian Anti Corruption Commission (MACC) to address the problem.[17] The interesting part is that even when it is just a fictional reinterpretation of these scenes, the theme of the indignation against corruption is consistent with Malaysian public opinion. Other videos from *Nasi Lemak 2020* dwelled on the themes of social justice and good governance in general.

By using scenes from famous movies and reinterpreting it into the Malaysian context by dubbing it with new conversations, *NasiLemak2020* helps to broach the subject of politics, corruption and social justice amongst the Internet-savvy general public. What distinguishes *NasiLemak2020* from *That Effing Show* is the language used which is mainly Cantonese, a dialect spoken widely among Malaysian Chinese, and this accessibility is reinforced by the selection of famous Chinese movies. It is often the case that the struggles that the protagonist faces in the movies are reinterpreted empathetically for the Malaysian context. In general, the political commentary embodied in both *That Effing Show* and *NasiLemak 2020* are often hilarious and it easily attracts viewers' attention. Most importantly, such satirical videos manage to magnify political issues and draw the viewers' attention in ways where traditional media can never do, albeit with a tinge of deliberate bias.

Putting aside the objectivity of these videos, it still serves the purpose of keeping various issues at the fore of public consciousness. Even when it was meant to be sarcastic, the brilliance of the sarcasm lies in the fact that it managed to reduce complicated issues into dimensions that are easier to understand through creative humor. On a different note, as most of these videos largely push an anti-establishment slant, the growth and popularity of these initiatives also have the potential to undermine the credibility of the state as they continue to paint the state in a negative light. Satire also has the potential to influence its viewers to continue believing that almost everything that comes out from the BN politicians' mouths is negative, unreliable and consequently muddled.

Prospects, Limitations and Implications

The aforementioned examples have illustrated the varying degrees of Malaysian grassroots movements' dependency upon the new media platforms. The new media terrain is used by these assorted movements to sustain their presence, to mobilize, to state their views as well as to raise issues to the fore of public discourse. While Bersih 2.0 used the new media for mobilization, other movements such as *That Effing Show* is entirely dependent on the new media to lampoon contemporary issues and trivialize them, whereas *Loyar Burok* has evolved into a movement that conducts other activities apart from just actively blogging. By and large, the new media is used as the alternative terrain by movements.

There are a few insightful prospects that this terrain offers. Firstly, new media enables the circumvention of the state's censorship. Without any gatekeepers in the realm of new media, the utilization of it by the aforementioned movements

17 http://www.youtube.com/watch?v=uDad1DgLjvU (Accessed 23 January 2014).

had indirectly played a check and balance role in terms of circulating non-conformist information and viewpoints in spite of the BN's hegemonic role in Malaysian government. While it is too ambitious to claim new media platforms as a comprehensive leveller against the mainstream media, new media does pose a significant threat to the credibility of the mainstream media. After all, new media has managed to raise issues that are considered sensitive by the ruling BN. Secondly, as the new media realm allowed free participation of ordinary citizens and organized political movements alike, it inculcates a more vibrant and vocal discourse, however limited it may be in relation to the wider population of Malaysia. This vibrancy is especially pronounced among readers who only consume their news through alternative news portals and when the public lacks faith in the mainstream media.

That aside, it is also interesting to note that when political movements utilize the new media and frame a powerful narrative to advocate a cause that can transcends narrow communal rights, it can enhance the solidarity of the supporters as exemplified by the diasporic supporters of the Bersih 2.0 movement. This virtual space, when used strategically, can facilitate supporters of a particular movement coming together and crossing racial boundaries to advocate a particular cause. For instance, the solidarity exemplified by the diasporic Malaysians for the Bersih 2.0 movement was not only unprecedented, it also roused a new sense of nationalism among Malaysians, manifesting in the aspiration towards free and fair elections. In other words, new media provides an alternative space for the people to imagine a different and normative possibility.

That said, despite the prospects and opportunities that new media offers, it is not without its limitations. Firstly, in a minimally governed electronic public sphere where information can be flawed and biased, consumers of information may not necessarily receive objective and reliable information. Similar to the mainstream media, it is also not entirely reliable and it can potentially sway the public towards believing one sided narratives. Secondly, the realm of public information will get more complicated when the definition of users of new media becomes increasingly blurred. As stated earlier, anyone who possesses a hand held device that allows its users to go online can be a participant in the public space of information. They can blog, comment and start creating and sharing videos that lampoon the current issues of the day on a whim, and therefore such new media participants can glibly and unthinkingly produce misleading perceptions, instead of sharing progressive or objective ideas. In general, what most people know about the current affairs of the state is from the media that they consume, hence, when the public only accepts what the new media offers just because they have lost their confidence in the mainstream media, it will reinforce either their scepticism or mistaken beliefs in the affairs of the state. Within the same line of argument, this means that the new media's prime limitation may simply lie in its possibility of preaching merely to the converted. This is especially true among the loyal supporters of certain movements such as Bersih 2.0. Supporters tune in to what they are already predisposed to believe and try to sway the uncommitted netizens to believe likewise.

Other than that, the question of just how far and wide such prospects could be inclusive towards the rural or semi-rural population of new media users needs to be addressed. Although Malaysia has experienced a steady rate of urbanization in recent decades, along with an increase in Internet users, it is important to note that there is still a huge number of Malaysians who may not have been connected to the Web. This is especially the case with the older generations who are residing in rural or semi-rural areas where the access to new media is still considered a luxury, while the higher Internet penetration rate is still confined to the urban and semi-urban areas. This may mean that the opportunities and prospects offered by the new media is still largely an urban and middle class phenomenon. For instance, it is interesting to note while Bersih 2.0 received its support from the city dwellers and diasporic Malaysians of diverse racial and economic backgrounds, there is a lack of equivalent solidarity from the *Orang Asli* (aboriginal) community as well as from the various tribes from East Malaysia. It is also the case that *Loyar Burok* remained consistently popular among the young, hip and urban. One simple explanation is they just do not have access to the new media and they are just not privileged enough to know about the existence of such movements.

On a different note, even when movements managed to attract supporters, to what extent this support can be translated into sustained concrete action is extremely difficult to gauge. It does not take much to support a movement's cause such as writing an insightful article at *Loyar Burok* or sharing the movement's updates through one's personal social media account. However, these actions will likely remain as ostracized online activities if there is a shortage of concrete platforms beyond the new media to push forward significant political campaigns offline. There could be a possibility that many of the participants of the new media realm will probably remain as just keyboard warriors.

Conclusion

This chapter has broadly sketched the growth of new media in Malaysia and its importance in the current social and political spheres. It has also discussed how different movements utilized new media in different ways. While Bersih 2.0 has largely used it for offline mobilization, *Loyar Burok*'s unprecedented growth from a blog to a movement that sports various human rights initiatives, showcased the potential of new media initiatives to blossom into full fledged civil society. Conversely, notwithstanding its biasness, satirical videos such as the effort of *That Effing Show* and *Nasi Lemak 2020* helped to magnify political or social issues in ways where traditional media cannot. All in all, these movements utilized the new media realm to contest the social and political issues in contemporary Malaysia.

This trend suggests that the new media space allows a seemingly more democratic sphere for the public to participate in its discourse since participation is really just a few clicks away. It seems to suggest that Malaysia is heading towards becoming a more democratic society since anyone who has the luxury to consume new media can participate in the market place of discourse and exercise freedom of expression in the literal sense. However, one should not confuse the online sphere with the offline sphere as there is still a significant gap between the two. When one logs out from the new media sphere, one is still required to live within the structural and legal restrictions on expression and action. Despite all the encouragement one gets from the online sphere, where one can find like-minded idealistic Malaysians, the reality is that Malaysia, as a nation-state, has yet to be transformed into a liberal democratic state that welcomes anti-establishment ideas or actions. As illustrated by the case study of Bersih, when one manifests social action on the street, one needs to pay the price of facing the chemical-laced water and tear gas cannons of riot police. The ideals in the online sphere are starkly different when implemented offline, unless protest is implemented subtly.

Nonetheless, the new media remains a strategic virtual space for movements to begin to challenge the incumbent's discourse and policies and for the purpose of mobilization and validation (Gamson and Wolfsfeld 1993). It is the terrain of alterity for citizens who prefer a more secular and democratic country. Additionally, the embrace of new media appears largely to be an urban centric phenomenon. Yet despite its limitations, one cannot deny that this trend definitely spurs the advancement of democracy in Malaysia through various nimble ways and unpredictable implications such as those attending to *Loyar Burok.* In the final analysis, the nexus of new media and grassroots political movements will remain critical in affecting the dynamics in the public discourse and serves as a safe haven for the active online community. However, its growth will likely be slow. It may trigger unpredictable rhizomatic political effects amongst the younger generations, or it may inspire a few to take their cause (however distinct from the BN-run state) further, yet it is unlikely to be immediately revolutionary (Weiss 2013) even when it struggles to democratize the offline Malaysia that is their target.

References

Anuar, M.K., 2005. "Journalism, National Development and Social Justice in Malaysia," *Asia Pacific Media Educator*, 16(9), Universiti Sains Malaysia.

Bell, Daniel A., Brown, David, Jayasuriya, K. and Jones, David M., 1995. *Towards Illiberal Democracy in Pacific Asia*. New York: St Martin's Press.

Case, William, 2005, "Southeast Asia's Hybrid Regimes: When Do Votes Change Them?", *Journal of East Asian Studies* 5, 2005, pp 21–216.

Chin, James, 2003, "MalaysiaKini.com and its Impact on Journalism and Politics in Malaysia," in K.C Ho, Randy Kluver, C.C Yang (eds), *Asia.com: Asia Encounters the Internet*. New York, London: RoutledgeCurzon.

Gamson, W. and Wolfsfeld, G., 1993. "Movements and Media as Interacting Systems." *Annals of the American Academy of Political and Social Science* 528:114–125.

Gowing, Nik, 2009, *"Skyful of Lies" and Black Swans: The New Tyranny of Shifting Information Power.* Oxford: Reuters Institute for the Institute of Journalism https://reutersinstitute.politics.ox.ac.uk/fileadmin/documents/Publications/Skyful_of_Lies.pdf (Accessed 14 January 2014).

Liow, J.C. and Pasuni, A., 2010. "Debating the Conduct and nature of Malaysian Politics: Communalism and New Media Post-March 2008," *Journal of Current Southeast Asian Affairs*, 29(4), pp39–65.

Means, G.P., 1991. *Malaysian Politics: The Second Generation.* Singapore: Oxford University Press.

Rodan, G., 2005. *Transparency and Authoritarian Rule in Southeast Asia: Singapore and Malaysia.* New York: Routledge.

Weiss, Meredith L., 2009. "Edging Toward a New Politics in Malaysia: Civil Society at the Gate?" *Asian Survey,* 48(5), pp.741–758.

Weiss, Meredith L., 2013. "Parsing the Power of 'New Media' in Malaysia," *Journal of Contemporary Asia*, 43(4), pp 591–610.

Zakaria, F., 1997. "The Rise of Illiberal Democracy," *Foreign Affairs* 76(6) http://fareedzakaria.com/1997/11/01/the-rise-of-illiberal-democracy/ (Accessed 12 January 2014).

PART II
Governmental Steering and Policy Alterity

Chapter 5
Hacking, Nationalism, Democracy and Cyberwarfare in the People's Republic of China: A Centre/Margin Perspective

Kay Hearn

Hacking and the disruption of networks is of concern to all nations as the Internet forms a new space in which international relations are played out and viewed. The Internet is both a resource to be protected and a space in which war can be waged both physically and in terms of propaganda. Governments are physically trying to protect networks while at the same time many countries are developing the tools to carry out attacks on other networks. In addition, non-government hackers are involved in both criminal and political hacking. China has been host to a number of hack attacks that have been reported in the media, the most spectacular of these was carried out by Falun Gong in 2002, when sect members hacked into satellite and cable networks to broadcast messages. Claims have also been made in the western media of officially sanctioned hack attacks against the sect's websites in the USA, Canada, the United Kingdom and Australia.[1] In 2001, there was a spate of tit for tat attacks between the USA and China following the spy plane incident that year. There were suggestions during the hack attacks associated with the spy plane incident that they were officially sanctioned. The hack attacks carried out by Falun Gong were beyond the control of the government and therefore unofficial. Hacking in this context represents another forum in which centre/margin relationships between the PRC and other countries are visualized through media reports of these incidents. In this regard, hacking constitutes a virtual form of interaction between the CCP as the central authority of the PRC and other groups such as democracy dissidents and nations. This chapter also looks at the way that time, as an official dialogue, is managed in response to hacking. Essentially, this chapter explores the relationship between hackers and Chinese government policy through a centre margin analysis which allows for an examination of the interaction between hackers and the government. This is the interplay between the official and the unofficial as played out via the Internet through hacking. I will also include two illustrations of hacker nationalism in action over Taiwan and Tibet.

---

1 For more details see Michael Chase and James Mulvenon (2002) You've Got Dissent! Chinese Dissidents Use of the Internet and Beijing's Counter-Strategies.

Hacking usually refers to someone who tries to disrupt or gain unauthorized access to a computer system. Patrice Riemens (2002, n.p.) argues that:

> Hackers, also often, but inexactly referred to as "computer pirates" or other derogatory terms, constitute without doubt the first social movement that was intrinsic to the electronic technology that spawned our networked society. Hackers, both through their savvy and their actions, have hit the imagination and have been in the news right from the onset of the "information age", being either hyped up as bearers of an independent and autonomous technological mastery, or demonized as potential "cyber-terrorists" in the process. More recently they have been hailed in certain "alternative" intellectual and cultural circles as a countervailing power of sorts against the increasingly oppressive onslaught of both monopolistic ICT corporations and regulation-obsessed governments and their experts. Transformed into role-models as effective resistance fighters against "the system", their garb has been assumed with various degrees of (de)merit by a plethora of cultural and political activists associated, closely or loosely, with the "counter-globalization movement".

Though this definition is aimed at western notions of hacking and hacking culture, it is still useful as a starting point to discuss the kinds of activities that characterize the incidents that are covered in this chapter. This kind of definition is also significant because it encompasses one of the themes that underscore the debates about the social implications of the Internet in western scholarship. That is the mythology of the democratising prospects of the Internet. However, what the above definition fails to take into account more generally though are the various kinds of official and officially sanctioned hacking and crime based hacking that goes on internationally.

To date, the literature on the Internet in China largely reflects the paradoxes that surround the development of the Internet. Some of the literature suggests that the Internet is a catalyst for change that is facilitating private citizens' participation in politics, while at the same time other sectors of the literature claim that the CCP has been successful in controlling the medium. *Dark Guests and Great Firewalls: The Internet and Chinese Security* (2002) by Ronald J. Deibert looked at the debate surrounding the impact of the Internet on Chinese politics and security policy. Deibert separates the debate into two camps, cyber libertarians, and a more pessimistic group who argue that the technology of the Internet has surveillance qualities and therefore represents a threat to privacy and reinforces the authority of the state. The cyber libertarians argue that the Internet is uncontrollable and they accentuate the contradiction between the attempts to control territorial space and the challenge that the Internet represents to this because of the spread of the technology around the globe. Deibert's work is important in that it clearly outlines the dichotomy of freedom and control that permeates much of the literature in this area. The myth that the Internet is uncontrollable is in part perpetuated through the vulnerability of networks to hacking. Hacking has been used by groups for both political and criminal purposes. However, my position is that the Internet in

China is managed and shaped by the government, often in response to what they perceive as negative uses of the technology by groups outside the government. Though there is a level of tolerance for some forms of dissent, there are still topics that are banned from discussion on the Internet, such as the causes of corruption, democracy and the Tiananmen crackdown of 1989. Dissidents are still harassed and detained, with even the most outspoken and seemingly untouchable dissident, Ai Weiwei, detained for 81 days in 2011, and his blog shut down in 2009. During 2012, Ai has been unable to leave China. In April 2012, he was ordered to remove webcams from his home. And though he is still talking to the international press and continues to update on Twitter, and has moved his blog offshore to the United States of America, within China access to his online activities remain blocked. Other dissidents, such as Hu Jia and Feng Zhengghu remain under house arrest as do many others. Liu Xiaobo lingers in jail, while his wife is under house arrest.

Other studies have specifically focused on the intensification of nationalism on the Internet in China (Liu, 2006; Wu, 2006; Zhou, 2005). These studies have focused on protests following incidents such as the spy plane incident of 2001, the bombing of China's Belgrade embassy in 1999, and the unresolved Diaoyu islands dispute. Both Zhou Yonming and Xu Wu argue that the emergence of nationalism on the Internet in China is independent of state-sponsored nationalism. However, nationalist sentiments have been allowed to flourish at different times, such as during the disputes named above, and have been tapped into by the state to advance their negotiations in those disputes, and toned down when the disputes were no longer of great significance to the CCP.

The theoretical framework used in this chapter is medium theory, particularly the work of Harold Innis (1951, 1952, 1972) and Ronald Deibert (1997). Innis was concerned with the interaction between the interests of those who controlled the flow of knowledge and the mechanisms used in the dissemination of information. Deibert is interested in the way in which social actors have adapted to changing media environments. This framework allows for a centre/margin approach for an analysis that looks at the interaction between online and offline politics. Online politics cannot be separated from offline politics in China as the CCP is the final arbiter of politics in that country. There are limited mechanisms for political participation outside of the CCP and as such all online activity is moulded to conform to the CCP's views.

It is often assumed by medium theorists (Carey; Comor; R.J. Deibert; Drache and Beyer; Innis; M. McLuhan and Fiore) that the introduction of a new form of communications technology into a society will directly affect and alter a country and/or culture both socially, cognitively, economically, and politically. For example, Marshall McLuhan (1997; 1967; 1989) argues that innovations in communications technology directly influence and change a country, and/or its culture and society, politically, and economically. The medium also changes the way in which people process information. This media effect is a limited technologically deterministic one. My view is that the introduction of the Internet into China cannot be studied in isolation, or from a technologically determinist position, but must be studied within the context of the social and knowledge flows that comprise modern China. Innis's ideas are useful here because his work was concerned with the interaction between the interests of those who controlled the flow of knowledge and the vehicle for the dissemination of information. Innis (1951) argued that communications technologies are used to exert influence over time and space, and that they are subject to the interests of a particular group who, in his words, represent a "monopoly of knowledge". He asserts that:

> The concepts of time and space reflect the significance of media to civilization. Media that emphasize time are those that are durable in character, such as parchment, clay and stone. The heavy materials are suited to the development of architecture and sculpture. Media that emphasize space are apt to be less durable and light in character, such as papyrus and paper. The latter are suited to wide areas of administration and trade. The conquest of Egypt by Rome gave access to supplies of papyrus, which became the basis of a large administrative empire. Materials that emphasize time favour decentralization and hierarchical types of institutions, while those that emphasize space favour centralization and systems of government less hierarchical in character. (1972, p.7)

Innis was not arguing the case for technological determinism, but rather through his examination of different media within different historical moments, showed a certain interaction between the management of time and space and communications technology which he always saw as having a contradictory potential (Drache and Beyer, 1996). Innis (1951, p.75) states that in regard to the Middle Ages:

> A balance between concern with space or extent of territory and duration of time appears to depend on a dual arrangement in which the church is subordinated to the state and ensures that the mobilization of the intellectual resources of the civilization concerned by religion or by the state, will be at the disposal of both and that they will be used in the planning for a calculated future in relation to the government of territory of definite extent.

It is also worth noting that Innis (1993) was interested in communication in China, especially the impact of Western technologies on traditional Chinese communication patterns that remained an amalgam of the oral and the written until very recently. This interest focused on the manner in which perceptions of time and space changed in China after the introduction of the modern press and the manner in which the Western-style press disrupted the balance between traditional orality and written communication.

As such, the maintenance of time and space are dependent upon networks, networks of association and communication networks. The Internet facilitates both and can also be used to challenge networks, physically through hacking, and organizationally through the development of oppositional networks. In the context of modern China it is important to look at the way in which the Internet has been utilized by state and non-state actors and in order to understand China's adaptation to a changing media environment. The latter is an environment that the government actively seeks to mould, and which, at the same time forces the government to respond to the uses of the medium that they actively seek to discourage. It is also an environment where the government constructs networks, both physically and socially, and acts as a site in which online and offline networks interact.

Online causes are completely dependent upon the offline political process as one informs the other. Goubin Yang (2009, p.1) argues that "online activism derives its forms and dynamics from a broad spectrum of converging and contending forces, technological, cultural, social and economic and political". However if the position of a cause online is not consistent with the view of the CCP, it will then be erased from Chinese cyberspace by the army of surveillance volunteers whose job it is to trawl and remove comments from cyberspace which are deemed inappropriate. In China the Internet is managed via code content and legislation. Code referrers to the code used to construct the Internet and the way in which code is used to manage access and online behaviour, it is in this sense that Lawrence Lessig (2006) argues that "code is law". Examples of code as law include the use of passwords to access email or networks. The technological means to manage the Internet is known as the Golden Shield[2] Project and this is designed to ensure that the CCP's is the main voice on the Internet in China.

The activities of online communities are often appropriated by the government to bolster a line. For instance the vitriol that followed the riots in Tibet in 2008 and the Xinjiang riots in 2009 was used to justify and to advance the government crackdowns. Any comments generated in China that may have supported the Tibetans or Uyghurs were wiped clean from the Internet, so that all that remains is a version of the events that reflects the views of the CCP. Following the Xinjiang riots the Internet in that region was effectively shut down for several months.

For China, the Internet acts as a window on public opinion and that opinion can be tapped into to promote a government line. Another example of this is the case of the nail house in Chongqing, where a home owner who refused to make way for urban redevelopment became a big online story.[3] The case was resolved and coincided with the introduction of the Property Rights Laws. The story was used to make the point that the government supported the laws. The Black Kiln incident in 2007 played out in much the same way when a group of parents posted a message on Tianya claiming that their children had been kidnapped and forced into slavery. The story triggered outrage across Chinese cyberspace and was followed up by a national crackdown on illegal mines and brick kilns. In addition, it appears that the activities of Chinese hackers often echo the opinions of the CCP.

---

2 For more details of the Golden Shield Project see China's Golden Shield Corporations and the Development of Surveillance Technology in the Peoples Republic of China (2001), by Greg Walton.

3 For a more detailed anlaysis of the Nail House incident see Hearn (2010) Official/ Unofficial: Information Management and Social Association.

Regardless of the intention of a hacker, whether they are hacking for political or "criminal" reasons, many of the methods remain the same. These activities include the use of junk email to flood and disrupt websites, the writing of viruses to disrupt a network, or the changing of content on a website. So, it is within this context that it becomes important to look at who is hacking for whom, in much the same way that Lessig (2006, p. 6) argues we must look at who the code writers are and who they work for. Before looking at that aspect in more detail, I will first outline the legal framework that is used to manage hacking as one of the strategies for managing the Internet.

Legal Framework

The first laws that were directly aimed at the prevention of hacking were endorsed at the 19th session of the Ninth National People's Congress (NPC) Standing Committee in December 2000. The resolution made it illegal for the following activities ("First Net Security Law Endorsed", 2000):

- To enter networks concerned with national security;
- To create and spread computer viruses and to interrupt computer networks or communication services;
- To spread rumours and slanders or publicize harmful information on Internet;
- To steal or disclose state secrets, intelligence or military secrets through Internet;
- To stir up ethnic hatred and discrimination, and sabotage national unity through Internet;
- Using Internet to organize a cult organization and keep in tough with members of the cult organization, undermining the enforcement of state laws and regulations;
- Using Internet to sell fake and substandard products or advertise goods and services in a deceitful way;
- Using Internet to damage other people's business reputation and commodity reputation;
- Using Internet to infringe upon other people's intellectual property;
- Using Internet to fabricate false information affecting securities and futures trading or disturbing financial order;
- To set up pornographic websites or web pages, provide access to pornographic websites, or spread pornographic books, movies, video products and photos on Internet;
- To defame other people on Internet;
- To illegally intercept, alter or delete other people's email or other data, infringing upon citizens' freedom and confidentiality of communications; and
- Using Internet to commit theft, fraud and atrocities.

The regulations were updated in 2006 when the Ministry of Public Security (MPS) aimed to prevent the spread of computer viruses, junk emails, spam and pornography. Wu Heping, a spokesman with the MPS, wrote on the China Internet Information Centre website that "more than 80 per cent of the domestic computers were once infected by viruses annually in recent years and the daily junk mails flowing to domestic users exceeds 60 million, making China a giant country of sending and receiving junk mails" ("New Regulations to Ensure Internet Safety", 2005).

In 2001, there were calls to strengthen network security through the development of Internet technology within China. Bai Yi, director of China National Laboratory of Computer Network and Information Security, said on June 5 in 2001 "that China should develop its own information industry on the one hand and stipulate strict regulations on management and prevention on the other in order to strengthen the management of information security" ("Dual Tactics Adopted to Ensure Information Security in China", 2001). Bai Yi also said that "China should develop its own information industry to gradually take the place of imported products with homemade ones, such as the operating system, router and chip [sic]" ("Dual Tactics Adopted to Ensure Information Security in China", 2001). At the time, these kinds of statements also had a lot to do with concerns about back door programs placed inside foreign software for the purposes of spying on China. In February 2000, the government banned the importation of foreign encryption software, though by March they had backed down from this position ("Government to Ban Trade in Foreign Encryption Software", 2000; Olesen, 2000). The laws relating to cybercrime were updated again in February 2009. The regulations widen further the definition of cybercrime and have extended the maximum sentence for those found guilty of such crimes from three years to seven (McMillan, 2009).

Military and Cyber Warfare

The management of information flows and the protection of networks were built into the Internet from its inception. The Internet also acts a space in which international relations are played out.[4] Protecting information and networks from external threats and attacks is a part of national security and this is a consideration for all nations connected to the Internet. There were reports in the Jiefangjun Bao (*PLA Daily*) that the army was preparing for cyber warfare as early as 1999, and that there was to be a new branch or "network army" ("China's PLA Prepares For Network Warfare", 1999). The paper said that "the invasion of the 'network space' will be considered a violation of national sovereignty, and the gravity of the crime will not be treated any less than a territorial violation by land, sea and sky …

4 This argument is detailed in Hearn, K., Williams, P.A.H., and Mahncke, R.J. (2010) International Relations and Cyber Attacks: Official and Unofficial Discourse.

Network sovereignty has the same economic, political and military significance as territorial land, sea and sky sovereignty" ("China's PLA Prepares For Network Warfare", 1999).

Network protection is still an important feature of the PRC's overall military strategy. In November 2006 Liberation Army Daily commentator argued that: (Office of the Secretary of Defense, 2007):

> [The] mechanism to get the upper hand of the enemy in a war under conditions of informatization finds prominent expression in whether or not we are capable of using various means to obtain information and of ensuring the effective circulation of information; whether or not we are capable of making full use of the permeability, sharable property, and connection of information to realize the organic merging of materials, energy, and information to form a combined fighting strength; [and,] whether or not we are capable of applying effective means to weaken the enemy side's information superiority and lower the operational efficiency of enemy information equipment.

The 2002 Chinese White Paper on Defence recognizes the importance of information warfare and the significance of electronic networks in the management of information in military situations. The paper outlines China's strategy in relation to network based warfare and says that "rapid and drastic changes are taking place in the military field around the world, and a new serious disequilibrium has occurred in the balance of military power. The extensive applications in the military field of new and high technologies led by IT have stretched the battlefield into multidimensional space which includes the land, sea, air, outer space and electron" (PLA, 2002). It can be assumed that the term "electron" refers to the information sphere. Finally, the White Paper acknowledged that the PLA was studying and had done training that investigated models of integrated network electronic warfare (INEW) (Thomas, 2005). The USA also has cyber warfare plans including a unit of hackers (Lasker, 2004).

China is often identified as the origin of hack attacks on Western computer systems and as such the United States Government takes seriously the potential threat China may pose to American network security. Toshi Yoshihara, from the Institute for Strategic Studies, writes that "it is therefore conceivable that information warfare (IW) could provide China with the capacity to hinder American military operations in the Asia-Pacific, a region of central importance to US national security interests. Hence, the direction of China's IW strategy has direct policy relevance to the United States" (Yoshihara, 2001). In 2000, the Department of Defence warned that, "China has the capability to penetrate poorly protected US computer systems and potentially could use CNA [computer network attacks] to attack specific US civilian and military infrastructures" (Farrell, 2002).

According to the annual report to United States Congress on Military Power of the People's Republic of China 2007 the PLA is investing in electronic counter measures. The report says that (Office of the Secretary of Defense, 2007):

> China's computer network operations (CNO) concepts include computer network attack, computer network defence, and computer network exploitation. The PLA sees CNO as critical to achieving "electromagnetic dominance" early in a conflict. Although there is no evidence of a formal Chinese CNO doctrine, PLA theorists have coined the term "Integrated Network Electronic Warfare" to prescribe the use of electronic warfare, CNO, and kinetic strikes to disrupt battlefield network information systems. The PLA has established information warfare units to develop viruses to attack enemy computer systems and networks, and tactics and measures to protect friendly computer systems and networks. In 2005, the PLA began to incorporate offensive CNO into its exercises, primarily in first strikes against enemy networks.

There have been a number of media stories about hack attacks on Western military networks and government websites. The most widely reported were the attacks following the bombing of the Chinese embassy in Belgrade in 1999, and again in 2001, following the spy plane incident. In the case of the spy plane incident, there was the suggestion that the attacks were officially sanctioned by the Chinese government, in particular the attacks carried out by the Red Honker Union. It is plausible that the group did have official sanctioning as they had a website in China and were never arrested for their activities. In addition, the State Council sponsored website of the China Internet Information Centre[5] reported the breakup of the Red Honkers in 2005, and dubbed them the "guardians" of Chinese cyberspace. According to the report "membership of the group was once as high as 80,000 and it organized many website attacks on overseas government sites as well as those of schools and private companies, and engaged in virtual skirmishes with groups of foreign hackers" ("Largest Hacker Group in China Dissolves", 2005). The re-grouping of Red Honkers later that year was reported by the People's Daily who said that "the task of the alliance was to prevent hacking attacks from foreign countries" ("China's anti-hacking alliance regrouped", 2005). The appearance of the story on a website with such a strong connection to the State Council, headed by the Premier Wen Jiabao, and in the People's Daily itself, means that the Red Honkers are sanctioned by the CCP at the highest levels.[6]

---

5 China Internet Information Centre's runs an authorized government website, www.china.org.cn which is published under the auspices of the State Council Information Office and the China International Publishing Group in Beijing. The State Council Information Office is run by the State Council, the highest administrative authority in the PRC.

6 For a more detailed analysis of Chinese Cyber nationalism see Wu Xu (2006) Chinese Cyber Nationalism: evolution characteristics and implications.

In 2007, there were a number of reports in the Western media alleging hack attacks that originated in the PRC. An official with the Naval Network Warfare Command in the US suggested that the majority of hack attacks on Department of Defence websites and networks came from China, and that the frequency and intensity of attacks "has reached the level of a campaign-style, force-on-force engagement" (Rogin, 2007). As is often the case it was also suggested that there was a high probability that the attacks were officially backed by the government, based on the number of attacks and the allegation that the attacks were very deliberate.

In August 2007, multiple accusations were levelled against the Chinese government's involvement in a number of hack attacks on Germany, Australia, New Zealand, France, the USA and the United Kingdom. The story first broke when the German Chancellor Angela Merkel visited Beijing. Her trip was shadowed by allegations from *Der Spiegel* that the Chinese government had hacked into "a large number of computers in the German chancellery [and the] the foreign, economy and research ministries had been infected with Chinese spy software" ("Merkel's China Visit Marred by Hacking Allegations", 2007). Trojan Horses[7] were used to infect the computers and the attacks were launched from the north western province of Lanzhou and in the South in Guangdong province ("Merkel's China Visit Marred by Hacking Allegations", 2007). According to *Der Spiegel*, "German officials believe the hackers were being directed by the People's Liberation Army and that the programs were redirected via computers in South Korea to disguise their origin" ("Merkel's China Visit Marred by Hacking Allegations", 2007). Premier Wen Jiabao denied the claims and said that "the Chinese government attaches great importance to the hacker attack on the German government networks. China would take 'determined' and 'forceful' measures to combat hacker activities" ("Premier Wen tells Merkel China opposes hackers", 2007).

In early September 2007 the British newspaper the *Financial Times* alleged that the Pentagon had been hacked by China's military and that 15,000 computers had to be checked and cleaned. According to the London-based publication Computing, a former Pentagon official was quoted as saying that "the PLA has demonstrated the ability to conduct attacks that disable our system ... and the ability in a conflict situation to re-enter and disrupt on a very large scale" (Thomson, 2007). According to the *Financial Times*, a senior "US official said the Pentagon had pinpointed the exact origins of the attack. Another person familiar with the event said there was a 'very high level of confidence ... trending towards total certainty' that the PLA was responsible" (Sevastopuloin and McGregor, 2007). The Chinese government denied the charge and a Foreign Ministry spokeswoman, Jiang Yu, said in Beijing that "the Chinese government has consistently opposed and vigorously attacked according to the law all Internet-wrecking crimes, including hacking. Some people are making wild accusations against China ... They are totally groundless and also reflect

7 Trojan Horse is a malevolent program that poses as legitimate program with a back door allowing hackers to make changes to the systems it has infected.

a Cold War mentality. China would like to work with other countries to take measures to crack down on web crime" ("China denies US charge it hacked Pentagon network", 2007). When the attacks on Britain were denied in the Chinese Press, Yang Yi, Director of the Institute of Strategic Studies under the National Defence University was quoted as saying that "China is a responsible country and we never do this kind of despicable thing ... As a matter of fact, China has never had so called military hackers. Although we stick to the road of peaceful development, many countries still see China with suspicion and guess subjectively if anything strange happens. China pursues a defensive strategy and will never be the first to launch an attack. Any military move is conducted in line with this strategy" ("Military expert: international cooperation to fight hackers", 2007).

More allegations of officially backed Chinese hack attacks emerged in May 2008 from South Korea and India. South Korea also alleged that China was responsible for 54 per cent of the attacks on the country ("Gov't transparency in quake relief not 'forced reaction' for hosting Olympics", 2008). *The Times of India* reported that there were attacks on Indian government and private computer networks (Bagchi, 2008).

By far, the most serious allegations surfaced in February 2013 when a report released by Mandiant claimed to have uncovered a military cyber unit, based in Shanghai, that had been carrying out attacks on the American government and corporations. The hackers, identified as Unit 61398, reportedly attacked Coca-Cola, aerospace firms, military contractors, mining companies, telecommunications corporations and chemical plants. Potentially, Unit 61398 has maintained a staff of thousands of members and are claimed by the report to be one of "the most prolific cyber espionage groups in terms of the information stolen" (Mandiant, 2013, p.2). In August 2013, the Unit, under the nickname of Comment Crew, were accused of targeting American military contractors developing drone technology (Wong, 2013). The Chinese government vigorously denied the allegations. In response, President Obama signed a directive that would allow the government to share intelligence about the digital signatures of the major hacking groups from China, including Unit 61398 ("Chinese Army Unit Is Seen as Tied to Hacking Against US", 2013).

These kinds of incidents are to a large extent played out in the international media. There are few instances where direct conversations between officials from China and the countries they are supposed to have hacked into are reported in the media, and in general these are confined to official visits and are thus stage managed events by all concerned. That is not to say that Merkel did not say anything to Wen during their discussions. However, if they did discuss the hack attacks on German websites, it was not reported in the media. The point I am making is that international relations are played out in the arena of the Internet through websites and news portals. The media becomes a forum that charts and visualizes the relationship and it is via these outlets that centre/margin relations are played out through the discussion of events like hacking. The hacking of government websites by other governments also signifies a virtual war and has opened up a new space in which nations are able to spy on one another as well as a new space to fight over. Rather than just viewing international relations as being carried out in official meetings and communiqués, it can just as well be depicted as taking place within the media and the Internet through official pronouncements on web sites and in press releases, press conferences and door stop comments. World leaders read the print media, watch the television and monitor news on the Internet. It is a way to communicate without a direct conversation.

Taiwan

There have been reports about a virtual war going on between Taiwan and the PRC since 1999 when Ian Buruma first reported on this (Buruma, 1999). In August 1999, there were 72,000 cyberspace attacks launched from mainland computers, 165 times with success (Buruma, 1999). At the time, a successful attack meant superimposing a picture of the PRC flag on the Taiwanese intelligence agency's website (Buruma, 1999). In the same year, the "Ministry of Public Security in Beijing set up a special unit to combat enemy hackers, or, as it was officially put, 'to prevent an invasion of hostile forces'" (Buruma, 1999). In that year many of the attacks were triggered by statements by the then Taiwanese President Lee Teng Hui, when he put forth the "two state theory" where he was suggesting that the Mainland and Taiwan should have a state to state relationship. This was seen by Beijing as a declaration of Taiwanese independence by Lee (Jame, 1999). In 2002, it appeared that Taiwan was the location from which hack attacks into Mainland television satellites were launched by Falun Gong ("Taiwan downplays China TV hacking", 2002). In 2006, The Taipei Times claimed that Taiwan had suffered 250,000 cyber-attacks between 1996 and 2006, making Taiwan the most hacked country in the world.

Hacking in Taiwan had become such a serious problem by 2003 that Taiwan sent a formal letter to the PRC to ask for help to track down hackers who had allegedly sent a virus to the Taiwan based Eha Technology Limited software company via an email ("Taiwan asks China to help track hackers", 2003). The sources of the emails were traced to four websites registered in Hubei and Fujian provinces. A letter of request for assistance was sent to the government in Beijing by the Straits Exchange Foundation, a semi official organization that handles Taiwan's relations with the mainland, as there are no formal ties between the two countries. The letter said "we would like the relevant authorities to help in quickly finding the motives, the aims and the true identities of the perpetrators" ("Taiwan asks China to help track hackers", 2003).

In 2004, Taiwan's Kuomintang website was hacked into by a man claiming to be a military veteran from the PRC. The website's homepage was replaced with pro-China photos and China's national anthem playing in the background.

The new photos were of a PLA soldier aiming a rifle at a target and another showed two men raising the PRC flag ("Hacker gives Kuomintang Web site pro-Chinese look with PRC photos", 2004). The hacker had also written "I'm proud of being a Chinese and a Chinese veteran" ("Hacker gives Kuomintang Web site pro-Chinese look with PRC photos", 2004).

The above represents some of the incidents that have been reported on hacking between Taiwan and the Mainland. The use of the Internet and hacking signifies an interaction between these two states and hacking in this way demonstrates another arena in which centre/margin relationships between the two countries is played out, and fought over. The negotiation of this relationship takes place on both an official and unofficial level and this arena is even more significant because there are no official channels of communication between Taiwan and the Mainland. The limits of this kind of interaction are difficult to gauge as there are no official figures on the number of hack attacks that are carried out officially or otherwise. The media's reporting of hacking in this instance provides a window on the way that the relationship is negotiated between Taipei and Beijing. The mainstream media becomes the forum in which these two countries discuss their differences and this is then rearticulated through the Internet with news from a wider number of sources that proliferate overnight, often on the same event.

The rituals of the state are also used in the centre/margin dialogue between the Mainland and Taiwan. By this, I mean rituals such as the opening of parliament or the national days or state visits. There is ritual involved in all of these kinds of events and they are reported in the media. These rituals of the state are also the foundations of what Anderson calls the "cultural products of nationalism" and these are the basis of what he called imagined communities (Anderson, 1993). For example, dialogue is orchestrated through official rituals such as the 17th Party Congress in October 2007 where Hu Jintao "called for a peace agreement with Taiwan under the one-China principle" ("Peace pact with Taiwan proposed", 2007). In a report to the 17th National Congress of the CCP, Hu said "we would like to make a solemn appeal: On the basis of the one-China principle, let us discuss a formal end to the state of hostility between the two sides, reach a peace agreement, construct a framework for peaceful development of cross-Straits relations, and thus usher in a new phase of peaceful development" ("Peace pact with Taiwan proposed", 2007). The party congress is the place in which these statements are articulated and the media is the vehicle through which they are disseminated for consumption beyond the borders of the PRC.

Because of the lack of official channels between Taiwan and the PRC, the relationship between the two is imagined in the media and these imagined communities slug it out in a virtual space, that of the Internet and mainstream media, and these discourses are then rebroadcast across the space of the Internet. On an even more fundamental level, the tensions of the relationship that are played out through hacking appears on some level to be officially sanctioned.

Tibet

Tibet is another sensitive topic on the Chinese Internet and the CCP go to great lengths to define the parameters of what can and cannot be said on this topic in the same way they define their relationship with Taiwan. There is no room for debate and so it is not surprising that there have been incidents of hacking into the websites of the Tibetan government in exile and the Tibetan Support Group (TSG) ("Tibetans allege cyber invasion", 2004). The TSG claimed that the source of the attacks was the official journal of the Tibetan administration in Beijing ("Tibetans allege cyber invasion", 2004). In 2002, the Chinese government was accused for the first time of hacking into the Dalai Lama's computer network. The charges were vigorously denied by the CCP whose response was "China opposes all forms of hacking".

A report in *The Times of India* in 2004 claimed that reports on the attacks upon Tibetan exile websites began in October 2003 ("Tibetans allege cyber invasion", 2004). In 2003, the computers of the Tibetan government in exile and their support groups around the world were gripped by a major virus attack and they alleged that it was the work of Chinese government officials ("Virus attacks on Tibetan network; Chinese blamed", 2003): "The International Campaign for Tibet said in a statement that it had traced email containing the virus to an Internet company based in Beijing. After the news of the attack spread, the attackers changed mailing addresses two weeks ago, making them appear to belong to Tibet support groups" ("Virus attacks on Tibetan network; Chinese blamed", 2003). At the time, the government in exile had a network of around 400 computers and was said to be well protected. In 2004, *The Times of India* ("Virus attacks on Tibetan network; Chinese blamed", 2003) reported that the Tibetan government in exile and support groups were attacked again. This time hackers sent emails that appeared to be from other official Tibetan websites, and they contained the Trojan Horse, which is a hidden program that installs malicious software on the recipient's computer. The hidden program can then be used to gain unauthorized access and do damage to a computer ("Trojan horse", 2006). Following the riots in Lhasa in March 2008, there was another round of reports of hack attacks on pro-Tibetan websites (Johnson, 2008).

In March 2009, the nongovernmental group Information Warfare Monitor released a report into hacking activity in Tibet titled *Tracking GhostNet*. Information Warfare Monitor is a sister project of the OpenNet Initiative who have carried out the most significant study on global Internet filtering. The OpenNet Initiative is a joint-venture between the Munk Centre for International Studies, University of Toronto, Berkman Center for Internet and Society at Harvard Law School, and the Advanced Networks Research Group at the Cambridge Security Program (Centre for International Studies) at the University of Cambridge. The research for the report was carried out over a ten month period from June 2008 to March 2009 and involved field work in Dharamsala in India with extensive access and cooperation with the Tibetan Government in exile. China's response to the report was to dismiss it as propaganda. In a written statement, the Chinese government said there was "no evidence" to back the report's claims and that the report was a part of "propaganda campaign" against China as the report was commissioned by the Tibetan Government in exile (Williams, 2009). The report goes on to say that "in China, it is against the law to hack into the computers of others, and we are victims of such cyber attacks. It is a global challenge that requires global co-operation. China is an active participant in such co-operation in the world" (Williams, 2009).

The relationship between Beijing and Tibet is very similar to Beijing's relationship with Taiwan in that there are no official channels for dialogue between the CCP and the Tibetan government in exile headed by the Dalai Lama. This apparently thorny communication, which reveals a subterranean form of sabotage and response, is a drama that is enacted via press statements, press conferences, and official websites. Hence, we might argue that the centre/margin relationship between these two groups is one of discursive militancy where no compromise is being offered by either protagonist.

China's relationship with Japan is also played out virtually in the arena of the Internet and hacking. In 2000, China was accused of hacking into Japanese government websites and posting messages condemning Japan for the 1937 Nanjing Massacre. The attack appears to have been triggered by an offline forum that was held in Osaka where there was a denial that Japanese soldiers killed 300,000 Chinese citizens after the fall of the city.

Interestingly, the Annual Report to Congress on the Military Power of the People's Republic of China addressed the future of nationalistic hacking in the PRC and concluded that:

> Nationalistic hacking is likely to occur during periods of tension or crises. Chinese hacking activities likely would involve extensive web page defacements with themes sympathetic to China. Although the extent of Chinese government involvement would be difficult to ascertain, official statements concerning the leveraging of China's growing presence on the Internet, and the application of the principles of "People's War" in "net warfare", suggest the government will have a stronger role in future nationalistic hacking. (Office of the Secretary of Defense, 2003)

According to the *Tracking GhostNet* report by Information Warfare Monitor, hack attacks on Taiwan and Tibet are cyclical and often occur around sensitive dates such as Taiwan elections (Ronald J. Deibert and Rohozinski, 2009, p.12–13).

Unofficial Nationalism and Hacking for the Nation

Hacktivism within the context of the PRC goes beyond the state and is mostly based on nationalistic sentiments. For example, a hacker defaced China's Nike website in 2004 and left wishes for a happy new year in bold red letters in both Chinese and

English ("Hackers Wreak Havoc with Nike", 2004). There was a suggestion at the time that the attack was in retaliation for a Nike television commercial featuring a famous American basketball player, LeBron James, battling animated dragons and Kung Fu masters. The advertisement had been banned in China, and was described as an "insult to the country's national dignity" ("Hackers Wreak Havoc with Nike", 2004). Nike had also just been found to have plagiarized the design of a Chinese flash animator and had been ordered to pay damages ("Hackers Wreak Havoc with Nike", 2004).

The Southern Metropolis ran a story in October 2007 on a computer virus known as the "patriotic virus". The Win32/KillDPT (the patriotic virus), an update of the W32.Welchia.B, is a virus that can decide to suspend the operating system of a computer or create intrusive damage based on different languages used on the computer (Zhang, 2007). The virus enters the computer and assesses what kind of operating system it has and what language the system is in. If the operating system is in simplified Chinese then the virus is completely benign and will have no effect. However, if the infected machine is running in Indonesian or Japanese, the virus then destroys the hard drive of the machine (Zhang, 2007). If the operating system is in English the virus leaves a pop up message that reads "Your luck's so good!". The virus also offers other nationalistic prongs such as declaring opposition to "Taiwan independence". If the virus is on a computer that uses traditional characters, such as those used in Taiwan, a pop up will appear with "Down With A-bian!" (Chen Shui-Bian's nick name) and other nationalistic pop-ups such as "Comrade Chen Shui-bian, you like Taiwan independence? Do you have any dignity or face? … You want to be condemned by history? Go away! We are Chinese! Even after death, our souls will belong to China" (Zhang, 2007).

Nationalism and Hacking

Nationalism incorporates a historical past into the imagining of a community and that is used to define and signify centre/margin relationships between nations. One way this has traditionally been done is through the method of reconstructing nationalist histories via an "ideological state apparatus" (ISA) (Althusser[8]), "official" discourses of events, and all the devices that construct a monopoly of knowledge. Interestingly, with regards to China, Japan, Taiwan and Tibet, this is played out beyond the borders of each nation and within their respective ISAs

8 ISA is defined by John Hartley as the various social institutions that arise in civil society (the sphere of the private, as opposed to the state). They perform regulatory functions and reproduce ideology on behalf of the state. They include education, the family, religion, and the legal system, culture and communication. They are characterized by consent rather than coercion, and by their relative autonomy from the dominant economic class or its representative in the state (O'Sullivan, John Hartley, Saunders, Montgomery, and Fiske, 1994).

via the hack attacks on these countries through the choice of target, or the date of attack, hence confusing and altering – in a style similar to tactics of culture jamming the official version of historical events that are sanctioned and subscribed to. For example, there were the competing versions *qua* "voices" of the Nanjing massacre that triggered the attack cited above. In the other nationalist hack attacks, the geopolitical role and sovereignty of Tibet or Taiwan have a historical context, and the dates that are chosen are evidence of the importance of the hegemonic use of history in the negotiation and contestation of centre/margin relationships, by ISAs, individual hackers and hacker collectives. The public complaints levelled by both the private security firm Mandiant Corporation and the Pentagon in the first half of 2013 against officially sanctioned Chinese hackers stealing corporate data, technological blueprints and military plans may be read as a virtual confirmation that patriotic hacking continues with sustained energy (Sanger, 2013).

Hacktivism and Democracy

Hacking for the nation is tolerated to some degree as the above incidents reveal. However, hacking is not tolerated when it directly challenges the CCP and their monopoly on political power. Apart from the Falun Gong hack attacks there have been few reports of hacking activity by democracy dissidents. The most notable hacking case involving a democracy activist is that of Blondie Wong and the Yellow Pages. In 1998, a group of North American hacktivists, the Cult of the Dead Cow (cDc), interviewed the reclusive leader Blondie Wong and the interview was published in *Wired* magazine and other places on the Internet. In 1997, Wong, a dissident astrophysicist living in Toronto, claimed to have disabled a Chinese satellite and was planning to establish a global network of hackers to protest Western investment in China (Hesseldahl, 1998). Wong is also alleged to have had "operatives stationed in Shanghai, Hong Kong, and Beijing – including three "highly placed" technicians working in Beijing, and a handful of government bureaucrats, many of whom lost family members at Tiananmen Square" (Hesseldahl, 1998). Blondie seems to have vanished into the ether, as I cannot, at the time of writing, find further details of his exploits.

The Boston based hacktivist group "Hactivismo", an international group of activists dedicated to hacking on behalf of human rights and free speech causes, claimed to have members in the PRC. In July 2001, they announced in the preamble to their declaration that:

> Hacktivismo and the CULT OF THE DEAD COW have decided that enough is too much. We are hackers and free speech advocates, and we are developing technologies to challenge state-sponsored censorship of the Internet. Most countries use intimidation and filtering of one, kind or another including the People's Republic of China, Cuba, and many Islamic countries. Most claim to be blocking pornographic content. But the real reason is to prevent challenging content from

> spreading through repressive regimes. This includes information ranging from political opinion, "foreign" news, women's issues, academic and scholarly works, religious information, information regarding ethnic groups in disfavor, news of human rights abuses, documents which present drugs in a positive light, and gay and lesbian content, among others. ("A Special Message of Hope", 2001)

Hactivismo aimed to have people in China, and other countries where there is heavy Internet censorship, post content using steganography that would otherwise be filtered in plain view by hiding the content in websites that would be acceptable to authorities. Ruffin, a member of Hactivismo, said that "Steganography is a kind of encryption that allows one to bury digital content in a digital content base. Think of a Web page displaying a picture of the Mona Lisa. Steganography would allow you to hide a copy of the Declaration of Independence, an MP3, or any other piece of content digitally rendered in Da Vinci's masterpiece" (Ruffin, 2004). The application was called "Camera/Shy" and was dedicated to the memory of Wang Ruowang, a former Chinese dissident leader.

Hactivismo has developed other tools to assist Chinese citizens in circumventing the Great firewall, one of those was called "Six/Four", a direct reference to the 1989 Tiananmen Demonstrations and the colloquial term for the massacre on June 4, "六四" literally "six four". The Six/Four protocol is a peer to peer system like those used to share music files across the Internet. This allows users to create a virtual network on the Internet that is invisible to all but its own members ("Hackers target web censorship", 2002). Another tool they have developed is ScatterChat, a secure instant messaging service. In Hactivismo's press release for the service, they said that:

> ScatterChat is unique in that it is intended for non-technical human rights activists and political dissidents operating behind oppressive national firewalls. It is an instant messaging client that provides end-to-end encryption over the Electronic Frontier Foundation-endorsed Tor network. Its security features include resiliency against partial compromise through perfect forward secrecy, immunity from replay attacks, and limited resistance to traffic analysis, all reinforced through a pro-actively secure design. ("Hacktivismo Launches ScatterChat for Secure, Private Communication", 2006)

In February 2006, Hactivismo also kicked off a campaign against Google and their censoring of the Chinese Internet by encouraging people to print up T-shirts with the graphic of an altered Google logo to read "Goolag, exporting censorship, one search at a time" ("cDc launches global campaign against Google", 2006).

There are also stories in the Western press that allege that Chinese authorities are hacking the email of dissidents. In 2005, the story of Chong Yiu-kwong, a key figure in the Civil Human Rights Front in Hong Kong, claimed that hackers from within the Mainland had been tampering with his email account ("Hong Kong Activist Says Chinese Hackers Read His E-mails", 2005). In 2005, Chong told Radio Free

Asia that his Internet activities had been monitored by someone within the Mainland since April 2004. He said "I didn't know that my computer had been monitored ever since [April 2004], until I found that all my emails from the account registered to the University of Hong Kong disappeared all of a sudden" ("Hong Kong Activist Says Chinese Hackers Read His E-mails", 2005). Following his discovery, Chong approached the computer centre of Hong Kong University. He said "they told me that my account had been monitored by three different IP addresses from China and that information from the account had been downloaded every few minutes" ("Hong Kong Activist Says Chinese Hackers Read His E-mails", 2005). Nevertheless, in the past few years, there have been many reports confirming that hacktivism has evolved into an all-pervasive culture across Chinese educational, corporate and government sectors. If the Chinese Ministry of Education, Universities and government-approved private companies can jointly sponsor hacking competitions, hacking services are surely available for hire on demand (Wong, 2013). Renowned dissident Ai Weiwei has alleged that his email account had been compromised prior to his arrest in 2011, whereupon police seized his computer equipment as well. It has also been alleged by *The New York Times* that China's local police departments do contract with private Chinese firms like "Xhunter" to trawl the Web and clamp down on subversive postings online (Wong, 2013). This is tantamount to hiring professional hackers to both hack and provide network defence through ironic turns in their interaction with the political centre. This may be said to undermine any sense that Chinese hackers are principled promoters of democracy online.

Conclusion

The writing of viruses and hacking into computer networks represent the most direct challenges to any network. In essence, hacking is about wreaking havoc on a network or triggering its breakdown. The challenge to code in this way comes from many groups, criminals, hacktivists and the military. I have attempted to draw together different ways in which hacking has been played out on the Internet in the context of China as a way of charting the interaction between the government and hackers using a centre/margin approach. The centre/margin approach allows us to analyse groups outside of China, as is the case with cDc and Hactivismo, nationalist groups within China, as well as China's interactions with other governments. Even though hacking is illegal in China and the government denies that there have been any officially authorized attacks, there still appears to be sufficient evidence to suggest that there are officially sanctioned hack attacks that have taken place. For example, the hack attacks by the Honker's Union appear to be officially sanctioned and highlight the relationship between the government and nationalist movements. Recent revelations by private security companies in the US about the scale and culpability of officially sanctioned Chinese hacking overseas add credible fuel to this alterity of centre/margin contestations in a greater, virtual China that exists between online and offline spheres (Sanger and Perlroth, 2013).

The Internet is ultimately a site in which nationalist sentiments are expressed and converge with those of governments. Nationalism has to some extent replaced Marxism as the popular dominant ideology in the country. The challenge for the CCP has been to reconcile the two. Nationalist sentiments spill over into international relations as well, and in the case studies presented in this chapter, disputes in international relations are the trigger for hack attacks. In this regard, nationalism as an offline mode of politics serves as a key motivation for controlling, or subverting, online political behaviour. The Internet, as it is viewed in China, is shaped and managed by the government and is a space in which China's relations with the international community are played out via news media and hack attacks, at both an official and unofficial level.

Tracing the activities of pro-democracy hacktivists is tantamount to tracing the negotiation of centre/margin relationships and the way that these have been reconfigured in space by the advent of the Internet. These groups are scattered across the globe and have come together with a common interest to test the limits of a centre identified as China/Beijing. Notably, the efforts of cDc and Hactivismo have not resulted in the overthrow of the CCP and the beginning of democracy despite their best efforts.

References

"A Special Message of Hope". (July 4, 2001). Retrieved from http://www.cultdeadcow.com/cDc_files/declaration.html.

Anderson, Benedict. (1993). *Imagined Communities Reflections on the Origin and Spread of Nationalism* (Revised ed.). London: Verso.

Bagchi, Indrani. (2008, 5/05/08). China mounts cyber attacks on Indian sites. Retrieved 5/5/08, 2008, from http://timesofindia.indiatimes.com/articleshow/msid-3010288,prtpage-1.cms.

Buruma, Ian. (1999). *China in Cyberspace*. November 4, 1999. Retrieved 29/10/1999, from http://www.nybooks.com/nyrev/wwwfeatdisplay.cgi?199991104009f.

Carey, James W. (1989). Space Time and Communications: A Tribute to Harold Innis. In Hyams (Ed.), *Communication as Culture: Essays on Media and Society*. London: Unwin.

cDc launches global campaign against Google. (2006). http://www.cultdeadcow.com/archives/2006/02/cdc_launches_global_.php3.

Chase, Michael, and Mulvenon, James. (2002). You've Got Dissent! Chinese Dissidencts Use of the Internet and Beijing's Counter-Strategies Santa Monica: RAND.

China denies U.S. charge it hacked Pentagon network. (2007). *People's Daily Online* (19:52, September 4, 2007). http://english.people.com.cn/90001/90776/6254757.html.

China's anti-hacking alliance regrouped. (2005). *People's Daily Online* (24/04/05). http://english.peopledaily.com.cn/200504/26/print20050426_182719.html.

China's PLA Prepares For Network Warfare (1999). ChinaOnline. http://www.chinaonline.com/industry/infotech/NewsArchive/Secure/1999/november/C9111102.asp.

Chinese Army Unit Is Seen as Tied to Hacking Against U.S. (February 18, 2013). *The New York Times*. Retrieved from http://www.nytimes.com/2013/02/19/technology/chinas-army-is-seen-as-tied-to-hacking-against-us.html?pagewanted=2&_r=1&.

Comor, Edward. (2001). Harold Innis and the Bias of Communication. *Information, Communication and Society*, 4(2), 274–294.

Deibert, Ronald J. (1997). *Parchment, Printing, and Hypermedia Communication in World Order Transformation*. New York: Columbia University Press.

Deibert, Ronald J., and Rohozinski, Rafal. (2009). *Tracking GhostNet: Investigating a Cyber Espionage Network* (pp. 53): Information Warfare Monitor.

Drache, Daniel, and Beyer, Robert. (1996). *States Against Markets: The Limits of Globalisation*. London: Routledge.

Dual Tactics Adopted to Ensure Information Security in China. (2001). China Internet Information Center (06/06/2001). http://www.china.org.cn/english/14157.htm.

Farrell, Nick. (2002). Chinese crackers prepare for cyber war. vnunet.com (23 May 2002). http://www.vnunet.com/articles/print/2118852.

First Net Security Law Endorsed. (2000). China.org.cn (2/12/2000). http://www.china.org.cn/english/2000/Dec/5888.htm.

Gov't transparency in quake relief not "forced reaction" for hosting Olympics (2008, 26/5/08). Retrieved 26/5/08, 2008, from http://news.xinhuanet.com/english/2008–05/26/content_8257840.htm.

Government to Ban Trade in Foreign Encryption Software (2000). *People's Daily Online* (February 24, 2000, updated at 16:58(GMT+8)). http://www.peopledaily.com.cn/english/200002/21/eng20000221T121.html.

Hacker gives Kuomintang Web site pro-Chinese look with PRC photos (2004). Information Warfare Monitor (2004–05–10). http://www.infowar-monitor.net/modules.php?op.=modload&name=News&file=article&sid=970&mode=thread&order=0&thold=0.

Hackers target web censorship. (2002, 20/20/07). BBC News. from http://news.bbc.co.uk/2/hi/science/nature/2129390.stm.

Hackers Wreak Havoc with Nike. (2004). China Internet Information Center (December 31, 2004). http://www.china.org.cn/english/2004/Dec/116507.htm.

Hacktivismo Launches ScatterChat for Secure, Private Communication. (July 21, 2006). Retrieved 12/10/07, from http://mediaserver.prweb.com/pdfdownload/414312/pr.pdf.

Hearn, Kay. (2010). Official/ Unofficial: Information Management and Social Association. *Journal of Current Chinese Affairs*, 39(3), 211–241.

Hearn, Kay, Williams, Patricia A.H., and Mahncke, Rachel J. (November 30–December 2, 2010). International Relations and Cyber Attacks: Official and Unofficial Discourse. Paper presented at the 11th Australian Information Warfare and Security Conference, Perth, Western Australia.

Hesseldahl, Arik. (1998). Hacking for Human Rights? *Wired News* (09:15 AM Jul. 14, 1998 PT). http://www.wired.com/news/politics/0,1283,13693,00.html.

Hong Kong Activist Says Chinese Hackers Read His E-mails (2005). Radio Free Asia. http://www.rfa.org/english/news/2005/07/02/china_Internet/.

Innis, Harold A. (1951). *The Bias of Communication.* Toronto: University of Toronto Press.

Innis, Harold A. (1952). *Changing Concepts of Time.* Toronto: University of Toronto Press.

Innis, Harold A. (1972). *Empire and Communication* (2nd edn). Toronto: University of Toronto Press.

Innis, Harold A. (1993). Printing in China in the 19th and 20th Century. *Continuum*, 7(1), 132–139.

Jame, Fred. (1999). China, Taiwan in Web hacking "war". MacWEEK.com (August 10, 1999, 5:00 PM PT). http://www.infowar-monitor.net/modules.php?op.=modload&name=News&file=article&sid=137.

Johnson, Bobbie. (2008). Hackers attack pro-Tibetan websites. *The Guardian* (April 10, 2008). http://www.guardian.co.uk/world/2008/apr/10/olympicgames2008.china2.

Largest Hacker Group in China Dissolves. (2005). China Internet Information Center (February 22, 2005). http://www.china.org.cn/english/2005/Feb/120819.htm.

Lasker, John. (2004). U.S. Military's Elite Hacker Crew. *Wired.* http://www.wired.com/print/politics/security/news/2005/04/67223.

Lessig, Lawrence. (2006). *Code Version 2.* New York: Basic Books.

Liu, Shih-Diing. (2006). China's popular nationalism on the Internet report on the 2005 anti-Japan network struggles. *Inter-Asia Cultural Studies*, 7(1).

Mandiant. (2013). APT1: Exposing One of China's Cyber Espionage Units: Mandiant.

McLuhan, Eric, and Zingrone, Frank (Eds.). (1997). *Essential McLuhan.* London: Routledge.

McLuhan, Marshall, and Fiore, Quentin. (1967). *The Medium is the Message.* Harmondsworth: Penguin.

McLuhan, Marshall, and Powers, Bruce R. (1989). *The Global Village: transformations in world life and media in the 21st century*. New York: Oxford University Press.

McMillan, Robert. (2009). As Hacking Hits Home, China Strengthens Cyber Laws. PC World. http://www.pcworld.com/businesscenter/article/164712/as_hacking_hits_home_china_strengthens_cyber_laws.html>.

Merkel's China Visit Marred by Hacking Allegations. (2007). Spiegel Online International (August 27, 2007). http://www.spiegel.de/international/world/0,1518,502169,00.html.

Military expert: international cooperation to fight hackers. (2007). China Internet Information Center (September 23, 2007). http://www.china.org.cn/english/China/225476.htm.

New Regulations to Ensure Internet Safety (2005). China Internet Information Center (December 30, 2005). http://www.china.org.cn/english/government/153719.htm.

O'Sullivan, Tim, Hartley, John, Saunders, Danny, Montgomery, Martin, and Fiske, John (Eds.). (1994). *Key Concepts in Communication and Cultural Studies* (2nd edn). London: Routledge.

Office of the Secretary of Defense. (2003). Military Power of the People's Republic of China. Office of the Secretary of Defense Retrieved from http://www.defenselink.mil/news/Jul2005/d20050719china.pdf.

Office of the Secretary of Defense. (2007). Military Power of the People's Republic of China 2007 Annual Report to Congress. Retrieved from www.defenselink.mil/pubs/pdfs/China%20Report%202006.pdf.

Olesen, Alexa. (2000). China Reverses Encryption Regulations. VirtualChina.com news (March 14, 2000). http://www.virtualchina.com/news/mar00/031400-cryptoreg-alo-jsl.html.

Peace pact with Taiwan proposed. (2007). *People's Daily Online* (08:18, October 16, 2007). http://english.people.com.cn/90001/90776/6283633.html.

PLA. (2002). Full text of China's defense white paper in 2002. Xinhua Retrieved from http://news.xinhuanet.com/english/2002–12/10/content_654851.htm.

Premier Wen tells Merkel China opposes hackers. (2007). Voice of China (2007–08–28 11:17:45). http://www.chinavoc.com.cn/NewsCenter/ShowArticle.aspx?Id=11523.

Riemens, Patrice. (2002). Some Thoughts On The Idea Of "Hacker Culture". [English translation in Cryptome on June 3, 2002.] *Multitudes*, 2(8).

Rogin, Josh. (2007). Cyber officials: Chinese hackers attack 'anything and everything' (February 13, 2007), http://www.fcw.com/online/news/97658–1.html?page=2.

Ruffin, Oxblood. (March 28, 2004). Hacktivism, From Here To There. Paper presented at the CyberCrime and Digital Law Enforcement Conference., Yale Law School.

Sevastopuloin, Demetri, and McGregor, Richard. (September 4, 2007). China "hacked" into Pentagon defence system, p. 1. Retrieved from http://search.ft.com/ftArticle?queryText=hacking+china&aje=true&id=070904000597&ct=0&nclick_check=1.

"A Special Message of Hope". (July 4, 2001). http://www.cultdeadcow.com/cDc_files/declaration.html.

Taiwan asks China to help track hackers. (2003). Information Warfare Monitor (September 24, 2003 11:53:17 AM). http://www.infowar-monitor.net/modules.php?op.=modload&name=News&file=article&sid=612&mode=thread&order=0&thold=0.

Taiwan downplays China TV hacking. (2002). CNN (September 25, 2002 Posted: 12:37 PM EDT (1637 GMT)). http://archives.cnn.com/2002/WORLD/asiapcf/east/09/25/taiwan.falungong/.

Thomas, Timothy L. (2005). Chinese and American network warfare. *Joint Force Quarterly*. October 18, 2007.

Thomson, Iain. (2007). US blames China for Pentagon hack People's Liberation Army responsible, say officials vnunet.com (September 4, 2007). http://www.computing.co.uk/vnunet/news/2197972/chinese-hackers-attack-pentagon.

Tibetans allege cyber invasion. (2004). *The Times of India* (January 29, 2004, 1801 hrs IST,IANS). http://timesofindia.indiatimes.com/articleshow/453079.cms.

Trojan horse. (2006). Retrieved 17/10/07, from SearchSecurity.com http://searchsecurity.techtarget.com/sDefinition/0,sid14_gci213221,00.html.

Virus attacks on Tibetan network; Chinese blamed. (2003). Information Warfare Monitor (October 31, 2003). http://www.infowar-monitor.net/modules.php?op.=modload&name=News&file=article&sid=728&mode=thread&order=0&thold=0.

Walton, Greg. (2001). China's Golden Shield Corporations and the Development of Surveillance Technology in the Peoples Republic of China: International Centre for Human Rights and Democratic Development.

Williams, Holly. (2009, 23/7/09). China: We Didn't Hack Into Foreign PCs. Retrieved from http://news.sky.com/skynews/Home/World-News/China-Denies-Internet-Hacking-Network-System-GhostNet-Used-Worldwide-On-Government-Computers/Article/200903415251712>.

Wong, Edward. (2013, 20/9/2013). Hacking U.S. Secrets, China Pushes for Drones, *The New York Times*. Retrieved from http://www.nytimes.com/2013/09/21/world/asia/hacking-us-secrets-china-pushes-for-drones.html?_r=0.

Wu, Xu. (2006). *Chinese Cyber Nationalism: evolution characteristics and implications*. Plymouth: Lexington Books.

Yang, Guobin. (2009). *The Power of the Internet in China: Citizens Activism Online*. New York: Columbia University Press.

Yoshihara, Toshi. (2001). Chinese Information Warfare: A Phantom Menace Or Emerging Threat?: Strategic Studies Institute, U.S. Army War College Retrieved from http://www.strategicstudiesinstitute.army.mil/pubs/display.cfm?PubID=62.

Zhang, Dongfeng. (2007). Can a Computer Virus be "Patriotic"?. *Southern Metropolis Daily*. http://chinadigitaltimes.net/2007/10/can_computer_virus_be_patriotic.php.

Zhou, Yongming. (2005). Informed Nationalism: military websites in Chinese cybersp.

Chapter 6
'Global City Foreign Policy': The Propaganda of Enlargement and Integration of an IT-Connected Asian City

Alan Chong

Global cities are often treated as analogous to the concrete foundations of globalization, and yet are obscured by the differing pathways to formation identified by geographers (Olds and Yeung, 2004). One of the classic works in this field, *The Global City – London, New York, Tokyo*, breathtakingly assigns four characteristics to the global city. Firstly, it functions as 'highly concentrated command points in the organization of the world economy'; secondly, such cities are 'key locations for finance and for specialized service firms, which have replaced manufacturing as the leading economic sectors'; thirdly, a global city has to be a site for 'the production of innovations'; and finally, such cities have to function 'as markets for the products and innovations produced' (Sassen, 1991, pp.3–4). Political economy processes have adduced one set of explanations for this phenomenon – changes in the nature of white collar work arising from the information technology (IT) revolution, the diversification and inner specialization of occupations within the financial sector and the course of evolution taken by the nature of stock markets that have differentiated into trading in futures denominated in bonds and currencies. Global cities are thus also 'commodityscapes' (Knox, 1995). Manuel Castells would however amplify the technological driving forces ignited by the IT revolution itself, leading to the patterning of global cities into what is known as the 'informational city' and 'network society' (1989; 1996). Most others (Friedmann, 1986; Taylor, 2003; Barber, 2013) would suggest that the typology itself reflects the myriad formations of globalization. The existing, and rather passive, analytical literature has yet to account for the political and intuitive *becoming* of global cities. This chapter argues instead that global cities need to be analysed through comprehending the political agencies behind making globalization work for the benefit of such localities and their populations whether one labels them generic 'global cities' or 'global city-states'. Essentially, what are the politics of promotion in the study of global and globalizing cities?

The chapter will proceed as follows. The concept of the global city will be related to the notion of foreign policy in International Relations theory in order to situate the global city as both agent *and* subject of promotional activity across geographical, economic and political boundaries. This argument will consciously stretch the notion of 'foreign policy' in relation to the city simply because the latter strives to promote its existence as an attraction to outsiders. The very act of promotion thus leads to the crux of my argument that a thorough understanding of the flourishing of global cities should be accomplished through the notion of propaganda. The three Asian global city candidates of Kuala Lumpur, Singapore and Taipei are chosen as case studies to substantiate the propaganda argument since these are latecomers to the category of the IT-connected, capitalism-propelled global city. These cities are even more worth selecting as case studies because they are presumably taking after the 'models' of London, New York, and Tokyo. Furthermore, all three have emerged as leading cities in the Pacific Rim only after the convulsions of postcolonial struggle, civil war and self-determination redrew the political and economic landscapes in Pacific Asia after World War Two. These cities are emblematic of the new Asia that is modernizing rapidly and integrating into global capitalism. Furthermore, they are each thickly embedded within national and statist projects that explicitly aspire to create vehicles for economic enhancement. It is also apt to note that these three cities have been granted extensive budgets by their respective host governments for promotion as proverbial 'jewels in the crown' of national development compared to other Asian cities outside Japan. Japan is contrasted favourably as a developed nation-state, against which the rest of modernizing Asia would prefer to benchmark. The conclusion would find that the fledgling global city foreign policy is manifested through complex forms that can be analysed as the *propaganda of enlargement and integration.*

Global City and Foreign Policy

It is hitherto conventional wisdom to articulate cities in terms of their locations as either natural geographical or man-made habitations that serve sustenance, defence and communication purposes. Most definitions from both dictionaries and the literatures covered in the present piece would concur that a city is a concentration of population for specific purposes of organizing the social life of individuals within a collective. New York can be defined in relation to its natural harbour and situation at the mouth of the Hudson; London in relation to the Thames, ancient Roman military considerations, and the history of river-borne commerce; and so forth. Asian cities too have similar echoes when one examines Singapore's dual commercial and military significance as a city that is largely coterminous with an island territory; Bangkok likewise can be defined in terms of symbolic, physiological and strategic needs; and Kuala Lumpur can justifiably be analysed from comparable histories of need-based settlement patterns.

It is also interesting to note that way before these cities came to be described as connected either in relation to international air travel connections, or in our contemporary case of IT connectivity, they were also conceived in terms of 'us' against 'them' identity formations. Charles Tilly and Wim Blockmans (1994) have edited a volume documenting the relations between cities and states in late medieval and early modern Europe showing that the city and the state did not always develop in politically and financially complementary ways. Tilly observed that

> The geography and timing of changes in Europe's systems of cities and states suggest that the positions of cities within market hierarchies (international markets, regional markets, exclusively local markets, and so on) *correlated approximately with their size, their demographic impact on their hinterlands, the extent of their capital accumulation, and their ability to build up and control an extended sphere of influence*. It seems that these, in turn, strongly affected the relative attractiveness of different cities as sources of capital for building armies and for state formation, the autonomy of their ruling classes with respect to would-be and actual state-makers, and the strength of their representative institutions. (Tilly, 1994, p.22; italics mine)

The collectives that had accumulated wealth and consolidated a materially sustainable lifestyle opted to extend political control over adjacent regions they regarded as vital for securing their existence. Italian cities in this period for instance 'strove systematically to eliminate all intermediary and indirect forms of government and to organize their territories into lower-level districts run by officials from the city …; the law, the legislation, and the fiscal, juridical, and administrative rules of the city were extended to the whole territory. This process formed a unitary body in which the city was the head (as in the famous image) and the countryside, organically and inseparably linked, the members' (Chittolini, 1994, p.31). These early cities asserted what the state would later claim as sovereign authority delineating the realm of the 'domestic' and 'external'.

Concomitant with these jurisdictional developments was, of course, the emergence of capitalism as a force for spatial transformation. Capitalism required the shaping of market relations within the city itself as well as between city and countryside. Marxist analyses do have a point when they repeatedly assert that cities extract surplus from manufacturing and other wage-earning activities. To ensure the regularization of extraction, owners of capital tended to systematize a hierarchical network of dependency among workers who needed to work in urbanized factories and suppliers of consumer goods and essentials for those very workers. Foreign capital would in most cases also be welcomed into this network of dependency insofar as the local owners of capital would act as intermediaries and co-extractors on their behalf. It is argued by many scholars of Third World urbanization that the dependency paradigm elaborated by Immanuel Wallerstein and Johan Galtung has left many indelible footprints in the deliberate underdevelopment of 'Third World cities' (Gilbert and Gugler, 1987). The latter are clearly integrated as 'the Periphery' in a world system of capitalism only on the basis of their technological and material inferiority to the cities of 'the Core'. But there is also the possibility that certain cities in the developing world aspire to graduating into the 'Semi-periphery' as a stepping stone into the Core. These cities are willing to take on some outsourced Core functions on the bases of political alignments with the existing Core, and the adoption of standards in labour skills and technological competence that closely approximate the socioeconomic profile of the Core. This is particularly true of many Asian cities that have touted their emergence as 'globalizing entities' within the rubric of climbing the ladder of high technology. In particular, these Asian globalizers tout their rise as a result of connecting to IT and its associated techno-pretensions. Connecting to IT and electronically-operated business ventures in turn requires that the connecting parties adapt to external partners' standards for technological sharing and business interoperability. The local parameters of operating an isolated city economy become intricately externalized and rendered dependent on whatever has been deemed 'global standards'.

Clearly implicit in all of these trends and literatures is the emergence of a field of promotional activity that is analogous to how International Relations scholars understand 'foreign policy'. Foreign policy as it is conventionally understood is the sum of all the external relations that a state controls through its sovereign governmental organs, and it concerns the total range of security interests involved in the operation of the state that impinge upon its external well-being (Wallace, 1971; Hill, 2003). Likewise, a city that aspires to globalize has to treat with a foreign sphere in relation to standards for interoperability clearly set elsewhere, or else negotiated with foreign partners. When it comes to understanding and rendering a city 'intelligent' in relation to the standards of IT in use abroad, that city has to collectively expand its intellectual horizons to manage expectations at home with those abroad towards some equilibrium. Therefore, it is relevant to hypothesize an argument in terms of a global city pursuing foreign policy in its attempt to strategize to take advantage of an electronic globalization that is underway. Sassen's definition of a global city acknowledges this when she articulates her criteria of cities serving as command points, financial markets, centres of innovation and other generic markets for a world economy; all of these functions require city planners, or promoters, to adapt to tastes and styles dictated geographically elsewhere (Sassen, 1991). Of course, one might object that innovation might mean that global cities can by themselves serve as dictators of new benchmarks in connectivity in business and IT. This is all possible but the grand game of capitalism filters innovation – how much demand can an innovation attract, and how reasonable are the costs of adapting or replacing current *modus operandi* with the innovation?

Therefore, when this chapter subsequently employs the phrase 'global city foreign policy' it is consciously *referring to the realm of promotional activity designed to attain for the city a significant degree of connectedness with cross-border flows of finance, production and information so as to achieve a commanding position in the global capitalist economy to extract surpluses from these very flows*. Global city foreign policy is not a straightforward process; it has to engage with, as well as suffer the interference from, the politics connected with globalizing in coordination with foreign partners.

Propaganda and IT

As is the case with the mainstream literature on foreign policy, an integral part of foreign policy involves propaganda. According to Harold Lasswell, propaganda is 'the technique of influencing human action by the manipulation of representations' (1995, p.13). Furthermore, propaganda as a practitioner's art assumes that while the world is the product of clear causation, it is only partly predictable. Propaganda plays upon the psychology of susceptibility in all human beings. It is not surprising that the infamous Nazi propagandist Josef Goebbels coined memorable principles of practice captured in phrases such as: 'propaganda must be planned and executed by only one authority'; 'credibility alone must determine whether propaganda output should be true or false'; 'propaganda may be facilitated by leaders with prestige'; and 'propaganda must label events and people with distinctive phrases or slogans' (Doob, 1995). That Nazi Germany lost the Second World War did not diminish the salience, and one might add, the timelessness of his advice.

The art of globalization-ready commercial advertising readily takes after Goebbels' principles. Janice Hirota's (1995) ruminations on sales formulas in advertising agencies argues that executives often have to draw upon their personal and embedded 'vocabularies of sentiment' to make products look heroic to tempt buyers through emotional affiliation. Likewise, Robert Jackall, the editor of one of the most widely-cited readers on propaganda, and himself a professor of sociology, argues that public relations executives tend to develop the innate ability to 'doublethink' – or the art of holding one reality in one's mind while being able to articulate as and when necessary completely contradictory versions of reality. Ethical considerations are not at issue, but the efficacy of selling one's case (1995, pp.381–382). Rather radically, other major scholars and advocates for the use of propaganda in democratic contexts base their arguments on the fact that mass nationalistic and industrial societies require the arts of propaganda for leaders at all levels to communicate with their followers. The market and politics cannot operate on the plane of idealistic face-to-face communication within a population of hundreds of thousands and millions. The writings of Walter Lippmann are a potent argument for vocal and charismatic democratic leadership in post-nineteenth century liberal states. Similarly, another widely acknowledged 'guru' of capitalist propaganda, Edward Bernays has stated that the First World War's manipulative practices on and off the battlefield have confirmed the permanence of modern mass-focussed propaganda:

> It takes account not merely of the individual, nor even of the mass mind alone, but also and especially of the anatomy of society, with its interlocking group formations and loyalties. It sees the individual not only as a cell in the social organism but as a cell organized into the social unit. Touch a nerve at a sensitive spot and you get an automatic response from certain specific members of the organism. (Bernays, 1928/2009, ch.2 online)

In the mass societies constructed by globalization's economic dictates and consumerist technologies, informational amplification is all the more relevant when one ponders how Japan, Taiwan, South Korea and China – East Asia's cutting edge computer manufacturing sites – have all at some point in the past two decades witnessed email-driven and website-initiated hysteria-filled felonies and nationalistic campaigns of outrage that are sometimes conducted independently of governmental preferences. When it comes to engaging IT and business mentalities to globalize cities, a certain level of hype must surely be integral to the success of attracting informational capital to reside in a particular locality, notwithstanding the presence of objective material factors. Manuel Castells' own formulation of the informational city recognizes that while the new IT and its derived technological forms contribute social impacts upon human organization, IT truly transforms economic geography only when it is inserted into the capitalist mode of development (Castells, 1989, p.17). IT needed an *articulation process* – hence the role of propaganda – for it to become decisive in developmental strategies. Firstly, Castells argued that human formations had to perceive how the rate of profit could be enhanced by streamlining the production process through the employment of microelectronics-based machines; facilitating intra-firm coordination through telecommunications; and positioning capital in a more commanding position vis-à-vis labour. Secondly, IT needed to be proven in 'weighting the accumulation and domination functions of state intervention'; the state could shift its administrative resources from traditional physical coercive forms of maintaining law and order to methods of control through electronic surveillance and reporting; furthermore, IT as a highly-refined mode of high technology 'draws the state to concentrate on providing the required infrastructure, downplaying its role in redistributional policies' (Castells, 1989, pp.29–30). Thirdly, IT had to demonstrate its 'effects on process[es that] condition the international competitiveness of countries and firms'. This meant that IT could dramatically encourage intra-firm vertical and horizontal dispersion of the production chain. IT could also remake calculations of the cost-benefit scenarios for enterprises of all sizes in terms of their output and input accessibilities in relation to consumer and raw material markets. In stark terms, the Headquarters of a Toyota or a Hewlett Packard Corporation could contemplate assembly operations in a second country, while assembling them in a third or fourth depending on the costs of coordinating operations in a continuous real time. Better still, thoroughly informational corporations such as banks, finance companies and data publishers could operate several connected service sites simultaneously, round the clock with very little need for staff to travel for interpersonal communication. Castells also noted that IT offered developmental economists an opportunity for promoting to the developing world the virtues of lowered barriers to entry for highly skill-intensive industries associated with IT. Indian and Philippine computer-aided call centres for instance are a profitable poverty-alleviating industry unto itself, but as Castells warned, these also meant that developing countries would ironically be positioned within a new but still unequal informational international division of labour despite leapfrogging the lower technological modes of development (Castells, 1989, p.30).

The following case studies of Taipei, Kuala Lumpur and Singapore intend to illustrate the propaganda behind the enlargement and integration of a connected Asian city as well as the limitations of such an effort. In order to provide some basis for comparison, each of the case studies will be structured according to the following themes – 'self-comprehension of becoming global', 'the role of IT and the knowledge industry' and 'the strategies of business attraction'. Through these case studies, one might tentatively glean how global cities in Asia have come into their own through image projection and management.

Taipei

Taipei – Self-comprehension of becoming global

The story of Taipei's evolution as a global city is tied inexorably to Taiwan's post-1949 history of external economic vulnerability and the management of dependence to mitigate that vulnerability. The modern state of Taiwan was essentially born of the Chinese Civil War (1945–9) between the Chinese Communist Party forces who captured the mainland in 1949, and the non-communist nationalist Kuomintang forces who fled to the island of Formosa to re-establish their authority. It was also a strategic pattern which coincided with the emerging Cold War between the new communist powers of the USSR and the People's Republic of China (PRC) on one side, and the western powers led by the United States and Britain on the other. The Kuomintang forces led by General Chiang Kai-shek renamed his territory on the island of Formosa the 'Republic of China on Taiwan' (henceforth, Taiwan). The Chinese Communists on the mainland declared their diplomatic policy of treating foreign states' recognition of the government of Taiwan, or any upgrading of their official presence in Taipei, the latter's capital city, as a zero sum game accompanied by a spectrum of protests and sanctions from Beijing. Having been closely associated with the western powers during the Second World War and throughout the 1945–9 period, the Kuomintang-ruled Taiwan became dependent on western, and specifically, American diplomatic, military and economic patronage to sustain Taiwan's position vis-à-vis the Kuomintang's foes on the mainland. Initially in the 1950s, the Taiwan government attempted import-substitution and self-subsistence development strategies not unlike most Third World states at the time. The military exigencies of the early Cold War inhibited other options. By the 1960s, there was a revamp when the government decided to take advantage of the liberal market access granted Taiwan by the US. Additionally, the influx of US and Japanese capital in starting up a sizable light industrial manufacturing sector enabled the option of export-oriented growth and investment (EOI). Taiwan's first export processing zone was established in 1966 just for this purpose. The 1970s and 1980s saw tremendous continuity with the EOI mode. Indigenous basic and heavy industries were induced into being since EOI in the previous decade had generated strong domestic demand for machinery and other intermediate materials.

This meant that local businesses could attempt to leverage on both local and foreign capital's demand for specialized suppliers and so-called producer services (CEPD, 2009, pp.8–9). The latter were services destined for manufacturers rather than final consumers, and included fields such as advertising, accounting, business law, and intermediate goods processing. These services easily attracted domestic entrepreneurship and seeded the future multinational corporations of Taiwan. The final push for Taiwan to fully liberalize its economy came in 1979 when the US relegated official diplomatic relations with Taiwan in favour of normalization of ties with its rival across the Taiwan Straits, the People's Republic of China. This led to two economic responses that cumulatively resulted in globalizing Taipei/Taiwan: firstly, the Taiwan government reacted by accelerating its liberalization of rules allowing the flow of goods, capital and services in and out of the island; secondly, it led to active measures to lessen Taiwan's disproportionate reliance on US market largesse by diversifying the island's trade options and partners (Wong, 1999, pp.16–18). Furthermore, one important result of the solid growth between the 1960s and 1980s was the commensurate increase in Taiwan's economic space despite the ongoing diplomatic strangulation practised by the PRC. One scholar described this enlargement of virtual diplomatic and brand recognition in the following manner:

> … the governments having trade with or receiving investments from Taiwan are, *with a view to increasing trade or promoting investment, bound to give each other necessary conveniences*. These conveniences may start out with facilitating visits by business people through shortening the time needed for obtaining visas and loosening the restrictions imposed on each other. While bilateral economic and trade relations are growing stronger, in order to promote business these countries have mostly approved of the expansion and change of name of Taiwan's representative offices and granted their personnel certain rights that are usually only given to formal diplomats. Increased exchange of goods and personnel naturally brings with it unavoidable frictions, necessitating bilateral official contact, negotiation … etc. According to Taiwan's official statistics, since the mid-1980s Taipei has recorded immense growth in the number of representative offices it has set up in foreign countries, in the number of high-level visits abroad and in the number of agreements it has signed with foreign governments. For example, in 1996 Taiwan had representative or administrative offices in 65 countries with which it had no diplomatic ties, up from 30 in 1991. (Wong, 1999, p.27)

In this way, we can glimpse the outlines of one successful outcome of a deliberate propaganda of enlargement and integration of Taiwan's political economy, and its corresponding effects on Taipei as its capital city and main investment funnel.

This narrative of enlargement and integration has continued unabated into the twenty-first century with Taiwan's increasing emphasis – plucked in all probability from the writings of Bill Gates, Manuel Castells, Saskia Sassen and Kenichi Ohmae – on promoting 'the i-Taiwan 12 Projects, which are designed to create a top-tier industrial development environment by, for example, promoting the development of high-tech industrial clusters, industrial innovation corridors, and an "intelligent Taiwan"' (CEPD, 2009, p.11). This narrative is recycled with an enthusiastic flourish by one of Taiwan's leading government-funded convention attraction portals, www.meettaiwan.com:

Excel Through the Building of Knowledge

> This is the Taiwanese philosophy and so in turn Taiwan has made the transition from manufacturing and production into design, research and development and is listed as the largest holder of patents for invention by the WEF (World Economic Forum) in its '2008 Global Competitiveness Report'.

A Hub of Innovation

> Taiwan is now at the forefront of research and development in all kinds of industries ranging from information and communication technology (ICT) through to biotechnology and powersports products. A hub of technological innovation, Taiwan has built its industrial excellence upon decades of working with businesses and consumers from places such as Japan, the United States and many European countries. It produces many high tech products that are typically first or second in terms of global market shares. (Meettaiwan, 2013)

These texts of promotion draw attention to a number of textures built into the propaganda effort in globalizing Taipei through literally the portal of branding Taiwan. They are forward looking and tinge the businessman's imagination with the expectation that 'Taipei/Taiwan' is a melding of a number of dimensions of strategic knowledge industry relevance. This author's interview with Chang Kuei-lin, Director-General of the Department of Urban and Housing Development, within the Taiwanese government's inter-ministerial Council for Economic Planning and Development, showed however that making any fine distinctions between Taipei and Taiwan are practically superfluous:

> Taipei is not ranked so high as a global city when compared with London, New York, Tokyo or Singapore, which are full service world cities. But within Asia, Taipei is globally connected, which plays an important role in the technology chain as well as regional trade, especially with mainland China, Japan and United States …
>
> As a global city, I am aware that there is increasing emphasis on [having investors at home and abroad] prompting internationalization and liberalization of our economic and social environment to be more friendly and accessible.

> However, it is extremely important to insist on Taiwan self-identity. It concerns about the 'glocalization'. Taiwan is always trying to differentiate itself from China's image. From time to time, identity branding is important. (Kuei-lin Chang, 2009)

Therefore, one might tentatively observe that Taipei's global city status might either be placed in doubt from an academic methodological angle, or be treated as an innovative publicity strategy by being blended into the image of Taiwan Incorporated. At the same time, Taiwan's governmental economic planners are keenly aware that Taiwan's corporate and cultural branding is a deliberate wedge against China's heavyweight diplomatic and economic worldwide presence. By trumpeting the virtues of associating global status with liberal economic postures, Taipei/Taiwan is already scoring in the public relations rivalry with China throughout the capitalist world notwithstanding the allure of China's market size.

Role of IT and the knowledge industry

In the understanding of the Taiwanese government's inter-ministerial Council for Economic Planning and Development (CEPD), the need for Taiwan to develop a knowledge-based economy is yet another stage in its evolution of a sustainable growth strategy. It has explained this plan as a reaction to a window of opportunity provided by the trends of 'Globalization' and 'Cyberization'. By 'Globalization', it is meant 'that cost-saving in production can no longer support continuous economic development. Therefore, *Taiwan must encourage innovation and foster new ventures as the way to maintain its global competitivness*' (CEPD, 2001; italics mine). 'Cyberization' refers to the understanding that the 'Internet expedites the distribution of information and knowledge, which makes it easier to combine with appropriate factors, and achieve better economic results. *Those advanced countries such as the US which make good use of cyberspaces to disseminate knowledge and information, have created impressive profits* (CEPD, 2001; italics mine). Therefore this opens up a window of opportunity for 'the application of knowledge and Internet as well as integration of knowledge and core competence of the existing industries' with a view towards sustaining Taiwan's international competitiveness and profitability. These are unremarkable statements that could have passed muster in any developing country industry minister's brief, but they also reveal that IT becomes the subject of a propaganda mill for improving development. There is firstly an appreciation that IT has been articulated into other states' models of economic success; and secondly, that the US is one such model which apparently employs cyberspace to create profit through knowledge dissemination. IT is recognized as a medium that inspires emulation and adaptation to existing national development plans. In a speech titled 'Deeply Cultivating Taiwan with a Global Perspective' in August 2001 spelling out his thoughts on Taiwan's future development, President Chen Shui-bian clarified that 'we will make Taiwan into a high value-added production center by promoting the "green silicon island" plan at full speed, improving R&D capabilities, and actively promoting the knowledge-based economy and industrial upgrading' (Chen, 2002, p.43). In these ways, IT appears to have been stretched into an elastic basket of meanings that is perhaps best described in terms of intellect-intensive economic activities and qualitative upgrading of existing industries. This interpretation appears to be supported by the latest 2009 initiative.

In 2009, following the further rearticulation of Taiwan's own interpretation of a blend of Castells' informational city and Sassen's global city, IT was transformed into a grand vision of an 'iTaiwan – 12 projects' (iTaiwan, 2009a). This comprised: a 'fast and convenient islandwide transportation network'; Kaohsiung Port-City Regeneration; Central Region New High-Tech Industrial Cluster Program; Taoyuan International Air City, 'Intelligent Taiwan'; industrial innovation corridors; urban and industrial park regeneration; farm village regeneration; coastal regeneration; 'green afforestation'; flood prevention and water management; and sewer construction. The augmentation of Taiwan's already renowned industrial technology parks along with the vision of industrial innovation corridors is obviously framed along the conventional IT-connected definition of a global city. However, the rest of 'iTaiwan' largely represents the enhancement of commonplace infrastructural features one would expect of any modern city. But the details of the upgrading of the islandwide transportation network suggest that Taipei is being enlarged by *word and deed* – the mass rapid transit of metropolitan Taipei would be extended into the immediate provinces. 'Intelligent Taiwan' is actually an extension of Taipei's ongoing official efforts to offer ubiquitous wireless connectivity to all other urban areas in Taiwan; broadband access would gradually become the default standard for Internet connections all over the island. A closer examination of the plan for industrial innovation corridors reveals that Taipei city's suburban Neihu Technology Park and Nankang Software Park would be connected by satellite parks linking Taipei city and its suburbs to the nearby cities of Keelung and Yilan. Each of these projects involving the enlargement and integration of the functions of Taipei is estimated to consume 58 per cent of the entire budget allocated for the iTaiwan project (iTaiwan, 2009b). The author's interview with a representative of the government-affiliated Taiwan Institute of Economic Research confirmed Taiwanese planners' appreciation of an expansive meaning of global-friendly knowledge economy: 'A few elements are crucial to a knowledge based economy (or a narrower definition as technology based economy): human capital, infrastructure (including education system), capital, capability, information and intelligence, and global connections (markets)' (Kao interview, 2009). By 2013, however, it was reported that Taiwan's IT industry was struggling to adapt to the demands of a tablet-driven format for computing, losing out to Samsung's domination of the market, while Apple Computer was fretting about Taiwan's slow adaptation to its outsourcing needs in relation to the production of the iPad (Bradsher, 2013). A follow up report in early 2014 even suggested that Taiwan's leading Smartphone manufacturer, HTC, ought to relearn the need for street-savvy propaganda in getting younger Smartphone aficionados to buy into its largely mid-market and low-end phones in the face of stiff competition from Samsung and Apple who typically fill the high end niche. The report noted that HTC's advertising for the phone they dubbed 'The One' was way too abstract to excite consumers! (Segal, 2014). HTC's woes mirror the ongoing challenge in branding Taipei the Global City.

The strategies of business attraction

As is evident from the preceding detail about Taipei's global city direction, the hand of the Taiwanese developmental state (Wang, 2003) is evident and often contributes to the obfuscation of Taipei's distinct global identity. This chameleon image may well be a matter of strategic necessity in integrating with the global capitalist economy through acting as a site of interface with global business firms. Jason Kao, Deputy Director of the Taiwan Institute of Economic Research (TIER) confirmed this need to demonstrate dovetailing with global business 'standards' in every possible manner.

There are several ways Taipei actively promotes its global status. For example:

- Establish sister city relationships for cultural exchange and building economic ties.
- Establish state-of-art science or industrial cluster (e.g. Neihu and Nankang science parks).
- Participate in important international city government organization such as IULA [International Union of Local Authorities].
- Host international conferences (such as APEC meetings), trade shows (Computex), exhibition and international games and competition (Deaflympics).
- Speed up building and renewing process of important infrastructure, such as MRT, Broadband Telecomm, water supply, roads, etc., and use major international languages for all traffic signs, posts and marks.
- Provide public services in major international language.
- Provide multiple language guiding information, including city government administrative information, practical living guide, travel guide etc.
- Promote Taipei's tourism through mass media (movies, foreign TV programmes, discovery channels, etc.).
- Attract foreign talents (Kao interview, 2009).

There was a very deliberate practice of enticement of firms into a logic of dispersal, especially in terms of attracting logistics and high technology firms into setting up some form of a base of operations in and around Taipei. Chang Kuei-lin of the Council for Economic Planning and Development explains it:

> More than 10 years ago, the Government of Taiwan set out to recreate the Taiwan economy into an Asia-Pacific Regional Operation Center (APROC). This objective was achievable because of the way multinational corporations (MNCs) operated across the Pacific Ocean's economic geography. *MNCs dispersed their 'Research & Development [R&D]', Value-Adding and Manufacturing processes to several locations. The supply chain overlapped across the entire Pacific Rim. Taiwan could take advantage of its location 'midway' across the chain.* Furthermore, the Taiwan Government implemented policies designed to shift the entire national economy towards technology-based industries.
>
> Taipei's location is the nearest hub in relation to the cities of the Pacific Rim. Taiwan encouraged European and North American firms to cluster in Taipei – specifically to set up their Regional Headquarters and International Procurement Offices there. This was a specific policy emphasis under the previous administration. However, the state of Cross-Straits relations remained an obstacle since it was a political minefield between Taipei and Beijing over Taiwan's international status then. The Regional Headquarters and International Procurement Offices set up by MNCs had to await a political breakthrough to achieve their maximum potential. (Chang interview, 2009; italics mine)

Additionally, the developmental state attempted to integrate the sociocultural niceties of becoming global into the planning and enlargement of the foreign business community in Taipei/Taiwan:

> Furthermore, the government then aimed to develop Taipei into an International Financial Centre. The Government was to address the issues of relatively high cost[s] of rental, employees and other costs of living, which the business community [had] concerns about. Furthermore, the Government was aware that Taiwan's society had to interface with a largely English-speaking business world. It was well known that the quality of Taiwan's bilingual education programs came under the scrutiny of western business circles. And a few private investors tried to recreate a high quality residential village to entice high-tech professionals to Taiwan. (Chang interview, 2009)

This created significant urban initiatives in Taipei, at the Taoyuan International Airport serving Taipei, and even in the bilingual signage on the Mass Rapid Transit in Taipei and the train systems around the island (Lewis, 2003). But these initiatives were not without their pitfalls. Chang admitted that Taiwan's past attempts to seed 'international villages' to aid the globalization of industrial sites were only partially successful due to weak conceptualization, and attempts to persuade European passenger airlines to build business hubs through Taipei failed to excite even large carriers such as Lufthansa and British Airways (Chang interview, 2009). The lesson learnt was that the propaganda of hubbing had to be concretized through the conviction of potential clients in planting tangible roots into the boldest of globalizing plans. Chang specifically warns that based on Taipei's attempt to generate IT connectivity via business promotion, attention to the offline aspects of making agents of globalization physically welcome are just as important:

> Talent, quality of living and knowledge intensive firms are successful factors in making a city competitive globally. These factors are more important than traditional factors of production like land. Of course, I have to clarify my point here – Capital is still important, but it will only flow into a country after talent, quality of life, and knowledge intensive service companies are entrenched in a location. It is imperative for Taiwan to establish a friendly environment to attract the multinational corporations to set up their regional headquarters and talent immigrants by deregulation and policy relaxation. (Chang interview, 2009)

Interviews with both the aforementioned Mr Chang of the Council for Economic Planning and Development, as well as Jason Kao of the TIER have revealed that the propaganda dimension of attracting hub businesses would also unfold according to the concept of 'agglomeration economies'. According to David McKendrick *et al.*, 'agglomeration economies' refer to 'the emergence of suppliers and a production and managerial work force with industry-specific experience and skills. Many of the benefits of location are collective in nature. Individual firms benefit from the physical proximity of related firms, even competitors' (2000, pp.11–12). A proximate gathering of interdependent, and alternately competing and complementary suppliers, manufacturers and marketers generate attraction momentum through secondary reputation and word-of-mouth transmission of co-locational advantages. This is the backbone of the continued flourishing presence of Neihu, Nankang, Hsinchu and other industrial parks in Taiwan that have gained from radial business attraction through the promotion of the 'Taipei/Taiwan' image. Taiwan's image-making has drawn considerable admiration from the Philippine IT industry (Saloma-Akpedonu, 2006, p.24). Although the contribution of the 'Knowledge Intensive Service Industries (KISI)' to Taiwan's Gross Domestic Product increased dramatically from 50 per cent in 1987 to 70.7 per cent by 2007 (CEPD, 2009, pp.20–21) some observers have warned that Taipei's global city status depends on keeping up with an existential technological relevance which in turn requires more propaganda efforts (Simon, 1996, pp.1222–1223). With the 'Tablet computer' and 'Android operating system' technological waves sweeping the IT industry and consumer markets in 2011–13, a report had recently warned that Taipei/Taiwan is confronted with a risk of losing its vaunted global city status over the long term if its home-grown IT firms and the business investors locating in Taipei do not innovate in the direction of flatter screens and portable designs that fuse mobile phone, video, camera and Internet-assisted computer capabilities. This same report warned that Taipei/Taiwan risked losing further credibility if its IT research personnel and university graduates increasingly fail to commercialize new digital innovations, or seek employment abroad due to increasingly competitive salaries across the Pacific and elsewhere (Bradsher, 2013). Faced with this challenge, the strategies of business attraction for Taipei/Taiwan ought to stay nimble either by focussing the propaganda of integration upon trends in technological change driven by foreign firms subcontracting to Taipei, or setting the pace in global technological fashion on its own.

Kuala Lumpur

Kuala Lumpur – Self-comprehension of becoming global

According to most interpretations, Kuala Lumpur's geographical importance has waxed and waned according to the varying political tides of its host nation-state, Malaysia (King, 2008). In fact, one treatment of the critical geography of the Malaysian capital suggests that its status is very much the product of consumption (Sardar, 2000). In this context, consumption refers to the construction of the status and design of the city to serve hegemonic purposes at a certain point in time. Consumption thus implies indeterminacy, and the infinite rendering of a work in progress. Indeed, historical evidence convincingly suggests that Kuala Lumpur became an urban settlement like almost any other in Malaysia that evolved at the confluence of rivers. As Sardar narrates it against the historical record, Kuala Lumpur (literally 'city at the muddy estuary') was 'chosen' as a Malay capital partly because of the waning of other Malay political kingdoms by the mid-1800s. Kuala Lumpur came into being in part due to the emergence of the tin mining community who assembled slightly upriver from the Klang and Gombak rivers in the Malay Peninsula. These tin miners were overwhelmingly the immigrant Chinese in a mostly Malay land. This insertion of a transient population rendered the Chinese community vulnerable to entanglement with the pre-existing Malay political rivalries on the Peninsula. With internecine civil war came conquest and the political strategy of holding symbolic political ground. Historians and geographers have henceforth described Kuala Lumpur as a development that was consequent upon British imperialism penetrating inland from 'toeholds' on the Peninsula's coast; this meant that the importance of 'inland' urban centres were secondary in relation to the more profitable British-controlled ports of Penang, Malacca and Singapore (Sardar, 2000, p.49). Having decided to go forward towards large scale territorial control after 1874, the British chose Kuala Lumpur as a well known Malay capital for 'cooptation' under a Residency system of indirect rule. The British subsequently reinforced the importance of Kuala Lumpur through further constitutional manoeuvres towards federation and the Malayan Union between 1895 and 1946. Taking this cue from the colonials, it is no wonder that when the disparate Malay, Chinese and Indian nationalisms on Malaysian soil were awakened after World War Two, the indigenous successor elites saw it fit to establish their seat of government in Kuala Lumpur, as well as to issue forth the cry of independence – 'Merdeka' – from a stadium within the city.

Finally, from the perspective of post independence history, Kuala Lumpur was the site for most of the intra-elite struggles for both the consolidation of authority and the venue for staging dissent. The catalogue of politically seismic events in Malaysia that emanated from Kuala Lumpur runs the gamut from the racial riots of 1969, to the pro-Anwar Ibrahim grassroots opposition protests of 1998–2000, through the Hindu Rights Action Forum protests which rocked the capital in 2007, and the anti-corruption ‘Bersih 2.0’ march in 2011, and again as the ‘Bersih 3.0’ demonstration in 2012.

Kuala Lumpur’s more recent reincarnation as a global city is also referenced from the political centre of gravity – the erstwhile administration of Prime Minister Mahathir Mohamad (1981–2003). As part of his vision for transforming Malaysia into a developed country by 2020, Premier Mahathir had officially interpreted a technological and communications-centred globalization as *the* national guiding principle. Buying into the inexorability of cheaper and more efficient potential in electronic technologies, Mahathir has an anecdote to preface his vision of revitalizing Kuala Lumpur:

> I remember the days of having to shout into the mouthpiece when making long-distance calls. Today, the reception is so clear that one does not know the speaker is 12,000 miles away. This poses a special problem for the user. He might think that he is calling someone in the same town when actually the person is on the other side of the world. The cost of his casual call would be very high. I still cannot figure how the callers are billed. It is no wonder that off and on someone gets a huge bill for calls he did not make. Maybe his foreign maid made it. (2002a, pp.3–4)

But Mahathir is also politically shrewd in partially acknowledging the dualistic political impact such globalizing information and communications technologies would have on local politics:

> Suddenly, all these marvels and more have become everyday things. The whole scenario has changed. Many people seem to be talking and gesturing, laughing and screwing up their faces all by themselves. They seem to me to be slightly mad. But, of course, they are all communicating as they have never communicated before. Maybe Mr George Soros was selling a billion dollars of Malaysian Ringgit and causing its exchange rate to plunge and impoverishing millions of people just by talking on handphone. That is now entirely possible with the new telecommunication technology. A word on the phone while walking along a street can make millions for the speaker while millions are thrown out of work, riot and destroy shops and vehicles. (Mahathir, 2002a, p.4)

Observers familiar with Malaysian politics will recall that Mahathir had politicized the debate over globalization in 1998–99 during the aftermath of the Asian financial crisis when he publicly pilloried financier George Soros as the personification of the nefarious intentions driving the activities of transnational investment funds. Nonetheless, Mahathir asserts that the intrinsic boldness of recreating virtually-oriented terrestrial developmental spaces can still discipline the politics of IT so as to earnestly lift Malaysians out of poverty:

> [W]e are not deterred, of course. It is not the technology which is bad. It is the people who apply the technology who are bad. And so Malaysia intends to make full use of the technology for its growth and development.
>
> First. We have launched the Multimedia Super Corridor (MSC), a chunk of land 15-by-50km extending between the Petronas twin towers in Kuala Lumpur to the spanking new, state-of-the-art Kuala Lumpur International Airport in Sepang. Within this area new policy, practices and laws which will facilitate the use of telecommunications for e-commerce and k-economy have been introduced. There will be incubators for small start-up companies and Research, Development and Operation centres for the big world-class companies. There will be software programmers and content producers.
>
> A university, the Multimedia University (MMU), will train the majority of the knowledge-workers and will do research in new technologies, and content production and will interact with the R&D facilities of the big companies. An entertainment village (e-village) will provide facilities for pre-production, production and post-production of animated and normal films and combinations of these. (2002a, pp.4–5)

As an addendum, Mahathir's Administration designated an 'information age' IT-friendly efficient and transparent Putrajaya to be built to house the major government offices within the corridor. Opposite Putrajaya, there would be a Cyberjaya to be built as a twin symbolic investment in the new IT-friendly era of governance and development. Since the groundbreaking ceremonies in 1995–6, the MSC is now a physical manifestation marked by a high speed express rail link connecting Kuala Lumpur's twin tower-studded city centre in the northern point of the MSC and the architecturally distinct Kuala Lumpur International Airport ('airport in the forest') in the southernmost tip; in the centre, the high-speed rail link and impressive highways connect Putrajaya and Cyberjaya to the relatively under-occupied parts of the MSC as well as to the rest of Malaysia.

Scholars of Kuala Lumpur's reinvented geography have argued that the MSC has indeed transformed Kuala Lumpur into something else but one that has yet to develop coherence. Ross King calls the new globalizing, greater Kuala Lumpur that is inclusive of the MSC as a 'city of contradictions, inconsistencies and resentments' (King, 2008, pp.xxiv). King describes a mega project that has forcibly displaced the poor and the racial minorities from the new IT-relevant landscapes while the architecture of Putrajaya exudes an idiosyncratic mix of traditional Middle Eastern domes, imported Islamic arches, and neo-western

Art Deco while the notion of the indigenous Malay *kampong* (village) has been marginalized in the grand image (King, 2008, ch.1; pp.209–212). Tim Bunnell describes the new MSC-appended Kuala Lumpur as an exaggerated attempt at constructing an '(IT) Intelligent landscape' that can only be comprehended partly as an attempt to invert western cartographies of becoming modern and global while asserting the nascent style of a new sense of synthesized 'glocal' content (2006, ch.2). The complex, global Kuala Lumpur is simultaneously a political statement of Mahathir's brave new Malaysia as well as one of nationalistic arrival in the twenty-first century. There is probably no stronger hint of propaganda at work than in the MSC's promotion.

Role of IT and the knowledge industry

If IT and nationalism can ever be alloyed, the MSC extension of Kuala Lumpur is its demonstration. Research by Tim Bunnell has argued that Mahathir's policies have framed the Kuala Lumpur-MSC city region as a monument to 'Information Age Malaysia' and its physical existence 'provides powerful symbolic resources for the imaginative construction of national space' (2002, p.294). Malaysia could not have been transformed into a nascent IT economy in the 1990s had it not been for the mobilization of an immense propaganda effort directed at home to convince its population to buy into the cult of preparation as knowledge workers, and abroad to excite the investment imaginations of high technology companies. Two acolytes of the Mahathir Administration have stated that the MSC vision was inspired by the direct advice of popular political economist Kenichi Ohmae who was closely associated with the thesis of the 'Region-State' (1995) as an ideal production scale locality for the era of globalization (Abdul and Pillai, 1996, pp.87–88). Ohmae advocated that the MSC should begin with offering financial advisory services, call centre services and direct mail services to gather momentum for expansion. Its technology had to be built upon the latest in fibre-optics emphasizing speed and volume in connectivity within the city-region, with the rest of the country and the world. Putrajaya ought to serve as a model for the possibilities of the latest form of electronic government through its façade and content. In these ways, the MSC would serve as a 'catalyst centre where world class, multimedia corporations will be invited to do business and locate their research and development facilities' (Abdul and Pillai, 1996, p.88).

Mahathir, on his part, articulated a more complex list of expectations for rendering Malaysian knowledge society a reality. To begin with, his obsession with cultivating present and future generations of IT-savvy citizens is an extension of his radical political philosophy contained in *The Malay Dilemma* which he authored in his younger days as an aspiring politician. He attributed Malay backwardness to the fact that the relaxed and cocooned rural setting of the traditional *kampong* was not conducive to self improvement and other rigorous intellectual endeavours. In contrast, the other Asian races resident in Malaysia were conditioned to struggle in urban settings. Urbanization 'alone involves a process of physical and psychological uprooting of the Malays from the traditional rural society. There can be no doubt that with this uprooting, old values and ways of life must give way to the new' (Mahathir, 1970, p.113). An IT culture must therefore be preceded with a fundamental embrace of a culture of change, creative destruction of old ways, and the staging of positive mental leaps. In Mahathirist language, cobbled ostensibly from Kenichi Ohmae, and perhaps also from Alvin Toffler's sensational *The Third Wave* (1980), he articulated the stages Malaysians had to progress to realize Vision 2020:

> It can be no accident that there is today no wealthy developed country that is information poor and no information-rich society that is poor and undeveloped ... There was a time when land was the most fundamental basis of prosperity and wealth. Then came the second wave, the age of industrialisation. Smokestacks rose where fields were once cultivated. Now, increasingly knowledge will not only be the basis of power, but also prosperity. (Summarized in Mahathir, 2002c, p.60)

This transformation was to be achieved through social engineering of human resources – 'What we have between our ears is much more important than what we have below our feet and around us' (Mahathir, 2002c, p.60). Therefore, Mahathir envisioned the need for an all-inclusive mobilization captured by neo-Churchillian and neo-Maoist discourse adapted to information age Malaysia:

> Our K-Economy Master Plan will not be drafted by the best and brightest, cloistered behind closed doors. The k-economy, the maximum application of knowledge to every Malaysian economic and business endeavour in every economic sector, is not an elitist process but one involving every Malaysian from the teacher in the classroom to his pupil, to his fisherman father and housewife mother, to the driver who drives the school bus, to the mechanic who maintains it, to the engineer who designs the vehicle, to the entrepreneur who owns the company, to his secretary, the janitor and the chairman of the Board ... It must belong to and be owned by all Malaysians. This is why in the process of drafting it, all segments of Malaysian society must participate. Before a full national consensus is reached, a thousand ideas must contend and a hundred flowers must bloom. (Mahathir, 2002c, p.62)

Since 1996, IT courses have been offered in virtually all of Malaysia's tertiary educational institutions and a dedicated Multimedia University (MMU) was even set up to spur IT education. To entice foreign investors and Malaysians, the MSC guaranteed a 'Bill of Rights' for MSC-status companies which promised amongst other things unrestricted employment of local and foreign knowledge workers, unrestricted capital sourcing from Malaysia and abroad, and exemptions from various local ownership requirements. The Malaysian Parliament reinforced these privileges by passing a number of Cyberlaws in 1997 to sweeten the deal for the MSC; they promised to protect intellectual property through online registration, licensing and royalty collection; the legalization of digital signatures for legal and business transactions; a Computer Crimes Bill punishing illegal access; as well as a Telemedicine Bill insuring doctors offering services from remote locations (Bunnell, 2006, p.95).

The Multimedia Development Corporation (MDC) was also set up to serve as a government-linked corporation cum super agency to facilitate joint ventures and advertise possibilities within the MSC. On its website, it claims to have empowered Malaysian lives in four ways: the implementation of a single Intelligent card electronic payments system interfacing with most public services such as road tolls to border control and payments of fees; E-government 'convenience at a click'; empowering learning in all schools; and enhancing health services. On the web page that spells out exactly how E-government has been transformative, it is proclaimed that 'whether voicing opinions, asking advice or applying for services, the e-Government applications has undoubtedly raised public service image and ease[d] citizens' transactions with the Government' (MDC, 2011). More recently, the MDC promised to enhance corporate entry into an optimistic digital future: 'The Creative Multimedia industry is making its mark as one of the most sought-after industries in the world, with prospects ranging from advertising, animation to computer games, publishing and also interactive media. Thus it would not be too bold to say that the Creative Multimedia industry acts as glue that bonds technology and arts together in harmony … MSC Malaysia give focus on the fundamentals of Creative Multimedia by investing in the long term prospect; namely by giving access to funding, discovering new talent, opening market opportunities and access; providing development infrastructure, policy intervention and also by forming strategic alliances with other companies' (MDC, 2013). This of course is a fine propaganda strategy that *attempts* to remake Malaysia into the image of a liberal electronic democracy. At the MSC's inception, Mahathir even pulled off a vast publicity coup by assembling a number of high technology luminaries on the MSC's International Advisory Panel such as Microsoft Corporation's Bill Gates, IBM's Louis Gerstner, James Barksdale from Netscape, Eckhard Pleiffer from Compaq, as well as Noboru Miyawaki from Nippon Telegraph and Telephone (Bunnell, 2006, pp.95–96). This level of hype was unfortunately knocked hard by the Asian financial crisis of 1997–8 when Mahathir's authoritarian measures to shore up his authority amidst an imploding economy provoked Alvin Toffler himself to publicly admonish Mahathirist policies and warn that Compaq and Hewlett Packard might have second thoughts about committing to the MSC. Currently, the MSC has plateaued at the level of offering basic IT business platforms at reasonable cost among a proximate cluster of complementary companies. Most observers agree that the level of investments have recovered from the Asian Financial Crisis attracting 7.12 billion Malaysian Ringgit in 2009–2011, compared to a total of 4.62 billion Ringgit between 1999 and 2009 (Tarrant, 2011). While the government is avidly promoting Cyberjaya abroad as a hub for companies involved in the creative content industry (i.e. producing original digital content), existing employees in Cyberjaya, such as those at the Hewlett Packard client servicing centre, claim that their IT work was getting repetitive and antithetical to skill enhancement (Tarrant, 2011). The 2013 second quarter report issued by Business Monitor International on the IT industry in Malaysia also hinted that a great deal of growth depended on sales and production in tandem with consumption, rather than creativity; it notes that 'Tablet sales are helping to compensate for the slowdown, and we believe lower priced ultrabooks and hybrids/convertibles, as well as new devices using Intel's Haswell chipsets, will boost sales later in 2013 and into 2014 and capitalize on the strong consumption story in Malaysia. Meanwhile, in the enterprise market growth will be slightly slower, with corporate customers more hesitant as a result of ongoing global economic uncertainty' (BMI, 2013).

The strategies of business attraction

In the Mahathirist vision, there is an elision of the tension between the nationalist aspirations of the new technologically-savvy Kuala Lumpur and the needs of foreign investors. In typical fashion, Mahathir argues that in recreating a hospitable space for IT businesses, he is in fact performing a special favour for existing and start-up IT-connected businesses:

> The MSC is envisioned to be a high-tech testbed that will allow companies to explore multimedia technologies without any limitations … This may seem somewhat audacious on the part of a small developing country … In fact, being a developing country helps. We offer a greenfield site, unencumbered by industrial practices and legacies or entrenched interests – a site dedicated to the full application of IT in the new age electronic commerce.
>
> We have before us the example of Britain and the United States, one fathered the Industrial Revolution, while the other brought it to its full development. America was then one huge greenfield site – providing the optimum conditions for technology and business to flourish, to fulfil the promise of industrialisation. We have taken this as a model. (Mahathir, 2002e, p.107)

This of course brings to mind the impression of incoherence generated by the architectural formations in Kuala Lumpur International Airport, Putrajaya, and the Petronas Twin Towers. An attempt at objectively reading business strategy out of Mahathir's statements would require appreciating his selling of the virtues of starting from a blank slate on the Malaysian side; for the foreign investor, the attraction would lie in possibility of a space for creative destruction – the 'greenfield' and 'testbed'. In one of his sharpest messages to a Malaysian audience, he invoked the metaphors of popular science fiction:

> I would like to see MIMOS [the Malaysian Institute for Microelectronics] and the MDC [Multimedia Development Corporation] working together to help a brave new breed of entrepreneurs: the cyberpreneurs or netpreneurs. Think of MIMOS as our *Starship Enterprise*, the flagship of a fleet of cyberbusinesses. The flag it carries is nothing less than the national consciousness for the knowledge society and knowledge-based industries.
>
> But more than that, this mother ship will actively encourage these fragile cybercraft. It will share its expertise, thereby giving cyberpreneurs the confidence to go where no businessman or woman has gone. And it will always be on standby to help its fleet establish new colonies in cyberspace … the idea is to create a self-supporting system that promotes everyone's existence. As a government-funded institution, MIMOS is not in the business of competition but of cooperation. It is here to develop a web of interdependent, mutually supportive cyberbusinesses working on the frontiers of the k-economy. (Mahathir, 2002d, pp.92–93)

Despite these grandiose imaginings of a fleet of e-businesses arising out of self-starting entrepreneurship, Mahathir articulated a significant note of caution in the wake of the Asian Financial Crisis. Amidst warnings about easy liquidity fuelling the financial bubble of the 'wonder of dotcoms' before 1998, he advised that

> … Malaysians must not place too high an expectation from this new business. There is a lot of money to be made from the right kind of application of data and knowledge, the right software and the right ideas … Start-up companies in the Internet-based business come fast and furious. They are really based on ideas for the application of data and the speed and directness of communication. But financing a new business will always be difficult despite the venture capitalists being willing to lose money on nine-tenth of their investments. But when a company hits paydirt the returns can be very, very considerable. Market capitalisation can grow very rapidly. E-commerce companies which are only a few years old have been known to buy up major corporations which are more than a century old.
>
> In e-commerce experience can even be a hindrance, especially experience in the old business and the old way of doing business. (Mahathir, 2002b, pp.14–15)

Propagandizing the global-friendly information age Kuala Lumpur with creative language is one thing, adjusting that discourse to reality and to survival through the tides of the worldwide cycles of capitalism are two to three different things. The IT-speeded currency turbulence and stock market panic that characterized the Asian Financial Crisis definitely rattled the nascent MSC and along with it Kuala Lumpur's image as the flagship of the confident new Malaysia. It seemed as if Mahathir the IT prophet was learning along with his countrymen the dangers posed by investment bubbles generated by the heady talk of techno-miracles amidst globalization. In the meantime, the inheritors of Mahathir's vision at the MMU argued that socio-political geography was still a significant obstacle to connectivity. MMU's president, Zaharin Yusof, lamented that connectivity throughout the MSC and within the rest of Malaysia was overly dependent upon the quality of pre-existing fibre-optic cables and traditional landlines of the traditional telecommunications provider, Telekom Malaysia. Furthermore, the Federal Government sitting in Putrajaya was weighed down by the need to devote resources to enhancing telecommunications infrastructure outside the Kuala Lumpur-MSC region. Additionally he argued that

> Cyberlaws here in general tend to be more 'protective' rather than 'proactive', and this may to some extent restrict innovations and creativity. Tax incentives and other generous forms of pro-investment legislation passed by the federal government in Kuala Lumpur also favour MSC-based companies as opposed to all companies. There is also the problem of which laws take precedence over which [others] when companies operate both within and outside of the MSC – you can refer to the MSC-specific laws, national cyberlaws, federal laws, state laws and religious laws to gauge the complexity of what I am referring to. IT companies residing in the MSC, a good example of which is the MMU that I preside over, spread their workers over several locations across Malaysia – Penang and Melaka are favoured locations for dispersal of IT operations.
>
> Furthermore, the IT laws somehow tend to be implemented at a very slow rate not only in Malaysia but also worldwide. Perhaps Singapore faces fewer constraints because of its implementation scale – Singapore is a city-state. Malaysia has a large hinterland to manage for IT development. (Zaharin and Zahid interview, 2009)

A 2001 report on the progress of the MSC by McKinsey and Associates that was commissioned by the Malaysian government had already warned that the MSC had not lived up to its promise within its first five years of operation. McKinsey and Associates criticized the persistence of 'red tape' in granting firms MSC status; there was conflict between the Multimedia Development Corporation and the companies they were supposed to assist; the quality and numbers of graduates produced by the MMU was short of expectation; the MSC had failed to attract sufficient 'world class' firms; and there was insufficient coordination between Malaysia Telekom and other Internet Service Providers on providing sufficient infrastructural support for the MSC (Huff, 2002, pp.253–254). Furthermore, analysts and critical journalists have alleged that the affirmative action policy of granting Malays *Bumiputra* ('sons of the soil') status for preferential entry into national universities have skewed the true capabilities of Malaysian intellectual capital for achieving the full potential of the k-economy (Huff, 2002, p.254; Bunnell, 2002b).

Some observers such as Toby Huff have however been quite willing to be cautiously optimistic in noting that if the MSC-appended Kuala Lumpur were compared with the rest of the Muslim world in 2001–2, Mahathir's vision had notched tangible achievements. When benchmarked against the rest of the world on a spectrum ranging from the high end 'Innovative leaders in E-Government' to the modest category of 'Platform Builders in E-Government', Malaysia ranks in the latter region together with Japan, Brazil, South Africa, Italy and Mexico. Even in terms of numbers of Internet hosts per 10,000 and Computers per 1,000 of population in 2001, Malaysia came in only fourth behind Singapore, Hong Kong and South Korea (Huff, 2002, pp.260–261). The IT leadership at the MMU take the philosophical view about the ultimate success of the Kuala Lumpur-MSC vision:

> It still holds true that in the IT age, a speedboat is still preferable to a tanker in navigating the proverbial seas of competition. But I would argue that the tanker is still not a lost cause. There are three roles in a technological economy: Enablers; Infrastructure providers; and Content creators. Therefore, I think of the technological economy as entirely driven by intellectual capital. In addition, these roles spell complementarity among knowledge hubs and intellectual capital production in various locations. The context we are operating in must be accounted for. One must complement one's 'competitors'; and one must accept that knowledge workers, such as IT professionals, are mobile in the borderless technological economy …
>
> It should be noted that Malaysia, animated by Mahathir's vision, is trying to obtain the lead in realising an Islamic Renaissance by creating a model of an Islamic knowledge hub in Malaysia. Prime Minister Abdullah, for instance, followed up by instituting 'Islam Hadari' – a vision of a progressive, technology-friendly and advanced Malaysia. It is a new philosophical framework prioritizing the exploration of new knowledge. The infostructure is ready, but execution has yet to be fully achieved …
>
> The Multimedia Development Corporation and the MSC project are both agents striving to transform Malaysia's current status, from being a net importer of software technology to a net exporter. Enabling space is one area where Malaysia may enjoy a competitive advantage internationally. Incrementally, Malaysia is exploiting this to good effect …
>
> The reversion in 2009 to *Bahasa Melayu* as the language of instruction in science and technology in tertiary education is a setback. But this does not necessarily mean that the Malaysian economy is hamstrung. Just look at the examples of Japan and South Korea – both managed to steer their economies into the high technology mould and become producers with 'world class' branding in spite of their societies' lack of facility in English. But Malaysia under Prime Ministers Mahathir and Najib are emphasising the need to produce thinking students, critical learning processes, and 'smart schools'. (Zaharin and Zahid interview, 2009)

In 2008, although 'Service Industries' contributed 58 per cent to Malaysian GDP as a sign of the Kuala Lumpur-MSC project's vitality, the Asian Development Bank noted that the obsession with IT-projects needed to be balanced with attention to the recognition that 'Growth in the future will increasingly depend both on a move into activities that are intensive in knowledge, skills, and technology, and on an increase in total factor productivity … [Additionally,] Eradicating poverty and reducing regional income disparities is another challenge' (ADB, 2009, p.6). Moreover, the Malaysian government's Department of Statistics admitted that in 2012, the information and communications sector contributed only a measly 7 per cent within the 54.6 per cent contribution by the Services Sector to overall GDP (DoS Malaysia, 2013). It is therefore not farfetched to conclude that the global city pretensions of Kuala Lumpur and its MSC appear to require a constant reconciliation between visionary propaganda and developmental reality.

Singapore

Singapore – Self-comprehension of becoming global

Historically, geopolitical designs upon Singapore have appeared to fix the island as a destination for the exchange of flows from either across the expanse of Asia, or more recently from across the world. The pre-modern history of the island suggested that it was a prize for regional empires based in neighbouring Java, Sumatra, the Malay Peninsula and Indochina. The British purchased the island from a local potentate in 1819 while on a quest for constructing a suitable 'free port' for their commerce and the commerce of the region. The British shaped Singapore's destiny indelibly as a global city with their philosophy of indirect taxation and profiteering from services attending to the trade that landed on Singaporean shores. The British were themselves enthusiastic traders who relished the advantages of reciprocal open access for themselves. Furthermore, Singapore would serve as the most efficient export outlet for Britain's raw material extractions from the Malayan colonies to the north. This attitude was notably distinct from Britain's colonial rivals in the region who pursued rigid policies of mercantilism and monopoly. For their differentiated perspective on open commercial access, the British, as well as their colonial subjects on the island, were amply rewarded with Singapore's reputation as the busiest centre for import and export traffic in manufactured goods and raw materials – the 'Clapham junction of the East' (Turnbull, 1988).

From then on, the debate between free trade and economic discrimination framed post-independence Singapore's foreign economic policies. There was an additional complication when both then-Malaya and Singapore attained formal independence from the British in 1957 and 1963 respectively – both successor states were now pursuing nationalistic policies across the entire range of their public life. The British policy had been to make the Malayan hinterland subservient upon the efficiency of Singapore's port. Now both the postcolonial elites in Kuala Lumpur and Singapore attempted to promise their respective peoples a higher standard of living through economic regeneration and eventually some form of material independence as well. Between 1963 and 1965 both states – Singapore and Malaya – tried federation for developmental goals, but the nature of ethno-nationalistic political currents worked at cross purposes with the goal of restoring the pattern of economic interdependence between trading hub and hinterland.

Singapore's policymakers faced the nightmare of trying to steer a developmental design for the fledgling city-state that no longer enjoyed a guaranteed hinterland. At the very least, it had the British design for a free trade hub for guidance. Fortunately, the Singaporean political elite correctly appraised the differences between nineteenth century geoeconomics and its assumptions of the singular dominance of the maritime trade, and the possibilities afforded by a judicious mix of geography and technology in the twentieth century. This evaluation by the People's Action Party (PAP) government that has ruled Singapore since independence is best articulated by its first foreign minister, S. Rajaratnam, in his speech on 'Singapore: The Global City' in 1972: the Global City 'is the child of modern technology. It is the city that electronic communications, supersonic planes, giant tankers and modern economic and industrial organization have made inevitable. Whether the Global City will be a happier place than the megalopolis out of whose crumbling ruins it is emerging will depend on how wisely and boldly we shape its direction and growth' (Rajaratnam, 1987, pp.225–226). Connectivity by telecommunications and the technological networks of finance would ensure Singapore's permanent communion with sister Global Cities such as London, Tokyo, and Hong Kong. Faith was placed in the global integration momentum fostered by multinational corporations to bind the Republic into a world hinterland of infinite resources and skills. Lopsided techno-financial dependency and its attendant implications for a sovereign foreign policy are likely outcomes of such an arrangement. But for Rajaratnam 'Singapore must be prepared to run these risks simply because the alternative to not moving into the global economic system is, for small Singapore, certain ruin' (Rajaratnam, 1987, p.230).

This was language that was remarkably prescient for a developmental city-state that predated the academic prognoses of Sassen and Castells by a decade and a half. To realize the global city vision, the PAP leaders embraced the concept of 'environmental possibilism', which treats the milieu for economic improvement 'only as a set of opportunities, limitations and possibilities' (Savage, 1992, p.189). They have alternately used convenient buzzwords of the likes of 'cosmopolitan city/cosmopolis', 'digital information society' and 'Singapore 21', to excite both domestic and foreign imaginations. In this regard, it is appropriate to conclude that virtually all of Singapore's 710 square kilometers have become discursively scripted into the terminology of constructed political and developmental landscapes (Kong and Yeoh, 2003). Indeed, the then-Minister for Information and the Arts, George Yeo breathtakingly described how Singapore had achieved the infrastructural foundations of digital information society by 1999:

> In 1991, we launched a long-term programme to promote the development of IT and establish Singapore as hub for e-commerce. This involves both hardware and software. The hardware includes the connection of every home, office and school in Singapore to a broadband network called Singapore One. Every home in Singapore already has access to broadband via existing telephone lines using ADSL technology. By the end of the year, every home in Singapore will also be connected by an optical fibre network to the kerbside, and by co-axial cable from the kerbside to the home. But even more important than the physical network is the legal and regulatory structure that we have put in place to facilitate the growth of e-commerce. For e-commerce to flourish, we need certainty in matters like authentication, intellectual property protection, contract definition, dispute resolution and privacy. (Yeo, 1999, para.12)

Singapore's elite-driven purposive anxiety in designing the global city has been regurgitated by most of its capitalist class. One sample from Mrs Lee Ju Song, the erstwhile Deputy Executive Director of the Singapore International Chamber of Commerce, is worth quoting here since is it spells out the link between techno-connectivity to the economics of becoming global in the IT era:

> Because Singapore is very small we have to look beyond the horizon and develop an external economy. In wanting to do so, we have to be able to identify niches. Speed is definitely going to be the key to success. It's not like in the past when you were talking about economies of scale to be successful. I think now that we are talking about the economics of scopes. We are setting up a set of international networks of satellite economic alliances to be successful. We have to be boutique-like in our approach to business. We must have effective market flexibility and speed in order to succeed and we are trying to use this strength that we have in tying up with our business partners outside the region for a joint presence in countries such as China, Vietnam and India, as well as in ASEAN (Association of Southeast Asian Nations). (Quoted in Murray and Perera, 1995, pp.3–4)

'Speed', 'economics of scopes' and 'joint presence' are variations upon the theme of Singaporean global city propaganda, but these remain illustrative even in the twenty-first century of the integral part played by IT connectivity in the Singaporean set-up.

Role of IT and the knowledge industry

Unlike Kuala Lumpur, and perhaps more like Taipei, IT in Singapore was originally conceived in official quarters as a strategic extension of economic growth strategies. It existentially reinforces an already attained 'global city' status. In the official 1985 White paper setting out a National IT Plan, the government noted in detached fashion that 'present trends indicate that IT will become a key technology in improving business efficiency and labour productivity, and generating new businesses' (NITPWC, 1985, p.ii). This observation was in fact a direct outcome of the highly publicized government postmortem on one of the city-state's worst recessions since the worldwide oil crisis of 1973–4. This larger post mortem noted that the growth in trade in banking, insurance, tourism, engineering, consultancy and other professional services had 'counterbalanced the slowdown in international merchandise trade'. This report on 'new directions' for the Singapore economy argued that services would be a leading growth sector 'provided we promote them aggressively' on the basis that 'we [already] have comprehensive transport and telecommunication links to the rest of the world. We have a well-educated, English-speaking workforce' (MTI, 1986, p.61). The prognosis for change that followed was deliberately not couched in draconian tones of paradigmatic displacement, but rather in the language of enhancement:

> The service sector is primarily knowledge-based ... Use of IT will result in improved service levels and higher productivity ... Singapore manufacturers must similarly exploit IT to reduce the labour content of their manufactured goods to remain competitive ... It is not enough to computerise. What is needed is strategic and creative exploitation of IT by our industries. Our companies must use IT to position themselves in the right market niches, and exploit IT applications in more far-reaching ways than our competitors. (NITPWC, 1985, p.ii)

The IT Plan of 1985 listed a seven-pronged approach to enhance the role of IT:

> IT Manpower – IT professionals were depicted as the extension of the City-state's relentless valuation of human resources. 'They must be developed into highly skilled champions who are experts in exploiting IT to enable our enterprises to gain [a] competitive edge and to introduce new IT related products and services'.
>
> IT culture – which meant the promotion of a 'supportive culture' for preparing citizens for engagement with the information economy.
>
> Information Communication Infrastructure – The 'backbone' of IT-associated businesses requires Singapore to develop 'the best telecommunications facilities in the world'.
>
> IT Application – All economic sectors ought to exploit IT. For those users that are reluctant to embrace it, 'new forms of handholding assistance must be provided to overcome their technological phobia'.
>
> IT Industry – A proper IT industry will be the 'main driving force to push the economy towards a higher level of performance'.

> Climate for Creativity and Entrepreneurship – 'We must develop indigenous capability in applied research in IT so that we can benefit from advanced technological applications'.
>
> Co-ordination and Collaboration – 'To realise the full potential of IT, we need to unite the individual efforts of various organisations under the leadership of a new National Committee on IT which will evolve from the present Committee on National Computerisation'. (Summarized and quoted from NITPWC, 1985, pp.vi–vii)

The art of socializing an entire economy and its workers into a culture of IT is typical of the Singaporean developmental city-state. The National IT Plan is as much about precipitating a mental shift as setting plans in concrete. Between 1982 and 1985, Singapore could boast a quadrupling of IT professionals from 1,500 to 4,300; as well as a nearly five-fold growth in sales of the numbers of microcomputers in the same period, from 5,977 to 19,901 (Motiwalla and Gilbert, 1989, p.882, Table 39.1). In an early survey of the outcomes of the 1985 IT Plan, it was noted that the central direction of the design of the Singaporean information society was an advantage wielded by the Singapore authorities. Nonetheless, it was observed that how much further could be achieved in economic growth depended upon external demand, i.e. the multinational corporations perceiving Singapore as attractive. Singapore, literally had to register as a connected Global City capable of allowing investors to capitalize upon the nexus of computers and communications enabling 'access to databases spaced across the country or even internationally' (Motiwalla and Gilbert, 1989, p.889). On the domestic front, statistics from the latest available comparison showed that between 2000 and 2005, the percentage of households with access to a computer at home rose from 61 per cent to 74 per cent, with Internet access rising from 50 to 66 per cent. Likewise, the description of Internet usage in the same period listed the following consolidation: sending or receiving emails; sourcing for information; downloading software; completing or lodging forms online; watching news Webcasts; downloading music; and Internet banking (Lee, 2006). In February 2009, a commercial Web traffic monitoring site reported that the Singaporean propaganda of a global IT-savvy city had worked rather successfully on the Singaporean public:

> Internet users in Singapore averaged 21 hours online per visitor during February, with online communication, entertainment, and social networking topping the list of how users were most likely to spend their time. Highlighting the particular significance of online communication in Singapore, Instant Messaging captured 24 percent of total minutes, making it the leading activity, while Web-based email accounted for 6 per cent. Singaporeans spent 14 percent of their online time at the Entertainment category, which includes popular Web brands like YouTube and MediaCorp, while social networking accounted for 8 percent. (Hartzer-Comscore, 2009)

Additionally, there were political side effects to this 'Global City Singapore' that track developments worldwide. Online political expression has proliferated in terms of blogs and alternative news sites such as *The Online Citizen* and *Temasek Review*, and much of this have compelled the ruling PAP government to accept a pluralistic political spectrum both online and offline, including the possibility that 'online social capital' exists (Skoric, Ying and Ng, 2009). Since 2002, there have been a number of instances where the government invoked laws on sedition to take down racist and blasphemous postings on Singapore-based blogs and Facebook pages stirring concerns from many libertarian advocacy groups based locally and abroad.[1] This is apparently an acceptable cost in the perception of the governing authorities for policing racial and religious harmony amongst a population comprising Chinese, Malay and Indian ethnicities situated within a politically volatile postcolonial region.

The strategies of business attraction

Although the National IT Plan of 1985 propagated the notion of IT as an efficient economic growth enhancer and suggested hazily that an IT industry could flourish autonomously on its own, it took a second report to fully sketch the 'Vision of an Intelligent Island'. This popularly dubbed *IT2000 Report* spelled out the importance of accentuating Singapore city's hub status in relation to all manner of information flows (NCB, 1992). It acknowledged that a 'new information order' was in play shaped by large multinational corporations 'competing and spawning alliances around the globe'; and equally important was the fact that Governments in the OECD grouping were investing heavily in research and development of IT products. As a result Singapore ought to foster specialization in highly demanded miniature IT devices, improving the speed and volume of broadband connections, explore the proliferation of multimedia applications and integrate 'tetherless computing' into transportation, work and lifestyle options (NCB, 1992, pp.11–13). The larger game was to get the city-state's economy,

> plugged into the global networks … Complementary use of resources across borders is becoming the basis for global competitive advantage … The NII [National Information Infrastructure] has an important role in this strategic economic thrust. It will help turn Singapore into a highly efficient switching centre for goods, services, capital, information and people. (NCB, 1992, p.20)

In concrete terms, a Singapore Business Hub would mean that when armed 'with high bandwidth communication, companies will be encouraged to base more high value added functions like product design, research and development, regional marketing and technical support in Singapore'. An IT-enabled 'Services Hub'

1 See Tan Kwoh-Jack's chapter in this volume for an in-depth examination of the Government of Singapore's political interventions in the cyber world.

could portend that 'our distance learning system could be projected overseas to turn Singapore into a regional education and corporate training centre. Similarly, our medical specialists, architects, engineers and other experts could provide consultancy services to counterparts in other countries, without having to do too much travelling'. The appended 'Transportation Hub' vision would mean that 'the NII will support the electronic exchange of data and sharing of information to make our air and sea ports most efficient in moving goods and providing convenience for passengers' (NCB, 1992, pp.20–22). In this way, traditional terrestrial shipping and airport service providers such as the PSA Corporation, the Civil Aviation Authority of Singapore, the Maritime Port Authority and Singapore Airlines would develop 'nth' capabilities to shorten transit and travel time through Singapore and for cooperating partners. This was to update the historic role of Singapore for the twenty-first century.

The IT2000 Report did however devote nearly 12 of its 54 pages to the importance of IT manpower couched in terms of education and training and ultimately empowerment of creativity (NCB, 1992, pp.25–36). In very elegant phrasing, the Ministry of Information, Communications and the Arts (MICA) subsequently linked creativity to IT policies in the following manner: 'Multi-dimensional creativity – artistic and literary creativity, design innovation, business entrepreneurship and technological innovation – will be the new currency of success'. In terms of tangible economics, the Creative Industries 'are defined as "industries which are inspired by *cultural and artistic creativity* and have the potential to create *economic value* through the *generation and exploitation of intellectual property*". This definition is adapted from the UK definition in the Creative Industries Mapping Document (Nov 1998) by the UK Creative Industries Taskforce. In Singapore, the Creative Industries are broadly classified into the arts, media, design and software and IT services' (MICA, 2009a). In line with this imported and synthesized vision, the Singaporean government drew up a *Creative Industries Development Strategy* in 2002 which comprised three components: 'Renaissance City 2.0', 'Design Singapore' and 'Media 21'.

Renaissance City 2.0 referred to the possibility of leveraging on present and potential intellectual and artistic strengths to generate a highly motivated and multitalented global city that would excel in arts and culture. The logic was that when locals and foreigners consume artistic products on and off stage, they would support the creative industries with their expenditure, along with multiplier benefits for the wider tourism industry, transportation industry, and arts education. In propagating this holistic strategy, Singapore's expenditure for the Arts was consciously contrasted to similar statistics for London, New York and Hong Kong which showed the Singaporeans under-funded (MICA, 2009b). In these ways, public and political enthusiasm would be generated for the new frontier of the Creative Industries.

Likewise the 'Design Singapore' dimension ingeniously states that 'design can be understood as material and conceptual innovation realized through the integration of arts, culture, business and technology, and experienced as beauty, value and meaning. It is therefore a misconception that design is just about look and feel and image makeover'. MICA illustrated this aspect by drawing attention to the profile of industrial and consumer product innovation associated with Finland, Ireland, Scotland, Hong Kong and South Korea. It added that design could also help 'brand' a city or state for global circulation in the informational marketplace; Singapore could be put on par with a brand like Sony, Philips and Samsung (MICA, 2009c). Placed in tandem, both the Renaissance City and Design Singapore concepts should help boost Singapore's lucrative pre-IT Meetings, Incentives, Conventions and Exhibitions services sub-sector. In May 2010, Steve Ballmer, the CEO of Microsoft Corporation, visited the Republic and declared it to be positioned to be at the forefront of the next major transformation in IT architecture – cloud computing. In Ballmer's vision, cloud computing eliminates the obstacles of start-up costs and geography by 'providing a platform for combining the convenience and power of smart digital devices with the computing and storage capacity of giant data centres' that can be physically remote from the user (Ballmer, 2010). In tune with this advice, between 2011 and 2014, the Government of Singapore has rolled out supplementary initiatives emphasizing fourth generation broadband connectivity for all homes and offices, cloud computing practices, and organized public-private sector partnerships to enhance cybersecurity for all firms operating in Singapore. In fact, Singapore is struggling assiduously to be the centre of excellence for cybersecurity practices in the Asia-Pacific following the worldwide trend of privately sponsored hacking attacks, as well as the rogue attacks of the so-called 'Anonymous' collective. Singapore's government websites were themselves the subjects of Anonymous attacks in 2013 and 2014, a trend that poses a significant new challenge to Singapore the IT-connected global city. As of mid-2014, cybersecurity professionals constitute a mere 0.8 per cent of the city's entire IT workforce (Leonal, 2014).

Finally 'Media 21' articulated a vision of 'Singapore as a Global Media City, where media services and projects are created, developed, traded and distributed to the international market. The vision anchors Singapore as Asia's leading media marketplace and financing hub, producing high quality content and digital media development. Media 21 seeks to increase the GDP contribution of the media cluster from the current 1.56 per cent to 3 per cent in 10 years, and creating over 10,000 new jobs for Singaporeans' (MICA, 2009d). This third dimension of creative industry is somewhat more straightforward in its projection of IT's translated economic value. Furthermore, its industrial imagination can be mapped to conventional industrial and business terminology – pre-production, production, post-production, packaging, marketing and distribution in relation to television and cinematic film-making, music recordings, singers and bands. It is also about hosting media awards events to precipitate a global presence to Singapore's aspirations. Currently, it should not go unnoticed that Singapore hosts more than 45 foreign press agencies, wire agencies, radio and satellite television broadcasters including CNBC Asia, BBC, Bloomberg and ZDF German television. *Reuters*,

International New York Times, *Asahi Shimbun* and the *Wall Street Journal* have all got correspondents based in Singapore to cover Southeast Asia.

It would therefore not be too much of a stretch of credibility to assert that Singapore as a global city is a thoroughly constructed endeavour across history, through to the IT-connected present. The discourse of IT has in fact intensified Singapore's need to propagandize its current status and potential. The late nineteenth century maritime port of efficiency has been politically upgraded into the twenty-first century equivalent of a cyberjunction of informational flows. The postcolonial developmental state, which has operated thus far according to authoritarian instincts, has acted as the visible hand of construction. This Singaporean Global City seems ironically to bear the hallmarks of guided planning and disciplined politics beneath the glossy images. This is perhaps where liberal critics have accused the city-state's governing class of underestimating the postmodern overlap in meaning between creative industry and 'creative rebelliousness' (Lim, 2002). Others point to the fact that the hitherto successful state-directed model of rendering Singapore into an economically-hospitable informational hub of design and production may ironically stifle long-term local creativity through the creation of architectural and policy grandeur inspired by overseas examples (Lee, 2007). In these ways, even the connected Asian global city's critics pay its planners a backhanded compliment for being overly successful in their propaganda for IT culture to the point where the developmental state might become a victim of its own success when future ounces of creativity might require more spontaneity from civil society.

Conclusion

In this chapter, the author had set out to argue that the very act of promotion has contributed to the actualization of global cities. In other words, the cases of Taipei, Kuala Lumpur and Singapore have demonstrated that in the era of IT connectivity, global cities do not come about in deterministic unilinear fashion. The models posited by Saskia Sassen, Manuel Castells and others have left a major gap in explanation that can be filled through a study of the propaganda aspects of IT connectivity. Becoming IT-ready in terms of getting the infrastructure right, schooling the populations in the use of electronic information, and the re-engineering of complete landscapes for the Information Age are acts of deliberate offline political will. The operationalization of political willpower requires that domestic and foreign opinions have to be aligned with elite aspirations at home, hence the need for the entire panoply of buzzwords, catchphrases, futuristic discourse, elaborate planning logic, business attraction logic, and in Kuala Lumpur's case, the role of a charismatic leader.

It should also be noted that so much of this promotional discourse resides within an implicitly urban logic – cities become global only when they can link with equivalently labelled IT-connected entities producing comparable and competing informational products. There is a 'foreign audience' in a borderless economic and social terrain 'out there' in the globalizing *terra electronica* that requires the operation of a global city foreign policy whose chief characteristic is clearly propagandizing the culture of IT. This foreign policy refers to the realm of promotional activity designed to attain for the city a significant degree of connectedness with cross-border flows of finance, production and information so as to achieve a commanding position in the global capitalist economy to extract surplus from these very flows. The brick and mortar formations of political bureaucracies are realigned to harmonize with the intangible effects of discourses to manifest the reality of a globally-linked IT architecture. Obviously, this study has been constrained by its deliberate consideration of postcolonial, or developmental, latecomer global cities in Asia. More non-Asian studies should be performed with the propaganda angle as a starting point. As has been quoted earlier, even Manuel Castells believes that IT does require an *articulation* of its utility in official discourse before it can be translated into implementation. It is the same with *becoming* a connected global city. Alterity exists therefore in the not-so-invisible hand propagandizing a global IT-connected city into existence.

References

Abdul, A.A.R. and Pillai, S. 1996. *Mahathir: leadership and vision in science and technology*. Kuala Lumpur: Academy of sciences Malaysia.

ADB. 2009. 'Asian Development Outlook 2009: Rebalancing Asia's Growth: Malaysia'. [online] Available at: <www.adb.org/Documents/books/ADO/2002/cam.asp> (Accessed 17 July 2009).

Ballmer, S. 2010. Cloud Computing Ushers in a Tech-driven Transformation. *Business Times* (Singapore) 27 May.

Barber, B. 2013. *If Mayors Ruled the World: Dysfunctional Nations, Rising Cities*. New Haven: Yale University Press.

Bernays, E. 1928/2009. *Propaganda*. New York: Horace Liveright, [online] Available at: <http://www.historyisaweapon.com/defcon1/bernprop.html> (Accessed 5 July 2013).

BMI. 2013. 'Malaysia Information Technology Report Q3 2013'. Presented by Business Monitor International. [online] Available at <http://www.marketresearch.com/Business-Monitor-International-v304/Malaysia-Information-Technology-Q3–7622269/> (Accessed 11 July 2013).

Bradsher, K. 2013. Taiwan Frets as its Electronics Industry Stumbles. *International Herald Tribune*. 14 May. pp.1,15.

Bunnell, T. 2002. 'Cities for Nations? Examining the City – Nation-State Relation in Information Age Malaysia'. *International Journal of Urban and Regional Research* 26(2), pp.284–298.

Bunnell, T. 2006. *Malaysia, Modernity and the Multimedia Super Corridor: A Critical Geography of Intelligent Landscapes*, 2nd edn. Abingdon: Routledge.

Castells, M. 1989. *The Informational City: Information technology, Economic Restructuring, and the Urban-Regional Process*. Oxford: Basil Blackwell.

CEPD 2001. 'Plan to Develop Knowledge-Based Economy in Taiwan – CEPD, Executive Yuan June 2001', available at http://www.cepd.gov.tw/encontent/dn.aspx?uid=2982 (Accessed 10 July 2012).

CEPD. 2009. *2008 Economic Development ROC (Taiwan)*. Taipei: Council for Economic Planning and Development, Executive Yuan ROC (Taiwan).

Chang, interview. 2009. Interview with Mr Kuei-Lin Chang, Director-General, Department Of Urban And Housing Development, Council For Economic Planning and Development, Executive Yuan, On 3 June 2009 at 0945H.

Chittolini, G. 1994. Cities, 'City-States', and Regional States in North-Central Italy. In: C. Tilly and W. Blockmans, eds. 1994. *Cities and the Rise of States in Europe, A.D. 1000 to 1800*. Boulder: Westview Press, pp.28–43.

DoS Malaysia. 2013. Statistics of Service Sector, Conference on Trade Competitiveness Analysis (Powerpoint Presentation), Department of Statistics, Malaysia, 12 March 2013. [online] Available at <http://www.epu.gov.my/documents/10124/ddf4d5c0-ff14–4df8-b90f-46fff8a982b3> (Accessed 12 July 2013).

Doob, L.W. 1995. Goebbels' Principles of Propaganda. In: R. Jackall, ed. 1995. *Propaganda*. New York: New York University Press, pp.190–216.

Friedmann, J. 1986. The World City Hypothesis. *Development and Change* 17(1), pp.69–84.

Gilbert, A. and Gugler, J. 1987. *Cities, Poverty, and Development: Urbanization in the Third World*. 4th edn. Oxford: Oxford University Press.

Hartzer-Comscore. 2009. 'ComScore Releases First Public Report of Online Usage in Singapore' available at http://www.billhartzer.com/pages/comscore-releases-first-public-report-of-online-usage-in-singapore/ (Accessed 21 July 2009).

Hill, C. 2003. *The Changing Politics of Foreign Policy*. Basingstoke: Macmillan.

Hirota, J.M. 1995. Making Products Heroes: Work in Advertising Agencies. In: R. Jackall, ed. 1995. *Propaganda*. New York: New York University Press, pp.329–350.

Huff, T. 2002. Malaysia's Multimedia Super Corridor and Its First Crisis of Confidence. *Asian Journal of Social Science* 30(2), pp.248–270.

iTaiwan. 2009a. iTaiwan 12 Projects. Pamphlet produced by the Council for Economic Planning and Development, Executive Yuan.

iTaiwan. 2009b. The i-Taiwan 12 Projects. (Powerpoint slides) via the Ministry of Economic Affairs, Taiwan website available at http://investintaiwan.nat.gov.tw/zh-tw/ (Accessed 10 July 2009).

Jackall, R. 1995. The Magic Lantern: the World of Public Relations. In: R. Jackall, ed. 1995. *Propaganda*. New York: New York University Press, pp.351–399.

Kao, interview. 2009. Interview with Dr Jason Kao, Deputy Director of the Taiwan Institute of Economic Research, on behalf of the Ministry of Economic Affairs, Taiwan, submitted as an electronic transcript in Microsoft Word format on 15 June 2009. Direct email communication with author.

King, R. 2008. *Kuala Lumpur and Putrajaya – Negotiating Urban Space in Malaysia.* Singapore: NUS Press and NIAS Press.

Lasswell, H. 1995. Propaganda. In: R. Jackall, ed. 1995. *Propaganda.* New York: New York University Press, pp.13–25.

Lee, M.C. 2006. Infocomm Usage by Households and Individuals 2000–2005. *Statistics Singapore Newsletter – March 2006.* Provided by the Infocomm Development Authority of Singapore. Available at: http://www.singstat.gov.sg/pubn/papers/people/ssnmar06-pg17–19.pdf (Accessed 21 July 2012).

Leonal, B. 2014. Bloomberg News: Cybersecurity Skills Shortage Poses Threat in Singapore, 22 June 2014. *Businessweek.com* available at http://www.businessweek.com/news/2014-06-22/cybersecurity-skills-shortage-poses-threat-in-singapore (Accessed 6 August 2014).

Lewis, S.W. 2003. The Media of New Public Spaces in Global Cities: subway advertising in Beijing, Hong Kong, Shanghai and Taipei. *Continuum: Journal of Media and Cultural Studies* 17(3), pp.261–272.

Mahathir, M. 1970. *The Malay Dilemma.* Singapore: Donald Moore for Asia Pacific Press.

Mahathir, M. 2002a. Advancements in Communications Technology. A speech delivered at the opening of the 40th Meeting of the Commonwealth Telecommunications Council in Kuala Lumpur on 6 November 2000. In: T.C. Ng, ed. 2002. *Mahathir Mohamad: a Visionary and his Vision of Malaysia's K-Economy.* Kuala Lumpur: Pelanduk Publications, pp.1–10.

Mahathir, M. 2002b. E-Migration: Rising to the Challenges of the New Economic Frontier. A speech delivered at the official opening of the Conference on Knowledge and the Twenty-First Century Economy in Petaling Jaya on 17 October 2000. In: T.C. Ng, ed. 2002. *Mahathir Mohamad: a Visionary and his Vision of Malaysia's K-Economy.* Kuala Lumpur: Pelanduk Publications, pp.11–16.

Mahathir, M. 2002c. Transcending the Divide. A speech delivered at the Second World Knowledge Conference in Kuala Lumpur on 8 March 2000. In: T.C. Ng, ed. 2002. *Mahathir Mohamad: a Visionary and his Vision of Malaysia's K-Economy.* Kuala Lumpur: Pelanduk Publications, pp.55–66.

Mahathir, M. 2002d. MIMOS's Role in Malaysia's Move towards a Knowledge-based Economy. A speech delivered during Prime Minister Mahathir's official visit to Mimos on 1 November 1999. In: T.C. Ng, ed. 2002. *Mahathir Mohamad: a Visionary and his Vision of Malaysia's K-Economy.* Kuala Lumpur: Pelanduk Publications, pp.87–94.

Mahathir, M. 2002e. Forces that will Shape Our Common Digital Future. A speech delivered at the MSC Investors Conference in Germany on 20 March 1998. In: T.C. Ng, ed. 2002. *Mahathir Mohamad: a Visionary and his Vision of Malaysia's K-Economy.* Kuala Lumpur: Pelanduk Publications, pp.105–115.

MDC. 2011. Empower your Life – Convenience at a Click. Presented by the Multimedia Development Corporation of Malaysia. [online] Available at <http://www.mscmalaysia.my/topic/Convenience+at+a+Click> (Accessed 10 July 2011).

MDC. 2013. 'Creative Multimedia'. [online] Available at <http://www.mscmalaysia.my/creative_multimedia> (Accessed 11 July 2013).

Meettaiwan. 2013. Why Taiwan. Where Business Meets Pleasure – Industrial Excellence. The official Taiwan convention promotion website operated by the government of Taiwan. [online] Available at: <http://www.meettaiwan.com/taiwan/taiwan_business.action?menuld=S001_04_04> [Accessed 11 July 2013].

MICA. 2009a. MICA – Creative Industries' available at http://app.mica.gov.sg/Default.aspx?tabid=66 (Accessed 22 July 2009).

MICA. 2009b. Chapter Two – Renaissance City 2.0. Available at http://app.mica.gov.sg/Data/0/PDF/1_ERC_SVS_CRE_Chapter2.pdf (Accessed 22 July 2009).

MICA. 2009c. Chapter Three – the 'Design Singapore' Initiative. Available at http://app.mica.gov.sg/Data/0/PDF/3_ERC_SVS_CRE_Chapter3.pdf (Accessed 22 July 2009).

MICA. 2009d. Media 21: Transforming Singapore into a Global Media City. Available at http://app.mica.gov.sg/Data/0/PDF/4_media21.pdf (Accessed 22 July 2009).

MTI. 1986. *Report of the Economic Committee – The Singapore Economy: New Directions*. Singapore: Ministry of Trade and Industry.

Murray, G. and Perera, A. 1995. *Singapore: The Global City State*. Folkestone: China Library.

NCB. 1992. *A Vision of an Intelligent Island. The IT2000 Report*. Singapore: National Computer Board.

NITPWC. 1985. *National IT Plan – A Strategic Framework. Prepared by the National IT Plan Working Committee*. Singapore: National IT Plan Working Committee.

Ohmae, K. 1995. *The End of the Nation State: the rise of regional economies*. New York: Harper Collins.

Rajaratnam, S. 1987. 3.5 (c) Singapore, Global City (1972). In: H.C. Chan and U.-H. Obaid, eds. 1987. *The Prophetic and the Political. Selected Speeches and Writings of S. Rajaratnam*. Singapore: Graham Brash; New York: St Martin's Press, pp.224–230.

Saloma-Akpedonu, C. 2006. *Possible Worlds in Impossible Spaces: Knowledge, Globality, Gender and Information Technology in the Philippines*. Manila: Ateneo de Manila University Press.

Sardar, Z. 2000. *The Consumption of Kuala Lumpur*. London: Reaktion Books.

Sassen, S. 1991. *The Global City: New York, London, Tokyo*. Princeton: Princeton University Press.

Savage, V. 1992. Human-Environment Relations: Singapore's Environmental Ideology. In: K.C. Ban, A. Pakir and C.K. Tong, eds. 1992. *Imagining Singapore.* Singapore: Times Academic Press, pp.187–217.

Segal, D. 2014. Leaks and Missteps Plague HTC. *International New York Times.* 24 March, pp.12,14.

Simon, D.F. 1996. Charting Taiwan's Technological Future: the Impact of Globalization and Regionalization. *The China Quarterly* 148 (Special Issue: Contemporary Taiwan), pp.1196–1223.

Skoric, M.M., D. Ying and Y. Ng. 2009. Bowling Online, Not Alone: Online Social Capital and Political Participation in Singapore. *Journal of Computer-Mediated Communication* 14, pp.414–433.

Tarrant, B. 2011. Malaysia's Dilemma: Can it Reform?. *Today* (Singapore), 8 July.

Taylor, P. 2003. *World City Network.* London: Routledge.

Tilly, C. 1994. Entanglements of European Cities and States. In: C. Tilly and W. Blockmans, eds. 1994. *Cities and the Rise of States in Europe, A.D. 1000 to 1800.* Boulder: Westview Press.

Toffler, A. 1980. *The Third Wave.* New York: Bantam Books.

Wallace, W. 1971. *Foreign Policy and the Political Process.* London: Macmillan.

Wang, C.-H. 2003. Taipei as a Global City: a Theoretical and Empirical Explanation. *Urban Studies* 40(2), pp.309–334.

Wong, T.K. 1999. *The Political Economy of Taiwan's Foreign Policy.* Hong Kong: Hong Kong Institute of Asia-Pacific Studies.

Yeo, G. 1999. Speech by George Yeo, Minister for Information and the Arts and Second Minister for Trade and Industry, at the *Yomiuri Shimbun* Symposium in Tokyo on 'Digital Information Society in the New Century' on 12 May 1999. Available at http://stars.nhb.gov.sg/stars/public/ (Accessed 21 July 2009).

Zaharin and Zahid 2009. Interview with Professor Zaharin Yusof, President And Chief Executive Officer of the Multimedia University, and Mr Zaid Hamzah, General Counsel (Research and Intellectual Capital) of the Multimedia University, at the Multimedia University Cyberjaya Campus, Selangor, Malaysia, on 29 July 2009 at 0930H.

Chapter 7
Biting Back Against Civil Society: IT, Media and Communication Regulations in South Korea

Byoung Won Min

Introduction

The emergence of South Korea as a leading country in information technology and wired broadband networks for the last decade has also cemented its reputation as a pioneer of both the new knowledge economy and democratization. In particular, the flourishing social activities of Korean citizens in every field of everyday life have become a symbol of the transformative power of information technologies. The candlelight demonstration in the spring of 2008 against the government-led negotiations for importing beef rumoured to be contaminated by mad cow disease, was regarded as one more instance of recalcitrant social movements in a democratizing Korea. This seems to have led the South Korean government of President Lee Myung-bak to lead a rejuvenated coalition among conservatives, to confront the 'smart mobs' who have equipped themselves with sophisticated IT-based technologies and ever expanding democratic aspirations.

Two cases are introduced in this chapter about this struggle between the Korean government and the civil society. They will show how the Korean government has been troubled by the uncompromising purposes of IT-related policies and regulations—between efficiency and publicity. The first case was about the establishment of the Korea Communications Commission (KCC) in 2008, which was to be an independent regulatory body for the information and communication sectors. The second case deals with the revision of media laws in 2009 that allowed big companies and foreign investors to acquire more shares in media industries. In both cases, the Korean government had accelerated institutional arrangements and legislation regarding the new IT-based social communication mechanisms. The core question in these cases should be: 'How well does the Korean government keep the balance between the two contradictory principles of efficiency and publicity?'

The answer, by now, is 'not very well'. It seems that the Korean government has been biased toward the logic of *efficiency* rather than toward the logic of *publicity*. It has kept the KCC as a government-backed, powerful regulatory body in response to the trend of convergence between media and communication technologies, even though many scholars have warned that they could not find any constitutional foundations for establishing the KCC (Lee, 2009; Kye, 2009). Moreover, the Korean National Assembly, dominated by the conservative Grand National Party, has passed a new media law that lifts the cross-ownership ban on newspapers and TV stations. Both cases tell us that the Korean government deregulated media industries for efficiency and competitiveness, while re-regulating a civil society that has expanded so much to threaten the government's authority despite criticisms that it would hamper policy publicity and the diversification of broadcasting industries. As such, the cases of the Korean government's biting back against civil society should be understood as a response by the conservative ruling elites who understand the instrumentality and utility of information and communication technologies, even though those technologies have transformed the landscapes of political institutions and democracy in South Korea during the last decade. The implications of the two case studies may still make sense as the conservative trends of Korean politics have been fundamentally sustained, even reinforced after Lee Myung-bak's government handed political power to another conservative leader, Park Geun-hye, in 2013.

The Background of New Commitments

South Korea has ranked among the top countries in Internet usage and broadband communication technologies. This has been backed up by IT-related hardware industries, which have accounted for one-third of South Korean exports. The national IT strategies were based upon government policies which had not only been adopted to promote related industries, but also adapted to the transformations of global and domestic societies (Shin, 2008). In 2007, more than 90 per cent of Korean families were using broadband services. As such, industries have been trying to meet increasing market demands with more sophisticated and user-friendly technologies. These technologies include convergence between telecommunications and broadcasting, voice and data services, wired and wireless services. Considering the high ratio of foreign trade in the South Korean economy and the potentials of IT industries in world trade, it seems reasonable for the South Korean government to encourage the development of information and media technologies and their ultimate convergence.

Information and knowledge have been regarded as two major resources of national wealth in the previous regimes under Presidents Kim Dae-jung and Roh Moo-hyun. This had been clear since the late 1990s. President Kim had suggested building a *creative knowledge-based nation* in 1998, when he initiated rescue plans to save his country from the Asia-wide financial crisis that had swept across many developing countries in the region. He thought that the fields of information and knowledge are areas where Koreans might enjoy a competitive advantage within the globalized world economy. Thus he established the Ministry of Information and Communication (MIC) and designated one of the elite business leaders as the first Minister of the MIC.[1] He also started the *Cyber-Korea 21* plan which was oriented toward four main goals: building infrastructures of information; encouraging productivity and transparency of government, enterprise and individuals using those information infrastructures; job promotion through information technologies; and nurturing IT commodities and services as strategic fields for South Korean industries.[2]

One example of the government-backed IT effort in South Korea was the former *IT839* master plan that had been implemented between 2004 and 2008 by President Roh Moo-hyun. Its economic and social impact on South Korea was much greater than expected. Having successfully pioneered the first-generation of the Code Division Multiple Access (CDMA) mobile telecommunications services in the 1990s, South Korea had deployed more sophisticated technologies such as Wideband CDMA and Orthogonal Frequency Division Multiplexing (OFDM) technologies under the *IT839* master plan. The result of these efforts has been to transform South Korea into an exceptionally strong leader in those IT dimensions that are essential to promoting national economic strategies in the age of globalization (Shin, 2007). As such, South Korea has become a model of government-led industrialization in the field of IT and media industries such as telecommunications companies, cable television operators, IT manufacturers and software developers.

On the other hand, the South Korean government has been pursuing a series of legal measures to block anti-governmental social networking movements through the Internet and newly emerging multimedia platforms. In 2008, one major target of the governmental drive was the Internet portal space, where a couple of forum chat rooms provided for the free exchange of opinion, including criticism of government policies. The South Korean government consequently suggested a bill that requires all Internet users to register with their real names. This is an easy measure to implement since the government controls major Internet Service Providers (ISPs) such as *Naver* and *Daum*. These companies cannot pursue independent policies since so many IT- and Internet-related commodities and services have been facilitated and encouraged by government. Moreover, the KCC, as an integrated government agency responsible for these monitoring duties, was established in early 2008 amidst much controversy.

1 President Kim Dae-jung's idea was that the only way for Korea to revive its economy under the threat of global financial crisis is to build an information- and knowledge-based society beyond the industrialization policy of the previous regimes such as Park Jung-hee's in the 1970s (Kim, 2010, pp.159–161).

2 He also tried to step up the level of information-based education as he thought human factors are the only resource for Koreans to build a wealthy economy without the benefit of plentiful natural resources and indigenous financial capitalization (Kim, 2010, pp. 439–443). As a result of these efforts, Seoul, the capital of South Korea, came in first in the evaluation of *e*-government performance among 100 cities in 2002.

Lee Myung-bak's government, which was essentially a conservative political faction that replaced the ten-year rule of progressives led by Presidents Roh Moo-hyun and Kim Dae-jung, had been troubled by the diffusion of social communication networks and real-time opinion exchanges among people since taking office. Mass demonstrations and critical opinions were quickly directed at the government arising from the re-import of American beef that were suspected to be tainted with mad-cow disease. The new South Korean government and the Grand National Party shared the impression that a lot of *misinformation* had been spread without any checks on the Internet, so the best measure against this conundrum was to control this diffusion mechanism at the infrastructural level. With Web controls in place, major social unrest and mass protests should no longer be influenced by wild rumours and unreasonable critiques on the Net. This control is exercised when the KCC monitors and checks the major ISPs which manage the Internet gateways for most Internet users in South Korea. These ISPs, having initially failed in facilitating a well-informed order on the Net, might now be transformed into filtering platforms for 'emotional, unfounded, and rampant messes' generated by unruly public opinion.

The Japanese government has also compelled ISPs to conduct self-regulation with more social responsibility. This has been criticized by civil societies as an anti-democratic measure that will ruin the principle of independent media. The situation in China is more serious than Korea's since the government there has banned the connections to some foreign-based Internet sites. This policy has been accompanied by high-tech monitoring and pre-emptive procedures against any anti-governmental propaganda and movements. In this process, of course, the burden of control and surveillance is shifted onto the ISPs, so they have to check whether any ideological, political, and non-acceptable contents are flowing through their platforms. Recently, the Chinese government has been focusing their scans on the information of human rights and democratization on the Web. All of these measures are conducted in the name of self-regulation. Lee's government, like Japan and China, had been actively considering Web monitoring as it had been criticized by Internet users angered over the resumption of imports of American beef.

The conservative mould of the Lee Myung-bak government signalled a transformation of policy orientation in media and communications. The Roh Tae Woo and Kim Young Sam regimes in the 1990s had kept the market-oriented paradigm in media regulations that focused on the principle of efficiency. This was reversed within a ten year period when the government was controlled by Presidents Kim Dae-jung and Roh Moo-hyun. These two Presidents had emphasized two points in their media policies: the integration of the KCC and the increasing numbers of Internet users and audiences. Their intention for a new KCC was to eliminate the 'bad habit' of governmental controls in communicating with the public, which had been managed by a government agency—the Bureau of Public Information—and criticized as thwarting any two-way communication between the government and the civil society. In this context, the emergence of the integrated KCC was deemed by many South Koreans as a legitimate extension of ongoing democratic institutionalization.

Although these efforts by Presidents Kim Dae-jung and Roh Moo-hyun were intended to achieve forward-oriented goals for Korean society, their implementation appears not to be deeply appreciated. The reason was that, even though these liberal Presidents were sincere in their intentions for media independence, the traditional opposition from conservatives, coupled with clashes within the liberal camp, had prevented institutionalization of electronic media freedoms. Specific policy guidelines and plans for new liberal media policies could not be initiated at this stage due to politicized social divisions. Market power was another obstacle for the Presidential aspiration to free up electronic media. Big business and capital investors had cooperated with the liberal governments to the bare minimum while publicizing the gap between them. In this context, the policies of Presidents Kim and Roh could not be efficiently implemented according to their original aims. Many policy plans had been controversial among interest groups and left vulnerable to the conservative critiques. As such, the former KBC could not coordinate or facilitate media-related policies among diverse stakeholders. Civil society, nurtured by the democratic currents in this period, had contributed to many social conflicts on media and communication issues.

Establishing a New Media Regulator

Building upon the experience of successful IT industries and burgeoning media regulations during the 1990s and the early 2000s, South Korea had attempted to introduce a new paradigm for managing convergent media technologies and social networks. Actually, the nerve centre of the newly integrated KCC was housed within the new government in 2008. One of the public commitments by Lee's party was the privatization of media, especially in broadcasting industries. The ruling party emphasized the *industrial* rather than *social* and *cultural* dimensions of broadcasting industries. In order to improve South Korean competitiveness and efficiency in world media markets, media industries should be nurtured by more investments and de-regulatory measures in the near future. Better quality media content would make broadcasting services more sustainable and profitable. The trend of convergence among IT, media, communications, and broadcasting services had made these arguments more persuasive. Thus, by the end of 2007 when the national election was looming for the new government, the environments were ready for the conservatives to finalize the establishment of the new KCC, with a different goal from the original one sought by the previous regimes.

However, the arguments for the new KCC had to endure severe criticisms from civil society. The most cited reason against the privatization of broadcasting services was that market-oriented policies had up till then created oligopolistic ownerships and excessive competition among media businesses. The *invisible hand* had not been working well, contradicting the argument of the Grand National Party and Lee's government, not only in the media sector in South Korea but also in terms of the image of Korean media companies overseas. Instead, the concentration of ownership had deepened as many liberals had worried. This again had reflected the old rivalry between the conservative and the liberal in South Korea. The concentration of ownership had the effect of discouraging, instead of encouraging, the diversity of messages and opinions. This could kill the buds of democracy in South Korea by limiting the spectrum of opinions among audiences and viewers.

The KCC was launched as a consolidated agency between the former Ministry of Information and Communication (MIC) and the former Korea Broadcasting Commission (KBC). It absorbed communication business license rights that had been supervised by the MIC, and was expected to manage broadcasting and communications policies and businesses as an office of the President. It was to promote and facilitate the convergence of broadcasting, telecommunications, and newly emerging media. This means, in a sense, a full renovation of regulatory bodies for technological, informational, and social changes in South Korea. As far as its purpose is concerned, the KCC was established as an integrated agency responsible for industrial promotions and regulations in broadcasting, communications, and media sectors. As a matter of fact, however, these purposes might not be acknowledged at their face value by many South Korean citizens. The KCC's legal position was proposed through several legal codes in South Korea, including the Broadcasting Act, the Internet Multimedia Broadcasting Business Act, the Telecommunications Business Act, the Law on the Protection and Use of Location Information, and the Information and Communications Construction Business Act.

South Korea has been a leading country in broadcasting services and has explored the convergence of media and information technologies as its primary industrial sector for the future. Digital convergence, which has been a new trend in this field, is one of the hottest targets in global information and communication industries. Lee's government in South Korea had also planned to promote and implement these convergence technologies and reshuffle governmental agencies for their promotions and regulations. Many programmes and projects have been launched in major industrial fields for this purpose. The KCC was expected to drive the growth of new convergence missions as it was intended to spend huge amounts of money in information and communication technologies in the near future. A number of de-regulatory measures were to be initiated to comply with the global standards and trends in IT-related industries and services.

However, there was another mission for the KCC—to regulate overall IT-related and media industries—in the age of technological convergence. This implies a much broader than expected influence by the KCC. Both the government and civil society knew this very well, so they have argued for and against the jurisdictions of the KCC. According to the theory of state capture, regulatory agencies are vulnerable to influence by their stakeholders (Laffont and Tirole, 1991). Ideally, independent regulators should avoid this situation. Major NGOs and civil society groups have argued for recruiting professional experts on media services. As expected, regardless of reasonable intentions and commitments laid upon the independent regulatory mission by previous regimes, the conflict around the role and status of the KCC has become more and more political.

The most important point regarding the political nature of the KCC is that all five candidates for the Commissioners are to be appointed by the President, two of them directly and the other three with the recommendations of the National Assembly. These latter three candidates require endorsements by the ruling party or by the opposition party. The ruling party holds one ticket while the opposition party holds two tickets for the candidates. This means that within the government of the day, whenever the President and his ruling party do cooperate, they can jointly monopolize media policy-making. This can become political regardless of any enlightened intentions stakeholders may have regarding media policy.

The problem of the KCC as a new integrated regulatory agency, as noted earlier, seems to be reformulated as a trade-off between efficiency and publicity. While Presidents Kim and Roh had intended to increase the level of independence of the regulatory role, the new government of Lee Myung Bak wanted to focus on the dimensions of industrial development and innovation when they were talking about a new regulatory agency. Their intention was to support media industry to gain in competitiveness and efficiency against the challenge of foreign companies. They chose *efficiency* rather than *publicity* for the new paradigm of media policy. Although the establishment of the KCC did not stir additional controversy aside from the aforementioned policy issues, the missionary goal had already been changed from the previous regimes. And this position would be continued in the case of revising media laws. The government aimed to de-regulate the media industry while monitoring Internet-based social movements.

Revising Media Laws

Since the inauguration of Lee's government in 2008, the ruling party and major opposition parties in the National Assembly have agreed to revise six media-related laws in order to adapt to the trend of convergence among broadcasting, Internet communication, and newspapers. The revision of media-related laws was composed of several elements. Firstly, cross-ownership between newspapers, news communications, and broadcasting is to be allowed. This had been imposed to block major newspaper owners from influencing the formation of public opinion. Ironically, several previous regimes of South Korea had confirmed this principle, but any real implementation of this could not be validated due to the limitations of South Korean democracy up till the late 1980s. The two progressive governments by Presidents Kim Dae-jung and Roh Moo-hyun might have tried to put this into action, but Lee's government closed the door on the necessity of deregulating this principle for the reasons mentioned above—i.e. the overwhelming need to sharpen the adaptive and competitive edges of South Korean media industries in the age of IT and globalization.

The revision also eliminated the clauses in the newspaper law that prohibited market-dominating companies from owning broadcasting or newspaper businesses. The regulatory measures in the ownership of media industries had been applied to business conglomerates, foreign investors, newspapers and news-service companies. These companies could hold only limited stocks in any broadcasting companies or channels, except satellite broadcasting, system operators, IPTV services, and programme providers. For example, big companies, foreign investors, newspaper owners could not hold any share in the stocks of terrestrial TV broadcasting services, general and news cable programming channels, according to previous laws. The new laws would allow them to hold up to 20 to 49 per cent of the ownership shares in these business fields. Additionally, the limit to the one-person-ownership in these businesses was extended from 30 to 49 per cent.[3]

The South Korean government had wanted these de-regulatory measures put in place in order for national industries to adapt to the changing environments of world business, such as the convergence among IT and broadcasting media. The situation, they argue, had changed since the regulatory clauses were incorporated into the legal code in the 1980s. In particular, the government and the ruling party of South Korea have hoped to remove any hurdles that might have blocked the development of media industries in tandem with the flow of huge investments. These logics for the de-regulation could not successfully be used to persuade the lobbies on the other side, such as civil rights groups and opposition parties. The latter worried over the potentially shrinking diversity in public opinion and the dominating power of conservative newspaper owners if these de-regulating measures are extended to broadcasting businesses.

Many Koreans have become aware of the bipolarization of newspapers between conservatives and progressives: the former have included *Chosun*, *Joong-Ang*, and *Dong-A* dailies, while the latter grouped the *Hankyoreh* and *Kyunghyang* dailies with some online newspapers such as *OhmyNews*. The impacts of conservative newspapers on the formation of public opinion have traditionally been deeply pronounced in South Korea as the conflicts between the North and the South have overshadowed the everyday lives of citizens.[4] This situation had changed since the late 1990s when the liberal regimes by Kim Dae-jung and Roh Moo-hyun accelerated the democratization of South Korean politics and pushed IT-based

---

3 The limits of ownership shares were set to forty-nine per cent for foreign investors to hold stocks in system operators, IPTV services, and programme providers in the revision.

4 According to a survey conducted by the Korea Press Foundation in July 2008, the circulation ratio of newspapers in South Korea was 36.8 per cent. The shares of major conservative newspapers are: 25.6 per cent for *Chosun*, 19.7 per cent for *Joong-Ang*, and 14.3 per cent for *Dong-A* dailies. The sum of these closes up to 60 per cent. On the other hand, *Hankyoreh* and *Kyunghyang* dailies take 5.8 per cent and 3.8 per cent, respectively. This means that the conservative South Koreans are relying more on newspapers than the liberals in getting information and exchanging opinions.

development policies for a decade.[5] This meant a louder voice for the liberals and the left, while there was less and less influence on public opinion by the conservatives and the right. In the field of Korean newspaper industries, the political and commercial influences of major conservative newspapers dwindled away. In this situation, the de-regulation policy of Lee's regime—the cross-ownership between media groups—may rekindle the power of conservative newspapers.

Secondly, the revision of media laws allowed big companies to hold stocks of broadcasting services for up to 20 per cent in the case of terrestrial broadcasting; 30 per cent in case of general cable programming channels; 49 per cent in the case of cable news channels. It also removed the clause that regulated the ownership of satellite broadcasting services. These de-regulation measures were based upon the recognition that South Korea is the only country in the world that prohibits big companies from holding large shares of broadcasting companies. On the other hand, Lee's government and its business partners have argued for increased investments in broadcasting sectors in order for them to compete with global media groups. It was also considered that broadcasting contents would achieve higher quality with more financial investment. For these reasons, the de-regulation measures of media ownership by big companies were legitimized.

Many South Koreans hold Janus-faced opinions over big companies. On the one hand, they have thought that big business conglomerates, the so-called *Chaebul*, are the locomotive of the Korean economy in both domestic and foreign markets. This has convinced the previous regimes to set the priority of economic policy towards supporting and encouraging export-oriented industries, most of which have had to be big companies.[6] On the other hand, South Koreans have grown more suspicious of the *Chaebuls*' contributions to the national economy as they have been thought to violate transparency requirements and social responsibility while reinforcing unfair economic practices and class divisions. This has roused many social movements and NGOs to push both the National Assembly and the government to regulate *Chaebuls* to compel them to practice good corporate ethics.

The previous media laws that prohibited big companies from holding large shares were the result of these negative opinions in civil society. This trend had been intensified during the liberal regimes of Presidents Kim and Roh. However, big companies had argued against these negative images of themselves, claiming that they were doing their best in complying with the regulations. According to

---

5 Kim Dae-jung had been the President of South Korea between 1998 and 2003, and Roh Moo-hyun had followed him in the period between 2003 and 2008. In the early 2008, President Lee Myung-bak took over the presidential power with his conservative Grand National Party for the coming five years.

6 The South Korean government defines *big companies* or the *Chaebul* according to the size of company assets—one is the group of *20-trillion-won* (slightly less than 20 billion US dollars) or more, and the other is the group of *between-ten-trillion-and-20-trillion-won*. In 2009, 19 conglomerates were included in the first group—such as Samsung, Hyundai Motors, SK, LG, POSCO, GS, and KT. The second group held ten *Chaebuls* in the same year.

them, prior to 2008, South Korea had been the only country that did not allow large corporations to hold media ownerships. In their perception, this was not a fair policy, because the global trend has been to increase and concentrate investments in media industries for competitiveness and efficiency. On the contrary, they argued, big companies could upgrade the quality of media through building competitive edges and developing smarter business strategies. These arguments have been circulating among conservatives before they could join to fight for the revision of media laws. Table 7.1 shows major changes brought about by the revision of media laws.

Table 7.1 De-regulation of cross-ownership of media industries in South Korea

	One-Person Ownership		Big Companies		Daily Newspapers & News Services		Foreign Capital	
	Old	New	Old	New	Old	New	Old	New
Terrestrial Broadcasting	30%	40%	not allowed	10%	not allowed	10%	not allowed	not allowed
General Cable Channels	30%	40%	not allowed	30%	not allowed	30%	not allowed	20%
News Cable Channels	30%	40%	not allowed	30%	not allowed	30%	not allowed	10%
Satellite Broadcasting	—	—	49%	removed	33%	49%	33%	49%
System Operators	—	—	—	—	33%	49%	49%	49%
IPTV	—	—	—	—	49%	49%	49%	49%
General and News IPTV	—	—	not allowed	49%	not allowed	49%	not allowed	20%
General Programme Provider	—	—	—	—	—	—	49%	49%

In the end, in July 2009, the National Assembly of South Korea passed three bills that revised major clauses in existing laws. Lawmakers from minority parties blocked the paths to the assembly conference room to prevent the parliamentary leader from introducing the bills. But the voting took place despite multiple fights and shouting matches among lawmakers. This was another phase of transition that opened the door to social clashes after the long accumulation of ideological distrust and power struggle between liberals and conservatives in South Korea. Many liberal and progressive elites in South Korea bemoaned these fights and the uncompromising gaps between what appeared to be parallel ideological positions. The case of revising media laws in mid-2009 has thus represented the alterity of IT-based social transformation that is special and path-dependent for South Korea.

After one and half years of this social catastrophe, major media groups in South Korea applied for licenses to operate new television channels according to the new media law. The Lee government planned to choose new channel operators to increase the global competitiveness of the local media industry and encourage the content market, as well as to offer more variety in programming for TV viewers. The KCC would also plan to simultaneously select operators in two categories of general programming and news in 2010.[7] Like many other policy issues in South Korea, the case of revised media laws by the Lee government has openly exposed the latent seeds of social unrest. The South Korean government, having been determined to replace the Internet-induced social chaos with order, has thus only embarked upon its first step toward its own utopia of network society.

Concluding Remarks

The two cases mentioned above represent a new phase for South Korean efforts to adapt itself to the trend of technological convergence in media, broadcasting, information, and communications. While many South Koreans had voted for Lee's government in the election of 2007, they did not make an issue out of the full range of their contentious opinions over media regulation. This gap emerged as the conflict between the new government and civil society when the latter was incensed by the re-import of beef from America despite the population's worry about mad cow disease in 2008. Lee's government did adopt the position of *neoliberalism* since it had dominated government policies over the world during the late 1990s. Elites in the government had thought that liberal and market-oriented policies are an urgent panacea for the deteriorating South Korean economy, particularly in the field of converging media technologies.

One interesting point in this current phase of media policy in South Korea is that the country has flip-flopped from the liberal tone to the conservative one with the change of regimes, but its direction was different from other countries. Many countries, such as the United States and the EU member states, had switched their conservative governments with liberal ones at the ballot box over the past decade. But South Koreans chose a conservative one *after* a ten-year period of liberal governments. This seems strange, but understandable, as the regimes of Kim and Roh had focused on the democratic and public dimensions of the country's

---

7 The KCC will consider five factors in choosing the new channel operators: the new broadcaster's willingness to ensure fairness and act in the public interest; appropriateness of programming and production planning; human resources and business plans; financial and technical capability; and support for the development of the media industry. *Korea Herald*, December 1, 2010.

development, while Lee's new government tried to reset the economic mode toward a more market-friendly one. This change of policy environment produced impacts on the media-related businesses and policy formation. The KCC and the revision of media laws were the result of this change.

The experiences of the KCC and new media laws represent the path dependence of South Korea in its policy orientation. The Lee government started out in 2008 without expecting any social unrest due to beef re-imports. It was a shock to many politicians in the new government when civil society protested vehemently over the beef issue, so they tried to monitor and regulate any undesirable opinions on the Internet. The project of establishing a newly integrated regulatory agency—the KCC—would be a good starting point for implementing permanent controls. Although the project was initiated by Roh's government, President Lee had seized upon it to expand governmental control over the entire media and Internet sectors. At the same time, Lee's government tried to persuade the lawmakers and the public to support revision of media-related laws in order to broaden opportunities for increased investments and ease market entry for major newspaper companies and assorted big businesses. These episodes had the effect of hardening ideological divisions within South Korean society rendering them more non-negotiable than ever.

South Korea has chosen a different path from other developed countries in tuning its way to a more technological and democratic country. It does not depend only on the Lee government's policy orientation but on its own cumulative history of previous liberal government attitudes and highly developed IT industries. This has made a softer democracy available to a civil society which had never experienced political freedom in such abundance before the late 1980s. Ironically, the increasing power of civil society has grown its own competitor—the government—equipped with the same technology of information and communication. The government as well as civil society in South Korea had learned to face the challenge of new technologies and subsequent social transformations. In particular, conservatives in South Korea had resurfaced prominently after a decade of liberal regimes by Kim Dae-jung and Roh Moo-hyun. The Lee government represented the turning point of South Korean politics from a turbulent liberalism to a responsive conservatism after rounds of national political experiments in democratic consolidation. Since another conservative government led by Park Geun-hye succeeded the Lee government in March 2013, the two cases discussed in this chapter may still have significant implications for the tension between liberals and conservatives as well as in the workings of a 'strong state' biting back against the liberal society that has enlarged itself since democratization in the 1980s.

References

Kim, D.-J. 2010. *Autobiography II*. Seoul: Sam Inchulpansa.

Kye, K.M. 2009. The Korea Communications Commission: Its Legal Status and Authority. *Oi-Beop-Non-Jip*, 33(2), pp. 347–376 [In Korean].

Laffont, J.J. and Tirole, J. 1991. The Politics of Government Decision-Making: A Theory of Regulatory Capture. *Quarterly Journal of Economics*, 106(4), pp.1089–1127.

Lee, W.W. 2009. Legal Principles for Constructing Administrative Organizations and Their Operation Procedures. *Journal of Law and Economic Regulation*, 2(2), pp.96–118 [In Korean].

Shin, D.-H. 2007. A Critique of Korean National Information Strategy: Case of National Information Infrastructures. *Government Information Quarterly*, 24, pp.624–645.

Shin, D.-H. 2008. Next Generation of Information Infrastructure: A Comparative Case Study of Korea Versus the United States of America. *Journal of the American Society for Information Science and Technology*, 59(11), pp.1785–1800.

Chapter 8
Growth and Government: The Rise of Information Technology Enabled Services' Centres in India and the Philippines

Joefe B. Santarita[1]

Introduction

The rise of Information Technology Enabled Services[2] (ITeS) Centres in India and the Philippines is an indelible trend in the long 20th Century (National Statistical Coordination Board, 2007). Yet in the history of late industrialisation in East Asia and the emergence of the global technological revolution, the decisive role of government in the economy is evident in either establishing new industry, providing support mechanisms to private sectors, or implementing industrial policies.

By establishing new upstream industries, the government either handed the factories over to selected private entrepreneurs or ran them as public enterprises (Wade, 1990, p. 78). These happened to some key industries especially steel, chemicals and other service utility enterprises in the early years of nation-building. After several decades, such a role did not wane but was instead further reinforced with the emergence of the ITeS business. It was the government that promoted and incentivised the new corporate entrants into ITeS. Government also provided hard and soft infrastructures, as well as facilitated the diffusion of technology to local industry through public procurement projects involving foreign firms (Amsden, 1997, pp. 473–474). In fact, Amsden's observation on the diffusion of development in greater East Asia in the early 1990s highlights the states' developmentalism

---

1 I owe special thanks to Dr Faizal bin Yahya for his encouragement and support in making this chapter a reality as well as to the anonymous reviewers for their valuable comments.

2 ITeS is defined as 'the delegation of one or more IT-intensive business processes to an external provider that, in turn, owns, administrates, and manages the selected process or processes based on defined and measurable performance metrics'. It includes business processing outsourcing, and software development. ITeS expands its scope of services to include knowledge process outsourcing (KPO), legal process outsourcing (LPO), games process outsourcing (GPO) and design outsourcing, among others.

(Johnson, 1995, p. 67).[3] She noted that governments were not just subsidising business but also imposing performance standards upon them. Other than that, governments also developed, guided and supervised industry through policies by modifying the old-fashioned concept of comparative advantage to concentrate on industries with a high human-capital content such as steel, machine tools, semiconductors (Johnson, 1995, p. 65), and now contact centres. In the case of the Philippines, the industry has also benefited from targeted developmental efforts by the government and industry players including being sheltered by the state's early stewardship (Information and Technology-Business Process Outsourcing Association of the Philippines, 2012).

These interventions are necessary, especially for infant industries, by providing private investors with a battery of incentives that boil down to subsidies (Amsden, 1989, p. 13). Such support from the government eventually facilitated economic development. As growth increased, the state became more committed to economic development and allocated more resources to it, which increased development further (Amsden, 1991, p. 286). In the past two decades, the role of the government grew even more pronounced with the emergence of knowledge-based industries such as the ITeS. Such online businesses suddenly became a significant success especially with the active participation of the private sectors along with the occurrence of dynamic regionalisation. In fact, a significant number of similar centres were established in Asia particularly in India, China, Singapore, South Korea, Vietnam as well as the Philippines.

Contrary to the western countries' experience, however, the rise and growth of the ITeS' centres in Asia are still under the government's steering. This alterity is even exemplified in the case of India and the Philippines wherein political machineries and processes are essential elements in the growth of this industry. This recent development also redefines the outsourcing market with the presence of Indian and Filipino homegrown companies that are gradually grabbing considerable shares of the global information technology (IT) shared services and outsourcing (SSO) market that was previously controlled by western owned multinational corporations (MNCs).

Having said that, this chapter argues that in India and the Philippines, the ITeS business is inevitably supervised by some offline political mechanisms.

3 Chalmers Johnson called it as capitalist developmental state and likened it to a revolutionary state wherein legitimacy is not based in terms of the acquiescence of the subjects but instead on the historical projects they embodied. Johnson cited the example of Japanese state's imposition of its economic achievements on the people. It is also worthy to quote at length Manuel Castells' definition of developmental state as cited by Johnson. Castells believed that the state is developmental when it demonstrates legitimacy through its ability to promote and sustain development, and understand by development the combination of steady high rates of economic growth and structural change in the productive system, both domestically and in relationship to the international economy.

Given ITeS' significant contribution to the economy, the governments of India and the Philippines improved their respective infrastructure as well as introduced changes in educational, technological and manpower policies to accommodate and complement the industry's rapid growth. Utilising various industrial white papers, data banks and secondary sources, this chapter examines the extent of the state's involvement in the government and growth of the ITeS centres in Asia particularly in India and the Philippines.

The Growth of ITeS in India and the Philippines

The countries of India and the Philippines along with China, Vietnam and others greatly benefitted from the rapid growth of the global outsourcing industry. India and the Philippines even tried to outdo one another to be the top outsourcing destination. Looking at the figures in 2006, the global outsourcing industry's spending was only valued at US$ 930 billion (Ahlan, 2008, p. 167). In 2014, the value is estimated to reach US$ 3.8 trillion (Gartner, 2013).

These developments have been collectively precipitated by the swift expansion of online businesses, particularly in the contact centre services, software development, animation and medical transcription. This situation was brought about by the decisions of numerous MNCs in the United States of America (US) and Europe to increasingly outsource their peripheral and BPO work as part of cost cutting and competitiveness strategies. It should be noted, however, that outsourcing of jobs is not really a new phenomenon in the US. It began in the 1970s with the migration of America's manufacturing jobs in the textiles and heavy industries, such as steel and electronics (Martin, 1986).

Tremendous attention was given to outsourcing lately due to the increasing complaints of Americans losing their jobs when their country underwent financial depression in 2009. Despite the protests and setbacks, outsourcing remains strong due to the practical benefits such as the MNCs' ability to efficiently stage 24/7 operations; the opportunity to customise products and services to meet local needs; and the means of geographically deploying workers and facilities to succeed in globally dispersed, highly competitive markets (Tech America, 2010). Moreover, the cheaper wage rate of the outsourcing agents in various overseas delivery sites, measuring 20 to 50 per cent lower compared to US workers (Beauprez, 2003), also favoured business dispersal. Other factors that spurred this growth included digitisation, the Internet, high speed data and transmission networks (Engardio, 2003). A wide range of high tech jobs and service sector jobs were moving offshore to developing countries (Mann, 2005, p. 285).

Capitalising upon these trends, India and the Philippines eventually became two of the most popular outsourcing destinations in Asia. These low-cost ITeS hubs possessed several advantages over rival outsourcing and software development locations. Both countries have a large base of easily trainable English speaking human resources. While India obviously has a much larger human resource pool drawing on nearly a billion-strong population, it also has a low literacy rate of around 66 per cent compared to the Philippines at 93 per cent of their respective populations (World Bank, 2010, p. 378). Their time differences relative to the US, the biggest source of outsourcing work and software projects, have created a niche for both countries. Their respective experiences and exposure to American business culture also help entice investors. This is perhaps more applicable to the Philippines, but it was also a highly marketable fact that Indian software engineers also have a lot of working exposure to the US, such as in Silicon Valley (Economic Times, 2003). Additionally, both India and the Philippines have democratic systems of government which decreases the likelihood of political objections in relation to linkages with US businesses. The Philippines and India have also provided incentives and concessions for their respective IT sector such as tax breaks to encourage their expansion.

Thus, within a short period of time, the numbers of ITeS centres in India and the Philippines grew rapidly. As of 2013, the National Association of Software Services Companies (NASSCOM), a global trade body based in India, has registered more than 1,350 members, which include both Indian-owned companies and MNCs that maintain a presence in India (NASSCOM, 2013). The Philippines, on the other hand, has three national bodies that facilitate the growth of this industry, namely the Information and Technology-Business Process Outsourcing Association of the Philippines (IBPAP)[4] (2013), BPO Association Services Unlimited Philippines (BSA/U) (2013)[5] and the Contact Center Association of the Philippines[6] (CCAP). BPAP has 255 members, BSA/U has 200 and CCAP has 53.

Furthermore, improving telecommunications has also enabled various jobs to be outsourced from answering telephones to developing computer systems (Moran, 2003). The voice sector of the Philippine outsourcing industry, for instance, in 2011 generated 493,000 jobs (BPAP, 2012). As of 2013, the industry employed approximately 926,000 full-time employees (FTEs) (Periabras, 2013)

---

4 BPAP was founded in 2004, and is supported by many stakeholders such as the Philippine government, Philippine and foreign chambers of commerce, and allied industries such as property, telecommunications, and employee benefits.

5 BSA/U was formed in 2006 as a private-sector led organisation to aggregate the collective interests of Business Process Outsourcing (BPO) providers. It advances the BPO industry through advocacy, supporting BPO-related Government programmes and initiatives, promoting best practice and service excellence among its member-providers and by aiding in the establishment of mutually-beneficial relationships between Overseas Customers and BPO Providers.

6 The CCAP was established in 2001. Its mission is to promote the Philippines as the country-of-choice for contact centre services, develop professional standards and practices, organise learning and networking events, and work with various stakeholders to further the industry's contribution to the national economy and strengthen its market position worldwide. Established in October 2001 by seven founding member companies, CCAP now counts 53 outsource and in-house contact centres as members, representing more than 80 per cent of call centre seats in the Philippines.

from 475,000 FTEs in August 2009 (Board of Investments, 2012). Overall, the industry produced revenues amounting to US$ 16 billion in 2013 (Ibid.). In 2016, the industry is forecasted to provide direct employment to 1.3 million Filipinos and supporting 3.2 million indirect jobs as well as generate US$ 25 billion in revenues (Department of Trade and Industry, 2013).

The success story of the Philippines lies primarily with the MNCs' effectiveness in capitalising on medical transcription, animation, BPO and software development as main outsourcing areas. The Philippine government has also made good use of the differences in global time zones to its advantage. While the US and European BPO operations and call centres took up the evening and night shifts of Filipino firms, the daytime shifts could be utilised by serving the regional markets such as Australia (Lebihan, 2003). Australian call centre operator Salmat has already established a call centre in the Philippines. It would cost an Australian company US$ 23 per agent, per hour or US$7 million to operate an average call centre. In comparison, it costs US$ 15 per agent, per hour in the Philippines to run a call centre, a saving of 35 per cent or US$ 2.5 million per year (Ibid.).

It should be noted, however, that although the most significant factors for locating online businesses outside North America and Europe will be cost efficiency and English proficiency, the MNCs also cannot deny the fact that the quality of infrastructure greatly counts in the selection of prospective destinations. In the case of most, if not all countries in Asia, the infrastructure is not built and controlled primarily by the private sectors, but remains within the bureaucratic purview of governments.

The Role of the Government in Supplying ITeS Infrastructure

As a public sector good, infrastructure could be categorised as hard and soft infrastructure (Wakelin, 1992). Hard infrastructure refers to the systems of conveyance for people such as roads, ports and telecommunications, while soft infrastructure deals more with the pillars of the future economy such as education and governance. In the case of the ITeS industry, the establishment of hard infrastructure is important for the expansion of a techno–economic mainstream that is essential for utilisation by knowledge workers in an outsourcing centre. However, the establishment of an information environment through the comprehensive upgrading of an underdeveloped 'infostructure' is very expensive and could create more confusion for the existing socio-political system (Connors, 1993). The most crucial elements of this infostructure are telecommunications and electricity on demand.

Hard Infrastructure

The advancement of the ITeS industry in India and the Philippines is greatly contributed by the continuous improvement of the countries' telecommunications sector, stable supply of electricity and development of ITeS Hubs and 'New Wave' Cities.

Telecommunications

The governments of India and the Philippines focused their efforts and resources in the improvement of the telecommunications[7] sector through liberalisation in the early 1990s (International Telecommunication Union, 2012). They have undertaken a variety of restructuring activities to increase the pace of ICT development. Telecommunications itself has undergone a revolutionary change in its importance not only in the rapid growth of technology that has enabled rapid expansion and convergence of voice, data and image transmission, but also in its application to newly emerging sectors such as BPOs and software development. Modern telecommunications has the ability to facilitate the development, manufacturing and marketing for the sale of products (Williams, 1992). As rightly pointed out by Castells, telecommunications has become one form of processing information, transmission and linkage technologies which are at the same time increasingly diversified and integrated into the same network, operated by computers (Castells, 2010, p. 72).

As mentioned, telecommunications is of critical importance to knowledge based industries as organising and adapting information is critical to the operations handled by knowledge workers. That is why India and the Philippines poured considerable investments into the telecommunications sector ranging from basic (fixed), mobile and Internet services. India is the second fastest growing telecommunications' spender in the region after China. However, in absolute terms, compared with other big telecommunications spenders worldwide, India is ranked fourteenth (Singh, 2002). India spent US$ 12.5 billion in 2001 in telecommunications development which saw its global share of telecommunications' spending doubling from 0.6 per cent in 1993 to 1.2 per cent in 2002 (Ibid.). In August 2000, India ended the government's monopoly in domestic long distance telephone services (Kripalani, 2000). In 2010, the Indian telecommunications sector witnessed the investment of around US$ 40 billion, presided over by the Telecom Equipment and Services Export Promotion Council. With the development of 3G telephony, expansion of the current networks and the widening of the Broadband Wireless Access (BSA) network, the investment in the sector is likely to increase from the US$ 20 billion already achieved in 2009 (IBEF, 2010).

---

7 Telecommunications now includes any transmission, emission or reception of signs, signals, writing, images and sounds or intelligence of any nature by wire, radio, optical or other electromagnetic systems.

This advancement has been facilitated by a series of telecommunications deregulation measures introduced in the 1990s to attract foreign investors and joint venture collaboration with the break up of the state monopoly in the sector. Lately, the government has taken many proactive initiatives to facilitate the rapid growth of the Indian telecommunications industry. Foremost is the permission of 100 per cent foreign direct investment in the area of telecommunications equipment manufacturing and provision of IT-enabled services. The regulator also did not impose a cap on the number of access providers in any service area. In 2013, 240 new Unified Access Service (UAS) licenses were granted to 19 telecom circle service areas and four metro service areas (Department of Telecommunications, 2014). Moreover, the Indian government also issued the revised subscriber based criteria for allocation of the Global System of Mobile Communication (GSM) and Code Division Multiple Access (CDMA) spectra in January 2008. At the same time, the government also provided infrastructure support for mobile services and a scheme has been launched to provide support for setting up and managing 7,436 infrastructure sites spread over 500 districts in 27 states. In 2009, about 6,956 towers had been set up under the said scheme (Ibid.). In 2012, the Indian government announced its plan in constructing 10,000 more towers to connect the remote parts of the country (Overseas Indian Facilitation Centre, 2012). The total number of towers by 2015, according to Indian Telecom Industry, is expected to reach to 571,000 (IBEF 2013).

The Philippine telecommunications sector, on the other hand, has endured a long history of stagnation. Until the late 1980s, this sector was notorious for its poor telecommunications systems and services. Under the regime of President Ferdinand Marcos, four government companies held protected monopolies over all main aspects of telecommunications. The biggest monopoly was held by the Philippine Long Distance Telephone (PLDT) Company which monopolised international and domestic calls. Things began to change with the succeeding regime of President Corazon Aquino. Competition was deliberately introduced to improve service efficiency by pioneering the privatisation of public utilities such as electricity, water, sewerage and telecommunication. The Philippines has progressed quietly with economic reforms and transformed itself into a private sector run economy. For example, in the 1990s the share of government enterprises in total sales among its top 1,000 companies was around 20 per cent but this figure had fallen to five per cent in 2000 (Chong, 2000) and is continually decreasing through the years.

In the telecommunications sector, new licenses were issued for international call operators, cellular operators and cable television. The following regime of President Fidel Ramos continued liberalising the telecommunications sector and introduced a new legislation called the Public Telecommunications Policy Act, to improve the business climate for telecommunications growth and investment. While government liberalisation improved the telecommunications sector, fate also issued a blessing in disguise for Philippine telecommunications. When the US forces vacated Subic Naval and Clark Air Bases, the telecommunications infrastructure left behind was modern and quickly adapted to improve the Philippine telecommunications sector. As a result, approximately 4,670,824 fixed telephone lines have been installed by various carriers such as the Philippine Long Distance Telephone Company (PLDT), Globe Telecom (Globe) and Smart Communications (Smart). The PLDT remains a dominant force in the telecommunications sector with 80 per cent of the total telephone subscribers. The deregulation of Philippine telecommunications has attracted some US$ 3.25 billion of investment into the sector.

Table 8.1 Fixed lines telephone subscriptions in India and the Philippines, 2001–2012

	INDIA			PHILIPPINES		
	2001	**2006**	**2012**	**2001**	**2006**	**2012**
Fixed lines (in millions)	38.5	40.7	31.1	3.3	3.6	3.9
Fixed lines per 100 inhabitants	3.6	3.5	2.5	4.2	4.2	4.1

Data generated from International Telecommunication Union (2013)

The total number of main telephone lines increased from 785,000 in 1993 to 3.9 million in 2013. The Philippines National Telecommunications Commission (NTC) reported a teledensity rate of 7.2 installed telephones per 100 people in 2011, while the Department of Telecommunications in India reported a rate of 2.6 installed telephones per hundred people. Table 8.1 shows the rate of teledensity between India and the Philippines for fixed line phones. The Philippines teledensity for both fixed and mobile phones increased dramatically since 2000. India too experienced a whopping development in telecommunications. In recent decades, the Indian telecommunications industry is one of the fastest growing in the world. The number of telephone subscribers in India increased to almost 31.1 million in 2012 with an overall teledensity of 2.5 per cent (International Telecommunication Union, 2013).

Table 8.2 Mobile cellular subscription in India and the Philippines, 2000–2012

	INDIA			PHILIPPINES		
	2001	**2006**	**2012**	**2001**	**2006**	**2012**
Mobile cellular subscription (in Million) (post paid + pre-paid)	6.5	166.1	864.7	12.15	42.86	103
Mobile cellular subscription per 100 inhabitants	0.62	14.52	69.92	15.3	49.07	106.51

Data generated from International Telecommunication Union (2013)

Table 8.2 provides a comparison between India and the Philippines in relation to mobile phones. For the Philippines, by the end of 2003, 2.1 million GSM phone units including those with Wireless Application Protocol (WAP) were sold. The telecommunications infrastructure in the Philippines is fairly dependable, fast, reliable and cost comparable to any other Asian country. In 2012, the mobile cellular subscriber base registered 103 million subscribers with a teledensity of 106 per cent (Overseas Indian Facilitation Centre, 2012).[8] This only shows that cellular phones have proven more popular as it meets demands in areas of high growth, it is easier to acquire and subscription rates have fallen drastically since the late 1990s especially in the Philippines (International Telecommunication Union, 2002). The Philippines also has spare capacity in its fixed telecommunications lines, with less than half of the total fixed lines used. Telecommunications companies in the Philippines have also realised that cellular phones are highly preferred to fixed line phones and this has reduced the demand for fixed lines, and hence their increasing unprofitability (Reyes, 2001). In this regard, the Philippines has been identified as having one of the best telecommunications infrastructures in the Asian region today. The glut in the availability of fixed lines as of mid-2001, has led to demonstrated preferences by telecommunications operators in promoting mobile phones (Ibid.). This may offer advantages to Filipino IT companies by increasing the mobility of their software engineers (*Businessworld*, 2000). With their mobile phones and portable computers, these software engineers conducted their work in dispersed locations and reduced overhead costs such as rental and utilities' charges.

Table 8.3 Internet users in India and the Philippines, 2001–2012

	INDIA			PHILIPPINES		
	2001	**2006**	**2012**	**2001**	**2006**	**2012**
Estimated Internet Users (in millions)	5.5	27	150	1.5	4.6	33.6
Estimated Internet Users (%)	0.66	2.81	12.58	2.52	5.74	36.24

Data generated from International Telecommunication Union (2013)

It is also notable that Internet users in India have increased from 5.5 million in 2001 to 150 million in 2012 while in the Philippines, 1.5 million Filipinos used the Internet in 2001 and this figure increased to 33.6 million users in 2012 (International Telecommunication Union, 2013). This growth is recently fuelled by the increased access to services owing to the launch of newer telecommunications

8 The number of telephone subscribers in India increased to 944.81 million at the end of July 2012 with overall teledensity of 77.79 per cent. Wireless subscriber base, on the other hand, registered 913.49 million subscribers. Meanwhile, the total broadband subscriber base has 14.68 million as per Department of Industrial Policy and Promotion databank.

technologies such as 4G services, better devices, affordable broadband plans, changing consumer behaviour and the emergence of cloud technologies (Overseas Indian Facilitation Centre, 2012).

Electricity

The Philippines and India have also revealed similar concerns over the provision of reliable and stable electricity supplies and telecommunications for their BPO outsourcing sector and software development. As an archipelago of 7,107 islands, the Philippines exhibits different transportation problems compared to India as a landmass of three million square kilometres. However, both countries have grappled with the enormous challenges of liberalising their electricity generating and telecommunications sectors. Prior to 1987, electricity generation in the Philippines came under the sole purview of the government-owned National Power Corporation (NPC). Since 1995, the NPC still produces the bulk of electricity supplies but Independent Power Producers (IPPs) have been granted access to install capacity, power generation and transmission. According to the World Energy Council, by 1999, the IPPs' installed capacity stood at 50 per cent of overall generating capacities. However, with inadequate government funding and insufficient revenue income, the government further liberalised the sector to allow even more private players, thereby allowing the NPC to concentrate on delivering a more efficient and productive industry. The World Bank observed that a stable and credible regulatory framework is crucial for private companies providing services.

India's electricity generating sector also suffers from deteriorating government funding. Energy shortages averaged 7 per cent to 13 per cent at peak hours of total energy demand in 2001. The poor quality of supply in terms of low voltage and grid instability has led to software firms in India using their own captive electricity supplies produced by generators. For example, software technology parks (STPs) are generally equipped with their own electricity, water supplies and telecommunications facilities. In this regard, they are self-sufficient and not dependent on the Indian national grid for their electricity (Kripalani, 2001). The host states ensured uninterrupted power supply to the IT/Outsourcing destinations like Bangalore, Delhi, Chennai, Bombay, Pune and Calcutta. In addition, reforms in the power sector are continuously undertaken to improve power supply to ITeS companies (Greet Technologies, 2010).

ITeS hubs and new wave cities

In the Philippines, the Cyber Corridor is an information and communication technology (ICT) channel running the length of the Philippines that interconnects BPO services centres all over the country to efficiently bring together cyber services providers and BPO locators. A US$10 billion digital network and high-bandwidth fibre backbone supports the infrastructure. With Metro Manila as the centre of the Philippine BPO industry, the Cyber Corridor includes 31 'Next Wave Cities' (NWCs) (Llamas, 2010). These areas are Metro Laguna, Metro Cavite, Iloilo, Davao, Bacolod, Metro Pampanga, Metro Bulacan, Cagayan de Oro, Central Bulacan and Lipa City in Batangas. A major achievement of the Philippine Cyber Services Corridor is the establishment of the Philippine Silicon Alley based in the University of the Philippines Technology Park (Office of the President, 2010). This park houses 20 software and firmware outsourcing companies such as the JAVA Research and Development Center, SYSTEMA Computer Solutions Corp., MICOM and ASTRA. It also has a network of over 60 small and medium software companies being incubated around the area and was recently awarded by the World Bank Infodev project as the most successful incubation centre in Asia. A major centre of the corridor, Silicon Gulf, is also being constructed in Davao.

Likewise, the Indian government also undertook a similar initiative. At the request of the private sector, the government in recent years identified and created 'BPO hubs' that offer an enabling physical and social 'eco-system' to primarily drive BPO-led growth broader and deeper within India. In cooperation with the industry players, the government also planned to develop Tier 2/3 Cities as alternative BPO hubs. This eco-system includes elements of physical/hard (e.g., international connectivity, mass-transport system, telecommunications connectivity, power, housing) as well as social/soft (e.g., healthcare, education, shopping and entertainment, security, hotels) infrastructure. Furthermore, there may be an opportunity to shape the creation of infrastructure in a way that is based on skill availability and the domestic industry footprint within each BPO hub (NASSCOM-Everest, 2008, p. 7).

Soft Infrastructure

The rise of ITeS centres in India and the Philippines is banking primarily on the assumption that knowledge is the real currency. This is the reason why the governments of India and the Philippines have also invested in soft infrastructures and mechanisms to encourage this industry. These infrastructures include educated human resource pools, as well as governance to include IT-friendly fiscal policies, educational IT attuned curricula and other legal and bureaucratic mechanisms.

Human resource pool

The main feature of KBEs is knowledge workers who are highly skilled and well paid. These are professionals dealing with critical knowledge intensive work (Collin, 1995). The transformation of knowledge workers involved in ITeS tasks into assets working for value added projects would determine the creativity of KBEs. One of the key elements required by a KBE is the acquisition of new skills and competencies by its human resources (OECD, 1999). As of end 2011, the Philippines has approximately 2,247 higher educational institutions with only

27 per cent of them being state run universities and colleges (Commission on Higher Education, 2013) and one BPO training academy established in 2006. However, this is nothing compared to India. India's technical education is spearheaded by its seven Indian Institutes of Technologies or more commonly known as IITs. The qualifying examinations for India's IITs could be as many as 400,000 candidates per annum but the places are limited to just 3,000. Moreover, the Philippines produces only about ten per cent as many engineers as India (Srivastava, 2010).

On another level, while India's educational resources are concentrated at the tertiary level, the Philippines has managed to spread its educational funds more evenly. While the size and quality of the human resources is the major factor behind the creativity and spread of new technology (OECD), equally important is the ability to pool and organise these complementary resources. The competencies of a firm and its staff strength play a large part in its ability to undertake complex projects. For small and medium enterprises (SMEs), there is a lack of resources and competencies. In this regard India may have an edge over the Philippines because their software work revolves around large companies such as Infosys, Wipro, Satyam and Tata Consultancy Services.

The Philippine universities produce about 350,000 graduates per year compared to 1.5 million graduates in India. India produces about 70,000 to 80,000 skilled IT graduates per year compared to 20,000 in the Philippines (BPAP, 2009).[9] The archipelago requires about 35,000 to 40,000 skilled IT workers per annum[10] (Osorio, 2009) but the state colleges are unable to meet even half this requirement. The shortages are being filled by private IT colleges amounting to some 20,000 to 30,000 skilled IT workers. Nonetheless, the training received by Filipino software engineers carries on when they are hired by firms and they must undergo retraining (Lanzona, 2001). While Filipino engineers may have emigrated for Silicon Valley in the US as their preferred destination for work, the dwindling numbers of employment opportunities in the US have reversed the trend of the brain drain and more engineers have either returned or opted to remain in the Philippines. While emigration to Silicon Valley is an eternal dream for most Indian software programmers and IT workers, Indian industry officials estimated that as of 2000, India still has around four million IT workers who speak English residing in India (Chepesiuk, 2000). Since the early 1990s, India has increasingly been known as a choice location for numerous American and European firms to reduce their manpower costs by relocating their software product development and maintenance of their mainframes (Jatras, 2001). India, with its highly skilled workforce that speaks fluent English and technological infrastructure which supports software development, has an advantage over Russia and China as alternative outsourcing centres. The salary of a software engineer based in India is about one tenth that of a counterpart based in the US and Western Europe.

9 In 2008, more than 490,000 college-degree graduates and 66.6 per cent of which have courses suitable for the IT/BPO or cyber-services sector. The annual growth rate of tertiary level graduates is estimated at 3.8 per cent.

10 In 2009, there are 100,000 to 150,000 jobs available.

Offering IT-BPO specific curricula and policies

Aside from graduates of existing tertiary educational programmes, the government has also increased employability and access to untapped talent pools by creating greater linkages between the current education system and the needs of the BPO industry, as well as facilitated the development of BPO-specific education models. In India, for instance, the government in coordination with industry players brought in policy changes like the liberalisation of higher education, introduction of BPO-specific curriculum and improving students' access to funds for higher studies; as well as introducing coursework changes and teacher training at the school level in accordance with future requirements of the BPO industry (NASSCOM-Everest, p. 7).

The Philippine government too also realised the current mismatch of what is being taught in schools and what the ITeS industry is looking for to make the Philippines a leader in the offshore sector. To address this, the government of then President Gloria Arroyo, acted through the Technical Education and Skills Development Authority (TESDA) to offer the initial seed money of 20 million pesos to bankroll an education programme called SHIFT[11] (Society for Higher Information Technology Education) to train 'near-hires' in the BPO sector (Technical Education and Skills Development Authority, 2008). In March 2013, IBPAP and the Commission on Higher Education signed a memorandum of agreement to integrate the service management programme (SMP) course into the curriculum of 13 state universities and colleges. This specialised course aims to prepare students from all types of traditional courses, especially those taking business administration and information technology, for a career in the IT-BPO industry while still in college (IBPAP, 2013).

In India, NASSCOM has joined the National Skill Development Corporation (NSDC) in advancing the talent development initiatives. NSDC is a first-of-its-kind Public Private Partnership (PPP) in India set up to facilitate the development and upgrading of the skills of the growing Indian workforce through skill training programmes. This NSDC engagement is expected to help the industry scale the many pilot initiatives and also build technology as the enabler for skill development in the country (NASSCOM, 2010).

Tax and incentives

Moreover, the rise of the ITeS centres in India and the Philippines is also attributed to the attractive tax and other incentives offered to online related businesses. In India, for instance, the timely government policies and increased public-private participation have indeed played a key role in developing a constructive business environment for the Indian ITeS industry. The Indian government's proactive

11 The projective was initiated by Informatics Philippines, computer school system, in collaboration with the BPAP.

approach towards the IT-BPO industry was further highlighted in 2008 through actions such as the IT Act Amendment, extension of tax incentives by a year, and the removal of the Special Economic Zone (SEZ) Act anomalies (NASSCOM, 2009). In tandem, the government was also determined to maintain support to the industry through appropriate incentives and facilitate creation of infrastructure to ensure parity with other competing nations. These incentives and support mechanisms could include fiscal incentives (e.g., continuation of the tax benefits under the Software Technology Parks of India (STPI) scheme beyond 2009, stamp duty exemptions), infrastructure incentives (e.g., build infrastructure capacity ahead of demand in Tier 2/3 cities through incentives to direct and indirect participants and increased public-private partnerships), changes to labour laws, promotion of SMEs, and removal of some key telecommunications-related restrictions (NASSCOM-Everest, p. 7).

The Philippine government, on the other hand, through the Board of Investments (BOI), offered both the ITeS and BPO investors numerous fiscal and non-fiscal incentives. The fiscal incentives include four to eight years of an Income Tax Holiday (ITH); a special five per cent tax rate on gross income after the lapse of ITH (for IT Park/Eco-zone locators); tax and duty exemption on imported capital equipment (for IT Park/Eco-zone locators); duty-free importation of capital equipment (for BOI-registered firms under E.O. 528); exemption from 12 per cent input value added tax on allowable local purchases of goods and services, e.g., communication charges (for IT Park/Eco-zone locators); and additional deductions for labour expense. Non-fiscal incentives, on the other hand, consist of unrestricted use of consigned equipment; exemption from wharfage dues and export tax, duty, impost and fees; relaxed employment of foreign nationals; and the institution of the special investor's resident visa (BOI).

Government supported IT councils

Aside from the tax holidays and incentives, the governments of India and the Philippines also supported the establishment of national and local IT councils. The Philippine government, for instance, through the Commission on Information and Communications Technology (CICT) encouraged the establishment of local IT councils in the NWCs all over the archipelago and subsequently the formation of the national federation, the National ICT Confederation of the Philippines (NICP). This organisation is composed of 32 local government-based councils, federations and organisations all over the Philippines (BENEFIT, 2009).[12] These associations

12 These include Aurora ICT Council, Albay ICT Association, Inc., Bataan-Olongapo-Zambales Subic Educational Development Organization for IT, BPO/ITEs Council of Quezon City, Cagayan de Oro ICT Business Council, Cavite ICT Council, Cebu Educational Development Foundation for IT, City of San Fernando Pampanga ICT Council, ICT Association of Dumaguete and Negros Oriental, ICT Davao, Inc., Iligan City ICT Council, Laguna Industry Network for Knowledge, Innovation and Technology Foundation,

complement the private coordinating entities on ITeS concerns such as the BPAP, BSA\U and CCAP. Unlike the Philippines, India's ITeS industry is coordinated by a privately run entity based in New Delhi, NASSCOM. This organisation oversees six regional councils to address the local concerns of member companies operating in Andhra Pradesh, Eastern India, Gurgaon, Karnataka, Noida and Mumbai (NASSCOM, 2009).

Government organised exhibitions and talent caravan

The governments of both countries also facilitated the growing awareness and curiosity towards the ITeS industry by organising BPO exhibitions and a talent caravan. The Philippine government has for instance, arranged an exhibition of over 90 local and international participants for the annual e-Services Philippines exhibit since 2000. It also conducted a Cyber Corridor Roadshow 'Convergence 2009' in the Top 10 NWCs in the country. These roadshows were able to promote the Philippine Cyber Corridor and the NWCs, ensure the supply of talent for the ITeS industry, increase awareness on the use of information and communication technology, enable SMEs to encourage its growth through technology, increase awareness of investments as well as motivate entrepreneurs and local government units to provide local support for the ITeS industry (Commission on Information and Communications Technology, 2009). In 2012, the Information and Communications Technology Office, together with its key partners, IBPAP and the National ICT Confederation of the Philippines conducted series of roadshows in nine cities outside Metro Manila or NWCs. The said roadshows aimed to provide a proper venue for the government, the industry players, the academe and the stakeholders to present and discuss the prospects of the ITeS industry in providing job opportunities and economic development in the countryside (Cagayan De Oro ICT Business Council, 2013).

Problems

After decades of engaging with ITeS business, the governments and private sectors of India and the Philippines continue to face recurring challenges that affect the growth of ITeS industry. These include poor investment environment, scarcity of quality labour pool, jobs–skills mismatch as well as inadequate data security laws among others. Similar observations are also noted by Agarwal on Indian ITeS

Technology of Information and Communications in Koronadal, Lipa ICT Council, Tarlac ICT Council, Cagayan Development Federation for IT, Bohol ICT Council, Bulacan ICT Council, Dagupan ICT Council, Balanga ICT Council, Cabanatuan ICT Council, CARAGA ICT Council, Urdaneta City Council for ICT, Vigan City ICT Council, Metro Ilocos Norte ICT Council, ICT@Bicol Council, ICT Solutions Association of Region 12 – General Santos City and Pasay City ICT Council.

companies, which had moved some of their operations to the Philippines because of a shortage of skilled manpower, high attrition and rising costs in India, that are now facing related concerns in the archipelago (Agarwal, 2013).

One sector that is greatly affected by the inevitable rising costs is energy. Despite the government's initiative of liberalising the said sector more than a decade ago, the high electricity tariff in the Philippines poses greater risks for ITeS investments in the archipelago. The electricity rates in the Philippines at US$ 0.17 per kWh is now the second highest in Asia (Bautista, 2012), even higher than Japan's US$ 0.117 per kWh. India's electricity tariff, on the other hand, is between US$ 0.08–0.12 per kWh (Ministry of Power, 2013). It is, therefore, in the best interest of the Philippine government to address this concern as soon as possible before it completely discourages interested investors.

Another issue that contributed to the poor condition of the Philippine business environment is the perception of the high occurrence of bribery and corruption in business transactions with government, and of transparency in government policies. The time and cost, for instance, of starting a business in the country is a cause of concern. It takes about 58 days to start a business in the country as compared to the Asian average of 34 days. Nonetheless, it takes an average of 177 days to apply for a business license in the Philippines versus the global median of 195 days (Mira, 2008). While India has already implemented a one-stop shop for paper processing in coordination with NASSCOM, the Philippines is moving at a snail's pace with only the government as the initiator.

Other pressing concern is the shortage of qualified labour force that stems from the difficulty in hiring new entrants as well as in keeping ITeS experienced personnel. The hiring rate in the ITeS industry is very poor – among 100 applicants, only six per cent to ten per cent is effectively recruited and deployed for an entry level job. This is made even worse with the high exit rate in the industry estimated at 18 per cent annually for the whole of the ITeS industry primarily due to migration and work opportunities abroad, job mismatch, poor job performance, and conflict in work schedules and family life, among others. On the front of job mismatch, while most applicants in the ITeS sector are degree holders, there is an undersupply of workers with educational backgrounds in information technology, business (finance and accounting), computer engineering, communication arts, economics, mathematics, English and foreign languages, as well as electronic communications engineering (Ibid.). This concern was already noted five years earlier by the concerned parties but surprisingly recurring as the years progressed. Thus, the ITeS industry players, in close partnership with the academe and the education agencies of the government, need to ensure that the incoming workforce entrants are also trained in the right disciplines and in acquiring the employability skills sought after by Corporate Services Segment (CSS) firms. These segments include finance and accounting as well as insurance and human resources outsourcing. Moreover, expansion of the ITeS training programmes of the Technical Education and Skills Development Authority (TESDA) is imperative to cover a much wider area where traditional education has not kept pace with workplace requirements (Information and Communications Technology Office, 2012).

Furthermore, the negative domestic public perception about the ITeS industry also emerges as a challenge. The lack of proper understanding and knowledge as to the benefits and advantages the industry can offer to each employee working for it and the degree of earnings it contributes to the local economies poses serious problems (Cagayan De Oro ICT Business Council, 2013). Most fresh graduates are reluctant to join the industry after graduating from college due to various reasons. Employment in the ITeS sector often carries a pessimistic undertone with the industry being described as low-skilled, routinised, and with limited opportunities for upward labour mobility (Beerepoot and Hendriks, 2013, p. 837); working on a graveyard shift; high propensity for health risks; and the belief that the industry is being limited only to voice support functions. This concern has hopefully been addressed by the series of roadshows conducted recently by the ICTO and its key partners in various NWCs all over the archipelago.

Other than these, the Philippine ITeS players should also emulate the positive developments in India. These include data privacy/cyber security, labour laws and ease of set-up as partly mentioned earlier. NASSCOM, for example, has played an active role by establishing the Data Security Council to monitor closely the developments and legislation of the India IT Act. Moreover, the Indian players also considered the amendments on the Essential Services Amendment Act (ESMA) to offer more social security benefits and payment of additional wage to ITeS workers. The Indian government also supported NASSCOM in establishing a single-window clearance in cooperation with the Ministry of IT (CICT, 2010). However, according to Yahya, these efforts of the Indian government and Indian ITeS companies appear to be mere 'window dressing' intended to assuage clients' concerns. The said efforts to tighten data security are limited in technical and legislative areas only. Actual awareness and training to maintain the confidentiality of clients' data seem to be lacking. Punishment for breaches of security and cyber crime seem to be symbolically punitive at best and the legal recourse in India is infamous for its glacial pace. Thus, some client companies have reviewed their outsourcing requirements and have relocated most of the confidential data handling back to within their own borders (Yahya, 2012, p. 631).

Furthermore, there is inadequate Philippine government support in providing hard infrastructure projects to retain the momentum of the NWCs' initiatives. There is a pressing need to build ITeS-ready hard/soft social infrastructure such as integrated townships containing housing, schools, entertainment; 24/7 facilities as well as develop the local real estate and telecommunications ecosystem to meet the needs of the industry agents. At least in India, gated communities are already mushrooming in various cities, including Bangalore, that cater to the growing demands of ITeS related enterprises (Chacko and Varghase, 2009, p. 57). It is also suggested that all concerned parties are encouraged to build hubs through directed investments in talent strength areas such as Naga City for animation or Pune City for engineering services to create a regional distinctiveness as part of levelling up in the value chain.

Lastly, the presence of having multiple bodies negotiate with both the government and private sector is another challenge that the Philippines will be facing in the coming years. Unlike India's NASSCOM as the lone body devoted to ITeS concerns and activities, the Philippine industry is supervised by three competing associations. Thus, there is a need for iBPAP, CCAP, and BSA/U to consolidate as a single organisation responsible for looking after the concerns of all players, including the lobbying of various projects and programmes with the government and luring potential investors into the country.

Conclusion

There is no doubt that the rise of the ITeS industry globally has been driven by the active initiative of the private sector across the globe. In Asia, however, the rise of ITeS centres, particularly in India and the Philippines, should also be credited in large part to the supportive policy environment provided by the government. State developmentalism is obviously still prevalent in India and the Philippines, as manifested by the various interventions of each government in the ITeS industry such as the promotion of contact centre businesses' proliferation in numerous local government units, the provision of soft and hard infrastructures, as well as implementation of industrial policies. Amazingly, these interventions produced considerable results for a short period of time. The general public has gradually demonstrated increasing awareness and utmost respect towards the ITeS industry in these countries only because of the soaring job opportunities it has generated and several infrastructures that were constructed for this purpose. These welcome developments, to some extent, fit India and the Philippines to Chalmers Johnson's idea of the capitalist developmental state and thereby legitimise it through the ITeS industry serving as a model project (Johnson, 1995).

Thus, the governments of India and the Philippines are actively developing tier 2/3 cities, or NWCs, as viable ITeS service delivery locations while continuously strengthening the multidimensional infrastructural development of leading cities as ITeS hubs. To ensure uninterrupted growth of the industry, various bureaucratic machineries were employed to supervise the immediate provision of public services such as power, local transportation, security, and others. Furthermore, the government also extended holiday and tax incentives, offered subsidies on training and infrastructure costs, as well as removing procedural obstacles such as eliminating taxation on software products and providing service tax refunds.

As for local transportation and security, the government provided transportation services to the ITeS agents particularly those on night and early morning shifts. The Philippine government, for instance, experimented with a 'Metro Rail Transit 3' special service to cater to the ITeS workers by extending the commuter line's operation to 24 hours, seven days a week (Olchondra, 2009). Due to low ridership, the programme was ultimately cut short. Nevertheless, it showed that the government had something to offer in securing and improving the players who are basically running this industry as one of the big contributors to the national economy.

In India, specifically in Gurgaon City, the government authorities supported the Gurgaon Cyber City Welfare Society by offering a shuttle service in transporting the 80,000 employees from Sikandar Metro Station to the various offices in the cyber city. The service is called SmartRide; it operates five custom-made air-conditioned buses six days a week between 7 am to 9 pm (BPO Watch, 2010). The authorities are also planning to extend the service to employees residing in nearby Dwarka as well as Sectors 55–56 and DLF Phase 5 in the near future. Furthermore, the recent connection of Delhi and Gurgaon through metro rail services also persuaded the ITeS companies in the Delhi-National Capital Region to gradually replace the existing shuttle arrangement. These companies offered instead travel allowances and metro rail cards for day shift workers while maintaining the cab services for night shift employees (Mamgain and Puri, 2010). As for other Indian states, this 'mess' is still under the responsibility of the ITeS companies (Shelley Singh, 2010).[13]

Moreover, the Indian government also invested a lot on the soft infrastructure by improving the quality of graduate and post-graduate human resources, policy de-regulation and nurturing clusters of research institutes. Indian IITs, for instance, produce hundreds of thousands of engineers and professionals annually which guarantee sufficient numbers of qualified ITeS talents to run the ITeS industry. Similarly, the Philippine government also encouraged its higher educational institutions to offer ITeS-specified curricula to augment the workforce demands of the ITeS industry.

It is therefore undeniable that the strategic involvement of the government in the growth of the ITeS industry is indeed a critical booster in India and the Philippines. Despite the presence of active regionalisation and globalisation of business operations, the role of the government is definitely significant in the advancement of IT and its related sectors, particularly in the developing countries. This alterity between offline governance and online business will be likely to be sustained continuously until the hard and soft infrastructures are fully in place for the private sectors to generate their own growth momentum. Until then, this arrangement whereby governments supply the 'basic plumbing' to build industry will not only exist in India and the Philippines, but practically all over Asia.

---

13 Pramod Bhasin, president and CEO of Genpact called the arrangement of transport for employees as one of the 'mess' of the BPO business in India. The other mess includes security, power back-up in offices and basic infrastructures.

References

Agarwal, Surabhi. (2013) 'In Philippines, BPOs Face the Same Woes They Faced in India' *Live Mint* and *The Wall Street Journal*. 20 March. http://www.livemint.com/Industry/lfJ7iqXLDyPtFrNgsi3ojI/In-Philippines BPOs-face-the-samewoes-they-faced-in-India.html.

Ahlan, Abdul Rahman, et. al. (2008) 'Assessment of the Impact of IT Outsourcing on IT Education in Malaysian Institutions of Higher Learning' *International Journal of Education and Information Technologies*. 3.2.

Amsden, Alice. (1989) *Asia's Next Giant: South Korea and Late Industrialization*. New York: Oxford University Press.

Amsden, Alice. (1991) 'Diffusion of Development: The Late-Industrializing Model and Greater East Asia' *American Economic Association Papers and Proceedings*.

Amsden, Alice. (1997) 'Editorial: Bringing Production Back in- Understanding Government's Economic Role in Late Industrialization' *World Development*. 25.4.

Bautista, Cesar. (2012) PH Electricty Tariffs Still 2nd-Highest in Asia. *Philippine Daily Inquirer*. August.

Beauprez, J. (2003) 'TeleTech loses call-center contract to overseas operator', *The Denver Post*, US, 2 February.

Board of Investments, Philippines. (2012) Offshoring and Outsourcing Industry: Philippines' IT/BPO Services Sector. September.

BPAP. (2011). 'History'. http://www.bpap.org/index.php/about-us/history.

BPAP. (2012). 'About the IT-BPO and GIC in the Philippines'. http://www.bpap.org/investor/about-the-itbpo-and-gic-in-the-philippines.

BPAP. (2012). 'Contact Center Industry Poised for Sustained Growth'. http://www.bpap.org/mediaroom/643-contact-center-industry-poised-for sustained-growth.

BPO Watch India Bureau. (2010) 'Shuttle Service for BPO Employees in Gurgaon' http://www.bpowatchindia.com/bpo_news/gurgaonsafety/november-17 2010/shuttle_service_for_bpo_employees_in_gurgaon.html. 17 November.

BSA/U. (2011) 'About us' http://www.bsau.org/#ITBPOREPORT.

Business Process Outsourcing Association of the Philippines. (2009) 'Offshoring and Outsourcing Industry: Philippines' IT/BPO Services Sector, September.

Businessworld. (2000). 'Instant office business debuts in the Philippines', Philippines, 21 March.

Cagayan De Oro ICT Business Council. (2013) New Wave Cities. October. http://cdoict.org/ict-roadshow/.

Castells, Manuel. (2010) *The Rise of the Network Society*. Singapore: Wiley-Blackwell.

Catherine Mann. (2005) 'Ofshore Outsourcing and the Globalization of US Services: Why Now, How Important and What Policy Implications' *The United States and the World Economy*. C. Fred Bergsten and the Institute for International Economics (IIE). United States of America: IIE.

Chacko, Elizabeth and Paul Varghase. (2009) 'Identity and Representations of Gated Communities in Bangalore, India' *Open House International*. 34.3.
Chepesiuk, Ron. (2000) 'India's Global Talent'. *Asianweek*, 24–30 November.
Chong, F. (2000) 'Filipino bad news buries brighter prospects', *The Australian*, 26 October.
Collin, N. (1995) *Knowledge Workers and Information Technology: Managing a New Organizational Paradigm*, SRI International, Business Intelligence Program, May.
Commission on Higher Education, Philippines. (2011). 'Information on Higher Education System'. August. http://www.ched.gov.ph/chedwww/index.php/eng/Information.
Commission on Information and Communications Technology. (2009) Convergence 2009. http://www.cict.gov.ph/ictroadshow/rationale.htm.
Connors, M. (1993) *The Race To The Intelligent State. Towards the Global Information Economy of 2005*, Blackwell, Oxford, UK.
Economic Times. (2003). 'European firm sees India as big BPO destination', India, 5 September.
Greet Technologies. (2010) 'About Outsourcing' http://www.greettech.com/abouthroutsourcing_4new.shtml.
IBPAP. (2013) 'IBPAP, CHED sign agreement to integrate Service Management Program into SUC curricula' http://www.ibpap.org.
Indian Brand Equity Foundation (IBEF). (2010) 'Telecommunication' July. http://www.ibef.org/artdispview.aspx?in=72&art_id=28389&cat_id=470&page=2.
Indian Brand Equity Foundation (IBEF). (2013) Indian Telecommunications Industry: an overview. http://www.ibef.org/industry/telecommunication-snapshot. September 2013.
Information and Communications Technology Office. (2012) 'Study on the Corporate Services Segments of IT-BPM'. http://www.icto.dost.gov.ph/index.php/study-on the-corporate-services-segments.
International Telecommunication Union. http://www.itu.int/net/about/basic texts/constitution/annex.aspx.
Jatras, Todd. (2001) 'Stock Focus: Indian Software Companies' Forbes.com. 16 July.
Johnson, Chalmers. (1995) *Japan: Who Governs? The Rise of the Developmental State*. New York: W.W. Norton and Company.
Kripalani, Manjeet. (2000) 'The Wiring of India: Private Companies are Rushing to Cash in on Telecom Deregulation' *BusinessWeek*. 7 August.
Kripalani, Manjeet. (2001) 'India's Worsening Power Vacuum', *Businessweek*, 27 November.
Lanzona, L.A. Jr. (2001) 'Labor, HRD and Globalisation', in *The Filipino Worker in a Global Economy*, Lanzona Jr., L.A. (ed), APEC Philippine Center, Makati.
Lebihan, R. (2003) 'Philippines Pushes Outsource Advantages', *Australian Financial Review*, 8 April.

Llamas, Cora. (2010) 'Where the BPO Industry is Booming' *Manila Bulletin.* 29 August.
Mamgain, Pramugdha and Mahima Puri. (2010) 'Metro May Replace BPO Day-Cabs Soon' *Economic Times*. 5 August.
Martin, Philip. (1986) 'Illegal Immigration and the Colonization of the American Labour Market' Center for Immigration Studies. January. http://www.cis.org/AmericanLaborMarket%2526Immigration.
Ministry of Power. (2013). State-Wise/Utility Wise Average Rate of Electricity for Domestic and Industrial Consumers. http://data.gov.in/dataset/state-wise averagerateelectricity-domestic-and-industrial-consumers.
Mira, Ricardo. (2009) 'Philippine BPI-IT Industry: Performance and Prospects. *Policy Advisory*. Congressional Planning and Budget Department. House of Representatives, Republic of the Philippines.
Moran, N. (2003) 'Looking for savings on distant horizons', *Financial Times*, London, 2 July.
NASSCOM. (2009) 'Indian's IT-BPO Value Proposition' Strategic Review 2009 16 June. http://www.nasscom.in/Nasscom/templates/NormalPage.aspx?id=54929.
NASSCOM. (2010) Annual Report 2010–11, 1.
NASSCOM-Everest. (2008) India BPO Study 'Roadmap 2012' – Capitalizing on the Expanding BPO Landscape.
National Association of Software and Services Companies. (2012) 'About NASSCOM. July. http://www.nasscom.in/Nasscom/templates/NormalPage.aspx?id=5365.
National Statistical Coordination Board, Republic of the Philippines. (2007) 'Understanding the Business Process Outsourcing (BPO) Industry in the Philippines'. 9 November. http://www.nscb.gov.ph/factsheet/pdf07/FS-200711 ES2–01_BPO.asp#1. http://www.ibef.org/industry/ITenabledservices.aspx.
OECD Science, *Technology and Industry Scoreboard, Benchmarking Knowledge – based Economies.* (1999) Organisation for Economic Co-operation and Development, Paris.
Office of the President, Republic of the Philippines. (2010) 'Philippine Cyber Services Corridor' 28 April. http://www.ops.gov.ph.
Olchondra, Riza. (2009) '1st Overnight MRT Run Serves 5,774' *Philippine Daily Inquirer*. 29 May.
Osorio, Ma. Elisa. (2009) 'RP Eyes Piece of $5-Billion Business Processing Mart in Japan' *The Philippine Star*, 22 May.
Overseas Indian Facilitation Centre. (2012) 'Telecommunication in India' September. http://www.oifc.in/Sectors/ICT-(Information-%26-Communication technology)/Telecommunication.
Periabras, Rosalie. (2013) 'Philippines: The New Call Center Capital of the World' *The Manila Times*, October.
Pete Engardio, *et al*. (2003) 'The New Global Job Shift', *BusinessWeek*, 3 February.

Pinoy Internet: Philippines Case Study. (2002) International Telecommunications Union, Geneva, Geneva, Switzerland, March.

Reyes, Mary Ann. (2001) 'Philippines: The Numbers' Up for Fixed Lines' *Asia Times*, 18 July.

Singh, Gurbir. (2002) 'Deep Sockets: India Among Top 20 Telecom Spenders'. *Economic Times*. 24 August.

Singh, Shelley. (2010) 'Indian BPO Lose Voice to Philippines' *Economic Times*. 17 March.

Srivastava, Mehul. (2010) 'Philippine Call Centers Overtake India' Bloomberg *Businessweek*. 2 December.

Tech America. (2010). 'The Impact of Offshore IT Software and Services Outsourcing on the U.S. Economy and the IT Industry'.

Technical Education and Skills Development Authority. (2008) Joint TESDA-BPAP Circular. http://www.tesda.gov.ph.

Wade, Robert. (1990) *Governing the Market: Economic Theory and the Role of Government in East Asian Industrialization.* New Jersey: Princeton University Press.

Wakelin, M. (1992) 'Globalization of Regional Development', in *The Technopolis Phenomenon. Smart Cities, Fast Systems, Global Networks*, Gibson, D.V., Kozmetsky, G., and Smilor, R.W. (eds), Rowman and Littlefield Publishers, Inc., US.

Williams, F. (1992) 'The Information Infrastructure in Technopolis: The Intelligent Network', in *The Technopolis Phenomenon. Smart Cities, Fast Systems, Global Networks,* Gibson, D.V., Kozmetsky, G., and Smilor, R.W. (eds), Rowman and Littlefield Publishers, Inc., US.

World Bank. (2010) 'Key Indicators of Development' World Development Report 2010.

Yahya, Faizal. (2012) 'India and Its Maturing BPO IT Sector'. *Journal of Asian and African Studies*, 47.6.

Chapter 9
The Political Economy of Data Security in the BPO Industry in India

Faizal Bin Yahya

Introduction

India's Information Technology (IT) industry consists of three major components, they are; IT hardware, IT software and IT enabled services (ITeS) including outsourcing. The IT revolution in India which began in the 1980s and was initially centred in Bangalore, the state capital of Karnataka one of the four southern states in India but thereafter other IT hubs emerged such as in Hyderabad (HiTec City) and Chennai, the adjoining state capitals to Bangalore. Arguably, a majority of IT analysts did not give the government much credit for the rise of the IT sector in India and some even argued that the sector was able to expand because of the government's inability to understand and control the sector. The economic reforms and liberalisation of India in 1991 further boosted the expansion of the IT sector. Several global factors accelerated the expansion of the sector such as the Y2K phenomenon and the rise of free trade agreements (FTAs). The Millennium bug or Y2K created panic globally and a critical race to update antiquated software systems which was undertaken by scores of Indian IT techies which gave India prominence as an IT hub. The increasing convergence of economies through transboundary linkages such as free trade agreements (FTAs) further accelerated the phenomenon of outsourcing which boosted India's brand as an IT hub. In this regard, what has the Indian government undertaken to ensure the sustainability of the vital IT sector? It could be argued albeit unintentionally that when the government produced thousands of engineers for its aeronautical, satellites and nuclear research centres it created a large pool of educated and trained manpower that was tapped by the emerging IT sector. This untapped human capital potential then attracted multinational companies (MNCs) to leverage on this and establish a presence in India. In 2000, the government unveiled the Indian IT Act (Cyber Laws India website).[1]

---

1 This Act aims to provide the legal infrastructure for e-commerce in India. And the cyber laws have a major impact for e-businesses and the new economy in India. So, it is important to understand what are the various perspectives of the IT Act, 2000 and what it offers. Chapter-III of the Act details about Electronic Governance and provides inter alia amongst others that where any law provides that information or any other matter shall be in writing or in the typewritten or printed form, then, notwithstanding anything contained

In 2006, the Indian outsourcing industry which at the time was worth US$ 23.6 billion was flourishing but was inundated by a series of identity thefts, fraud and other cyber crimes that threatened the potential of this vital sector to the Indian economy (*The New York Times*, 5 October 2006). It could be argued that cyber crime occurs on a global dimension and not only in India, for example, in 2004, data broker Lexis Nexus reported that hundreds of thousands of personal information were stolen from its data base system (TBRNews.org, 12 April 2005) in the United States (US). However, the frequency with which these cyber crimes surfaced in India created the perception that India was an unsafe destination for outsourcing. What is at stake for India? The incidences of cyber crimes within its jurisdiction has grave political implications for the doubts that it raises in the minds of Western companies intending to outsource business to India. Coupled with the negative publicity that India carries through consumer groups and unions for allegedly stealing American and European jobs, the business process outsourcing (BPO) companies in India had to take action to salvage its reputation as a high-skilled and low cost location for outsourcing (*The New York Times*, 5 October 2006).

A year earlier in 2005, a trend was spotted when two incidents occurred among Indian BPO firms, Infinity e-Systems in New Delhi and Parsec Technologies that questioned the security of data management in India. In June 2005, an employee of BPO firm Infinity sold the account numbers and passwords of 1000 bank customers to a reporter from the British tabloid paper called *The Sun*. In the other incident, in November 2005, four former employees of Parsec technology were arrested for allegedly stealing classified information. The former Parsec employees then diverted the calls of potential customers which caused a sudden drop in the productivity of call centres managed by Parsec. While improvement needs to be undertaken as to how data security is being managed in India, some industry analysts believed that there was a deliberate attempt to manipulate news coverage by the media to discredit Indian outsourcing companies (*Financial Express*, 7 April 2005).

In 2006, a report by Boston based consultancy Forrester Research predicted that security concerns, regulatory pressures and customer backlash would undermine India's call centre expansion by as much as 30 per cent (*Insurance Networking News*, 1 August 2006). This is because financial firms would require a longer time to make outsourcing decisions, slowing down the implementation of large projects or forcing firms to establish their own call centres in India rather than utilising outsourcers. To avoid these developments, the Indian outsourcing industry joined forces with the National Association of Software Companies (NASSCOM) to develop and implement several security measures to restore confidence among client firms. This included a voluntary registry for call centre employees as a personnel reference for all BPO firms.

---

in such law, such requirement shall be deemed to have been satisfied if such information or matter is; Cyber Laws India http://www.cyberlawsindia.net/Information-technology-act-of-india.html.

The aim of this chapter is to examine the role of the state in regulating the outsourcing sectors in India. Given that the IT and ITeS sectors are crucial to the development of knowledge based industries (KBIs) in India, the state and key organisations such as NASSCOM have a keen interest in expanding these sectors. Furthermore, with greater economic integration through the linkages made by free trade agreements (FTAs) the KBIs are likely to be a key component of trade negotiations. Do India's BPO firms have adequate security measures to safely handle outsourcing work from other countries?

While, the "beefing up" of security measures was already under way for several years in India since early 2000, a famous incident of identity and fraud crime by a call centre managed by a company called Mphasis in Pune again questioned the rationale of outsourcing work to India. This case is all the more damaging because despite being a CMM level – 5 certified company (which is the gold standard for IT firms), Mphasis was also vulnerable to data theft and fraud. However, Mphasis took comfort in the incident by stating that the breach was caused by fraudulent employees who skimmed off money from Citibank customers by tricking them into revealing their passwords and not by a breach of their online systems. Nonetheless, the "silver lining" to the scandal was that it provided the necessary impetus and political clout to legislators to pass crucial amendments to enhance security procedures and security consciousness in the work practices of BPO firms (*Insurance Networking News*, 1 August 2006).

While, the Mphasis case resulted in positive measures, security problems in BPO companies continued and were accentuated by the following factors; the high employee turnover rate of 50 to 100 per cent for call centres in the outsourcing industry made monitoring of personnel difficult. This problem was compounded by high internal and external staff turnover by senior managers which deprives companies of continuity and accountability and poor employee screening procedures. Other problems included a corporate culture that sought to maximise financial gains from offshore outsourcing which permeated through the ranks; disengagement by the client community especially banks and finance companies; and finally, outdated and obsolete fraud detection and enforcement procedures (*E-Commerce News*, 21 October 2010).

The general level of labour attrition in the BPO-ITeS sector had increased steadily and for average firms is between 30 to 60 per cent and 15 per cent for top end firms per year. Nasscom accurately predicted that the outsourcing industry would face a shortage of 262,000 professionals by 2012 (BPO India website). The lower end of the attrition spectrum involves non-voice (transaction processing) tasks and the upper end involving voice related tasks (Goel and Thakur, January 2007, 3). What are the causes of increasing labour attrition? Table 9.1 below shows some of the internal and external causes for high labour attrition rates in the BPO industry.

Table 9.1 Causes of labour attrition in the BPO-ITES sector in India

S/No.	Internal	External
	Monetary Consideration	Concentration of demand for talent
	Slow career growth for internal talent	Limited talent pool supply
	Monotony	Shortage of management pool
	Shift timings	Career outlook
	Working environment	
	Limited training and development opportunities	
	Deficiencies in the recruitment process	
	Mismatched resources	

The future growth of the Indian BPO industry is dependent on the supply of human capital at all levels. The current strategy of hiring "ready to eat" talent has to be altered because this will lead to a shortage of 800 000 to 1.2 million entry level graduates by 2012 (Nasscom, 2008, 4). This shortage of talent will be further aggravated by domestic competition from the service sector in the Retail, Insurance, Telecom and Banking industries. Human capital in middle management with domain experience will be in short supply as well as those on sector specific skills such as actuaries for Insurance BPO. This will impact directly on recruitment and training costs. Another complication to hiring entry-level talent is access to these employable talents in remote locations.

In a survey conducted by NASSCOM and the Information Technology Association of America (ITAA), among the companies polled, the findings indicated that information security is perceived as a key differentiator. Greater than 75 per cent of respondents agreed that offering sophisticated information security provisions and practices provide a competitive advantage because security has become a critical selling point. The poll results showed that there is a growing concern about data security in the software industry. In general, researchers agreed that as a trend these security challenges would impact on outsourcing (Outsourcing Center, 1 December 2004). In Ernst & Young's 2004 Global Information Security Survey, companies surveyed have identified major viruses, spam and employee misconduct as the key concerns in India. The survey rated major viruses and Internet worms as the top concern in India.

Competition

Since the mid-2000, the BPO industry in India has been in the process of transforming itself from a cost arbitrage proposition dealing with low end back – office work into a high-value and knowledge based industry (KBI) supporting clients globally (*The Times of India*, 2 July 2012). In short it has ridden the wave from a BPO hub into a knowledge procession outsourcing hub (KPO). The industry feels that a curriculum needs to be developed specifically for the BPO industry and this would entail the training of college teachers. The call centre business has been transformed from making random sales pitches and servicing queries into more complex issues. Nonetheless, since 2010, the industry has stagnated and overseas clients remained wary over India's BPO tag (*The Times of India*, 2 July 2012). Is the BPO industry progressing? At a glance, the industry in 2012 employs domain experts such as accountants, tax consultants, lawyers, PhDs, doctors and other professionals. Therefore, at a glance it could be argued that the BPO industry is moving towards a KPO trajectory.

In 2012, the Indian BPO industry faced a number of challenges such as competition from rival BPO destinations like the Philippines. Competition from outside India is a given but is not in itself the main threat to the Indian BPO companies. It is more of a contributing and ever present factor. This is because market share will remain in perpetual flux influenced by price pressures, regulatory shifts and trends. Business plans have to account for such variability and allow nimble service providers to react accordingly (Global services, 7 April 2011). The required technology compliance of BPO companies is linked to copyright, patents and data security. Indian BPO companies are at a higher level of regulation than mandated by Indian regulations. Table 9.2 below compares Indian BPO companies against its greatest rivals, China and the Philippines.

Table 9.2 Indian BPO versus competition (China and Philippines)

Laws	India	China	Philippines
IPR			
Copyright	4	3	3
Patent	Product Patents 2005	x	x
Data Protection			
Data Protection Laws	Comprehensive Framework 2004	x	x
Vertical Specific Laws	x	x	x
CYBER			
Digital Signatures	3	3	3
Blackhat Hacking	3	3	3
Privacy	3	3*	3

*Privacy laws exist in China, but they are not comprehensive

Source: NASSCOM Indian ITES-BPO fact sheet (Evaluserve Analysis).

NASSCOM is working with the Indian government to bring regulations such as the Indian IT Act 2000 to be on par with regulations such as the EU Data Protection Directive. While US customers of Indian BPO feel that it is the ideal destination for high-end data services, they are also concerned about possible pitfalls. This is because the Indian IT-BPO value proposition to its customers rested on the following: continued focus on optimal cost efficiency, unparalleled human capital, unique customer centricity, scalable and secure environment and a supportive ecosystem.

From 2011 to 2012, the Indian software and services export including BPO exports was estimated to be worth US$ 68.7 billion. IT services exports was estimated at US$ 39.8 billion. IT services contributed 58 per cent of total IT-BPO exports and this was followed by the BPO sector at 23 per cent (*SME Times*, 31 July 2012). The IT-BPO sector has become one of the key sectors of the Indian economy because of the substantial share of its contribution to GDP. The sector was responsible for creating significant employment opportunities in the economy. Within the IT-BPO sector, employment reached 2.77 million with over 230 000 jobs created between 2011 and 2012 (*SME Times*, 31 July 2012). In 2012, the IT-BPO industry weathered uncertainties in the global business environment and aggregate IT software and services revenue excluding hardware reached an estimated US$ 88 billion (NASSCOM, 2012). As a proportion of national GDP, the sector's revenue has grown from 1.2 per cent in 1998 to 7.5 per cent in 2012. Moreover, the sector's share of total Indian exports increased from less than 4 per cent in 1998 to about 25 per cent in 2012.

Nonetheless, security remains a major concern. As a result of the negative coverage of the scandals among India's BPO firms, a report by Boston based Forrester Research predicted that security concerns, regulatory pressures and customer backlash would undermine Indian call centres' expansion by as much as 30 per cent (*Insurance Networking News*, 1 August 2006). This is because financial firms would require a longer time to make outsourcing decisions, slowing large projects or forcing firms to establish their own call centres in India rather than utilising outsourcers. To forestall these negative developments, the Indian outsourcing industry joined forces to develop and implement several security measures that included a voluntary registry for call centre employees. The beefing up of security measures was already under way for several years but the scandal involving Mphasis and Citibank customers provided the necessary impetus and political clout to get things done (*Insurance Networking News*, 1 August 2006).

Role of NASSCOM

A survey by global audit firm Pricewaterhouse Coopers and the Data Security Council of India (DSCI)[2] from 2009–2010 showed that 90 per cent of all security

2 DSCI is a focal body on data protection in India, setup as an independent Self-Regulatory Organisation (SRO) by NASSCOM®, to promote data protection; develop security and privacy best practices and standards; and encourage the Indian industries to implement the same. DSCI is engaged with the Indian IT/BPO industry, their clients

breaches at 13, small, mid-sized and large IT/ITes companies were insider jobs. Sidharth Vishwanath, an associate director of consulting at PwC said, "Insider-led issues have increased. They know the vulnerabilities of the organisation, and what is important and what is not. Partners, vendors and dissatisfied employees are also potential threats" (*The Times of India*, 29 June 2011). Respondents said that insiders at service provider organisations copied sensitive information on mobile devices like USB drives or PDAs, sent out information via email or even wrote information on paper. In order to monitor and regulate the IT-BPO sector, the Nasscom formed the Data Security Council of India (DSCI). The DSCI is an independent self-regulatory organisation that was established to promote data protection and develop security and privacy practices in the Indian industry (*The Times of India*, 29 June 2011).

The main law that affects Indian BPO companies is the Indian IT Act 2000. The IT Act 2000 did not cover issues on privacy, protection and regulated use of data. In its original form the Act only covered unauthorised access and data theft from computers and networks with a maximum penalty of about US$ 220 000 and did not have specific provisions related to the privacy of data. In general, Indian law at the time did not cover data interception and computer forgery. Data protection issues remained primarily in an unregulated Indian environment (Outsourcing Center, 1 December 2004).

Other legal regulations that affect the sector are the Indian Penal Code Act, Consumer Protection Act 1986, Indian Contract Act 1972, Specific Relief Act 1963, Indian Copyright Act 2000 and the Product Patent Act 2005. In comparison, to the laws in the United States (US) and United Kingdom (UK) the Indian Act IT 2000 was not considered to be adequate. Foreign companies outsourcing their jobs to India were insisting that BPO companies certified their operations under international standards such as BS 7799, SAS 70 and HIPAA (Rediff.com, 25 May 2005). In 2011, India introduced the Reasonable Security Practices and Procedures and Sensitive Personal Data or Information Rules 2011. The purpose was to alleviate fears that data such as credit card details were at risk because no data protection law existed. The new rule in section 43A of the Indian IT Act said, "that a corporate shall have to obtain permission through letter or fax or email from each client before collection of sensitive information, if they go by the new IT rules 2011" (ComputerWeekly.com).

However, there is a downside to enhancing legal controls. These regulations impose a major burden on the Indian BPO companies as it would create additional work hurdles for Indian companies to obtain consent from their customer clients. Sensitive information here refers to physical, physiological and mental health condition, medical records and history. All medical transcription firms operating in India must have access to medical records of patients from client firms in the US

worldwide, banking and telecom sectors, industry associations, data protection authorities and other government agencies in different countries. DSCI is focused on capacity building of Law Enforcement Agencies for combating cyber crimes in India and towards this it operates several cyber labs across India.

(*The Times of India*, 26 August 2011). Moreover, the rules also related to implementation of reasonable security practices by the corporate bodies for sensitive personal information which refers to financial details related to bank account, credit card or other payment methods. A large segment of BPO companies have clients such as American Express, Citibank, HSBC, Bank of America and it was the usual norm to collect financial information before undertaking any transaction (*The Times of India*, 26 August 2011). The new rules were effective 11 April 2011. Thus, the BPO firms would have to inform the client regarding the purpose of usage before collection of such information if they were following the new rules. The NASSCOM on behalf of the Indian BPO firms submitted a request for clarification by the government on the new rules as it would impact on Indian firms. The government clarified that the new rules won't apply to outsourcing providers located in India. In addition, consent could also be given by any mode of electronic communication such as SMS or calls and not restricted to consent provided through letter, fax or email. Nonetheless, the government also advised the BPO service providers to follow "reasonable security practices" for protecting sensitive personal information that they are processing (*The Times of India*, 26 August 2011).

Reaction from US Firms

It was thought that at the time of the fraud incident faced by Citibank in 2005; this would prompt client firms in the US to consider using smaller, better-managed facilities and exploring new outsourcing locations in India such as Kolkatta (*E-Commerce Times*, 4 December 2005). The fraud case prompted a reexamination of corporate cultures and corporate ethics. In 2006, there were fears from Indian companies that Western clients would hesitate to outsource to India if the country was depicted as a market susceptible to scams (*The New York Times*, 5 October 2006). Analysts in the industry were urging for data protective laws that would facilitate more client confidence in Indian companies and progression from low–end BPO work, such as at call centres, to high-end BPO work (*Business Line*, 27 July 2005). What has been the progression of the BPO sector in India? The BPO sector began as a call-centre hub leveraging on cost arbitrage. However, over the years it has migrated to high-value, knowledge-based industries that support global clients across multiple domains. The legions of call-centre agents have also transformed themselves into domain experts, specialists and analysts. Fast forward to 2012, the Indian BPOs are employing domain experts in areas like financial accounting and legal; specialists in analytics; professionals like doctors, PhDs, chartered accountants, tax consultants and lawyers (*The Times of India*, 2 July 2012). What were once seen as a stop-gap option for employees have become full-fledged career options (*The Times of India*, 2 July 2012).

In a survey undertaken by the DSCI and PwC among Indian BPO companies on how they are mitigating risks associated with insider threats such as social networking and credit card history check, it was found that the IT/BPO industry were exploring new and innovative security measures. In terms of framework, the survey used a three-pronged approach to understand the security environment of the Indian IT/BPO industry (PwC Press Release). The three pronged approach involved leveraging on industry survey and inputs, analysis of insider theft cases and insider threat secondary research. The key findings of the DSCI-PwC survey were;

- In 89 per cent of service providers firms, behavioural motivation to loosen existing norms is the primary motive leading to insider threat, while 75 per cent of client organisations believe personal financial gain is the prime motive at service provider organisations.
- All client organisations have authorised their service providers to conduct employee background; but the employee verification processes were not standardised as providers were subjected to client-driven data.
- All service provider organisations believed that their current employees were the primary source of insider incidents. More than 50 per cent of the service provider organisations revealed that insiders who were not working in the IT department, and do not have privileged access as a result, had carried out insider incidents at their organisations.
- All client organisations, along with 33 per cent of service provider organisations, were convinced that the lack of education and awareness was a major barrier in addressing insider threats.
- Over half of the respondents believed social engineering and "someone else's computer account" were used by insiders to commit a breach in service provider organisations.
- 89 per cent of service provider organisations were able to internally resolve cases of insider incidents without involving a legal agency. Only 22 per cent of service providers initiated legal action against perpetrators.
- Almost 67 per cent of service provider organisations and 75 per cent of client organisations believed unintentional exposure of private and sensitive information is still one of the major challenges faced by both service provider and client organisations.

The DSCI had undertaken another survey with auditing firm KPMG covering 50 organisations in association with the CERT-in process to assess the data security and privacy practices adopted by the Indian BPO industry to gain insights into how the industry is addressing security and privacy related issues. Nearly 50 per cent of the companies were negotiating contracts to ensure that any liability arising from vulnerabilities in the client's environment are borne by the client (*The Times of India*, 2 December 2010). The study highlighted that the Indian BPO industry is maturing because they are treating security as a "hygiene factor" instead of a competitive issue (*The Times of India*, 2 December 2010). In addition, 70 per cent of the BPO companies surveyed felt that the key threats to data security were internal by nature. As a result, the Chief Information Security Officers (CISOs) of the majority of the organisations were also spending significant amounts of time on strategic initiatives like identifying the security implications of new business initiatives (*The Times of India*, 2 December 2010).

The DSCI and KPMG report added that, there has been a paradigm shift in the management focus towards information security in the IT/BPO industry. The survey findings showed that none of the service provider companies identified "limited or no support" from their executive management as a barrier to good security measures. This indicated that information security has become a norm in the boardroom agenda. However, the techniques that could be used to address insider threats are different from those used to repel external threats. In order to address insider threats, the management has to implement a comprehensive approach that must include awareness, education, policy, culture and technology (DSCI and PwC Report).

Some of the recommendations by analysts to enforce strict data privacy for India BPO companies to remain competitive include stringent measures to control information leakage from the company via the Internet and other means. Other measures mandated using appropriate software to block attempts to download or copy files from the company's system and the prevention of unauthorised access. With data processing increasingly undertaken on cloud or the client's environment, information security is becoming a critical operational issue. Companies now move beyond internal security and have to ensure cloud security and network security to prevent any unauthorised access. In relation to employee management, the signing of the Non Disclosure Agreement (NDA) with employees reinforced internal security controls, along with blocking unnecessary Internet access and preventing employees from carrying information with devices such as paper, USBs, mobile phones and other recordable devices. The creation of a paperless environment and prohibiting people from bringing electronic devices to the office premises would assist in the prevention of information leakage (*BPO Insights*, 6 December 2011).

In another survey undertaken by Forrester Research, most security executives explained that they are in the process of achieving certifications, publishing policy statements and writing white papers as part of their initiatives to improve security (*Daily News and Analysis*, 6 April 2010). Their emphasis is client focused and seemed to be highlighting what they are developing to build client support and not to reduce threats. While most companies have a chief security officer, they will usually be given attention if a security breach has occurred (*Daily News and Analysis*, 6 April 2010).

Security procedures have been increased. In most BPO companies airport style frisking have become a routine. BPO workers are also required to surrender all their possessions such as mobile phones, PDAs, pens and notebooks. Access to personal email accounts is prohibited and firewalls block access to any website not necessary for work. After a day's work, workers in BPO companies have to shred notes of conversation with customers and workers are forbidden from socialising with non-employees during working hours. Collectively, Indian BPO companies do a lot of hiring through referrals from their current employees and this helps them to easily verify credentials. In the event that a data security breach should occur, the whole industry will be adversely affected. In this regard, the BPO industry also circulates a list of employees terminated on disciplinary grounds (ComputerWeekly.Com).

In terms of global certifications and standards, the majority of Indian BPOs are BS 7799 and ISO 17799 certified. According to Ernst & Young and the Indo-American Chamber of Commerce (IACC) Offshore Outsourcing Survey, 43 per cent of the BPO companies surveyed have BS 7799 and ISO 17799 security certifications. In addition, on the service management front, the IT Infrastructure Library (ITIL) is used as a foundation by most BPO companies. The effective use of ITIL meant that Indian BPOs would find it less daunting to be certified by future standards such as BS 15000 and the Control Objectives for Information and Related Technology (COBIT) framework (*Network Magazine*). The government encourages such security and standard certifications to prevent and mitigate against "offline temptations" such as the pilfering and sale of clients personal particulars.

Political Relations

Given that the BPO sector is a significant contributor to India's GDP, the sector has become a significant factor in India's trade negotiations. In negotiations for a free trade agreement (FTA) with the European Union, the Indian government has said that it will only agree to such an accord if the EU grants India data-secure destination status (ZDNet. 10 September 2012). India had no access to sensitive data such as intellectual property (IP) or patient information required for telemedicine from the EU because it was not considered a data secure market and data protection laws prohibited the transfer for such information. India's commerce secretary S.R. Rao said, "We have to gain data-secure business to get the EU's BPO business. This is the only way the bilateral agreement will be balanced between the two" (ZDNet, 10 September 2012). Rao added that, "we have to gain data-secure business to get the EU's BPO business. This is the only way the bilateral agreement will be balanced between the two". According to the DSCI, India's outsourcing business from the EU could increase from US$ 20 billion to US$ 50 billion annually should it be accorded data-secure status.

US President Barrack Obama is also not a fan of outsourcing. During his election campaign in 2008, he said that if reelected he would stop providing tax breaks for corporations that outsource jobs and reward those that create jobs in America (ZDNET, 21 January 2009). President Obama mentioned repeatedly in his 2012 reelection campaign that outsourcing had stolen several thousands of well-paying jobs from Americans and handed them over to cheaper Indian and Chinese labour. Notwithstanding such grandstanding rhetoric, an economic recovery plan for the US that does not include an outsourcing component may not be plausible (ZDNet, 21 January 2009). In today's business world, outsourcing is a necessity and an economic recovery plan for the US may not be feasible without an outsourcing component.

Conclusion

India is in an advantageous position to sustain its global leadership position. Its offshore IT-BPO industries can grow at an annual rate of 13 to14 per cent and it can sustain nearly 10 million direct jobs while generating export revenues of US$ 175 billion and domestic revenues of US$ 50 billion by 2020. However, the industry leaders and government have to convince BPO client companies especially in the US and Europe that their security procedures have met and surpassed standard requirements. Moreover, the authorities in India and leading BPO companies have to convince existing and potential clients that India is no more susceptible that its rivals, or even the US government, to data fraud and cyber crime, despite rampant coverage of such incidences by the Indian media. What is at stake? With the increased GDP growth of emerging markets and shrinking working age populations, a new set of untapped opportunities will present themselves that includes new verticals, service lines, geographic and customer segments. In 2020, the IT-BPO sector is likely to expand into a US$ 1.5 trillion industry worldwide. For India to continue exploiting this pool of wealth requires both the Government of India and its private corporations to recognise and practice techno-political alterity: the government provides assurances in policy and statute, while the private sector supplies services and employs the educated workforce.

References

Basu, I. (2005), "Indian BPO providers tighten data security", *SearchDataManagement.com*, URL: http://searchdatamanagement.techtarget.com/news/2240175894/Big-data-in-motion-Where-does-it-make-sense, 9 November.

Bhagwati, G. (2004), "India Responds to Growing Concerns Over Data Security" *Outsourcing Center,* 4 December, URL: http://outsourcing-center.com/2004–12-india-responds-to-growing-concerns-over-data-security-article-37883.html.

"Data security, client privacy biggest challenge for BPOs: Study" (2010), *The Times of India*, 2 December.

D'Souza, R. (2011), "5 Best Ways to Ensure Data Security in BPOs", *BPO Insights*, 6 December.

Flinders, K. (2011), "India confirms tough data law will not apply to Indian BPO suppliers, Inside Outsourcing", *ComputerWeekly.com*, 26 August, URL: http://www.computerweekly.com/.

"Indian IT, BPO face threat from insiders: Study" (2011), *The Times of India*, 29 June.

"Indian BPO units address security concerns" (2004), ComputerWeekly.com, URL: http://www.computerweekly.com/news/2240176194/Met-police-to-equip-officers-with-30000-mobile-devices, June.

Kwang, K. (2012), "India pushes for data-secure status from EU", *ZDNet*, 10 September, URL: http://www.zdnet.com/.

Mitchell, A., "Indian Call Center Fraud Case Highlights Need for Change", *E-Commerce Times* (4 December 2005), URL: http://www.ecommercetimes.com/story/Showrooming-Shoppers-Send-eBay-Soaring-77114.html.

Our Bureau, "Data security vital for BPO growth" (2005), *Business Line*, 29 July.

"Outsourcing" (2011), *The Times of India*, 26 August.

Patel, N. (2008), "Outsourcing: Data Security and Privacy Issues in India", *Issues in Information Systems*, Vol.IX, No.2.

Prasad, M/V.S. (2012), *SME Times*, URL: http://www.smetimes.in/smetimes/news/top-stories/2013/Jan/18/aepc-sets-up-research-centre-to-strengthen-smes628595.html, 31 July.

Rai, S. (2006), "Security Breaches Worry Outsourcing Industry", *The New York Times*, 5 October.

Rigby, B. and Kolker, T. (2005), "LexisNexis Uncovers More Consumer Data Breaches", *TBRNews.org*, 12 April, URL: http://www.trb.org/Main/Public/Blurbs.aspx?taxonomy=AnnouncementsNews.

"Security concerns hit BPO firms in India" (2005), *Rediff.com*, URL: http://www.rediff.com/, 25 May.

"Security 'only skin deep' in Indian IT-BPO" (2010), *DNA*, URL: http://www.dnaindia.com/, 6 April.

Tejaswi, M.J. (2012), "BPO sector calls for rebranding its offerings", *The Times of India*, 2 July.

"The Changing Face of Indian BPO Industry" (2011), *Global Services*, URL: http://www.globalservicesmedia.com/, 7 April.

"The IT-BPO Sector in India" (2012), NASSCOM, *Strategic Review*, India.

"The recent BPO scandal in India was manipulated, effect will be minimal" (2005), *The Financial Express*, 4 July.

"The threat within. A study on insider threat by DSCI in collaboration with PwC" (2011), DSCI & NASSCOM Initiative, Pricewaterhouse Coopers, India, URL: http://www.pwc.in/en_IN/in/assets/pdfs/publications-2011/The_Threat_Within.pdf.

Trombly, M. (2006), "India Tightens Security", *Insurance Networking News*, URL: http://www.insurancenetworking.com/, 1 August.

Conclusion
Alterity in the Landscape of Asian IT Politics

Alan Chong and Faizal Yahya

The chapters in this volume lay to rest any possibility of sweeping generalizations that IT impacts Asian politics by inexorably triggering democratic change in the nation-states it is introduced into. Admittedly, there are degrees of Asian democratization enabled through the proficiency in grassroots initiatives empowered by the availability of Internet access and social media platforms. And there are equally disciplinary requirements that are called into being when IT implementation demands a quality of infrastructural development and policing of the social peace that can only be supplied by government. This is the nature of alterity between online and offline politics.

Understanding alterity as a condition privileging the hitherto marginal and subterranean aspects of a capitalist world order through the capabilities of information and communications technologies becomes clearer when we summarize our authors' responses to the research questions we have set out in the introduction and reiterate some of the generic observations we made there.

Online Causes, Programmes and Businesses Rely Upon the Backbone of Offline Political Processes

Virtually every chapter traces the seemingly intuitive reliance of online activity upon the demands of offline social currents. Muslim students studying abroad respond to their encounter with otherness by resorting to online networks and other information sites to affirm their identities as adherents to their Faith. Filipino expatriates have found a role for mobile phones, and smart phones interfacing with Facebook, to exert long distance social controls over their families and their finances. The chapters by Nasya Bahfen and Fernando Paragas thus affirm that Benedict Anderson's thesis of imagined community (Anderson, 1991) remains very much applicable to the world of IT. Anderson had of course traced the impact of the printed newspaper as a framer of a common news frequency that all its readers tune into. Bahfen and Paragas suggest that IT has produced the Internet as the 'newspaper' of the twenty-first century, and furthermore, the online community of readers can interact by talking back and writing in their feedback for their fellow networked users to react to, often knitting a community together through the pattern of continuous information exchange. In the other examples of social politics in IT use, the chapters by Tan and Choong suggest that virtual communities can also form as subgroups within national communities. In the Singaporean and Malaysian cases, these subgroups have acted out roles of civil society by offering opinions which are contrarian to their sitting governments, and occasionally urging change for the better by producing satire, serious commentary blogs, and initiating causes of democratic and legal advocacy. What binds all of the social politics chapters is the lively discussion of interactive community online, responding to both the latent and active needs of the marginalized, the conservative and the idealistic younger generations that have grown up to embrace two way communication as a mainstream media norm.

Finally, when it comes to practising state sovereignty for the 'national interest', governments have no qualms rolling out 'pork barrel-like' incentives, infrastructural projects, policy coordination and legal accommodation to the needs of the foreign investor in the IT sector. In all these aspects, IT and its associated forms of socially-portable media are little different from their pre-electronic predecessors, in that the medium's impact can be most accurately comprehended from the perspective of their human, social and political contexts.

Do Offline Political and Social Formations Exert a Disproportionate Impact Upon Online Networks?

The picture is mixed in relation to how far offline politics and social formations exert a disproportionate impact upon online networks. The chapters by Bahfen, Paragas, Tan and Choong suggest that online social politics tend to develop a life of their own after the initial push from offline causes. Virtual communities often substitute for offline political and social absences for a variety of reasons. In the cases of Malaysia and Singapore, the nature of circumscribed offline democracy feeds netizens' discursive creativity and passion on blogs and other social media. In the case of Islam and the faith of adult students overseas, online explorations of the latter's faith is a major effort in permanently surmounting the barriers of distance and displacement, and obtaining spiritual affirmation in the process.

The second section of chapters dealing with governmental steering and alterity confirms that the alterity is in fact precipitated by governmental actions in controlling IT usage for the national interest. The chapters by Hearn and Min seem to suggest that governments deliberately want to control the Web because their imperative is to control either unbridled nationalism or democratization for what they perceive to be the long term public good. Necessarily, ideology is a guiding hand in these so-called repressive measures. Even where ideology is directed specifically for attracting IT-related investment and development, as Chong's chapter on global city foreign policy argues, the hand of the state is intended to control against the odds of marginalization in the electronic economy. The final two chapters on Indian and Philippine IT economy by Yahya and Santarita confirm that the economic fundamentals of the IT miracle are continuously state-led initiatives, or state supported policies urged on by business people.

How Do the Offline Progeny of Online Networks and Industries Impact the Wider Governance of IT-Connected Societies and Governments?

Whether it is civil society adapting to the Internet's spaces for complaint and dissent, or the Philippine diaspora's utilization of mobile and smart phones to exert long distance financial and emotional control over family, social behaviour tends to be patterned over time in reference to online activities. In this way, one can discuss the prospects of 'offline progeny' impacting wider society and government over a considerably longer period of time. Governments may learn to accept the 'facts' of online protest spaces, and additionally, learn to tolerate their existence as a social safety valve. This is the case in the Malaysia chapter treating grassroots movements' usage of social media to prolong their public presence in spite of the authorities' publicly stated disapproval of grassroots civic agendas. This official tolerance might well become the norm in Singapore over time as well, even as the authorities selectively invoke sedition clauses in the constitution and media legislation to rein in the politically rambunctious websites.

Even where the direct intervention of the government is publicly acclaimed as conducive to the growth of the knowledge economy or electronic commerce, established patterns of corporate reliance upon the government to structure the growth of the IT industry and its ancillary parts ironically laid ever deeper tracks for governments to step in to smoothen out the economic pathways when invited to do so. Business lobbies expect more of the same 'good interventions' whenever bottlenecks are encountered in the takeoff of the knowledge economy. Yet, as the Chong, Santarita and Yahya chapters also caution, corporate dependence upon government intervention may also contribute to the accidental problem of corporations' lack of initiative in branding themselves once the IT economy is underway within a borderless world. This is the case with global city Taipei and its Taiwanese IT firms. In Malaysia, it was a case of the inconsistency of branding and the knee jerk reactions of the Malaysian government to corporate players who counselled against draconian economic self-therapy and capital controls during the Asian financial crisis. Santarita also warns that the Philippine government's 'new wave cities' may well undercut their future promise if their growth is not managed in terms of timing and scale while taking into account workers' living density and availability for adaptation. Yahya's chapter also warns that the problem of data theft or insecurity within business process outsourcing firms cannot be handled from the insides of corporations alone. These financially successful firms still need to partner with the Indian government to restructure the landscape for penalizing data theft, and ultimately deterring it.

What is the Shape of IT-Revolutionized Social and Political Entities in Asia?

Although this entire exploration of the impact of IT on Asian states and societies could have been more comprehensive, for instance, by picking a case study each from every subregion of the Asian continent, it is possible to argue that Asia will pioneer very divergent paths that lead away from the premise of a liberal perspective of IT sketched by Al Gore's vision at the International Telecommunication Union conference in Buenos Aires more than 20 years ago. After all, this volume can modestly claim to be one among a wave of pioneering studies focussing on the politics of IT in Asia. First of all, the ever present Asian 'love-hate romance' with the role of government, often treated synonymously with the 'state' and 'nation-state' in popular discourse, is a fact of the IT landscape. In most public imaginations, the government is rarely distinguished from the 'state' and 'nation-state' for a good reason: the nationalism that animates development is truly well and alive and the various national populations look to government to define the national interest *qua* state interest *qua* collective good. Even civil society rarely wishes to completely overthrow sitting governments. Nonetheless, civil society, as seen in the chapters under the section labelled the social politics of IT, is not averse to resorting to tactics verging on sedition to get their way. In the chapters focussing on governmental patrolling of the Web in China and South Korea, some degree of ideological loyalty, a limited sense of entrusting a vile government with economic responsibility, together with the spirit of patriotism, may contribute to reining in the excesses of democratizing society through Web-based means. The Asia-wide romance with the collectivist project is not yet over: government is still called upon to deliver more and more welfare-oriented directed development, while being at the same time hated and admonished for insufficient consultation with the populations they govern. Web activism in Asia, while effervescent, will therefore be likely to be both self-restrained and other restrained for the foreseeable future. We can still dub this pattern as positing the centrality of authoritarian politics in IT impacts in Asia.

Secondly, the 'Asian paths' towards embracing IT in state and society are still plural and inchoate. Asians are experimenting indefinitely with the political and business possibilities of IT. As the chapters on Singaporean and Malaysian bloggers and social media usage suggest, these Web-savvy netizens are mostly middle class and elitist. In contrast, the studies of Muslim students and Filipino expatriates abroad utilizing IT-facilitated means of communication suggest a more classless experience: the use of IT is motivated by piousness, fidelity, frugality and family. One might add that Kay Hearn's chapter on the 'centre-margin' relationship between the government in Beijing and Chinese bloggers reflects an Asian value logic where government ought not to be dethroned even if it is tyrannical in some aspects. The rest of the chapters treating the political economy of IT also point to the ultimate reliance upon government as the preferred helm of providing infrastructure. In a recent reflection on 'e-frictions' plaguing Asian IT usage, the vice-president for Asia at the Internet Corporation for Assigned Names and Numbers (ICANN) admits to the fact that tracking Asian e-commerce is a particularly elusive endeavour:

> There is evidence to suggest that the diversity of Asia's Internet economy is not fully captured in the study [by Boston Consulting Group entitled 'The Connected World: Greasing the Wheels of the Internet Economy'] … [M] any Asian entrepreneurs do not register websites at all, preferring to host their content on intermediaries such as social media sites like Tumblr or Facebook. Or they may open virtual shops made available on AliBaba, Qoo10, Rakuten or eBay. When they do register a company domain, the preference is to register a generic top level domain [such as .com, .info, .net and .org].
>
> Other measures may not have fully captured the explosive growth and dynamism of Asian Internet platforms, and their use. Counting the number of micro-messages made in home languages on Twitter bypasses the Asian galaxy of China's Weibo. And measuring the share of population using social networks misses the flourishing volume of China's RenRen, Vietnam's Tamtay, South Korea's Line, Indonesia's Detik and Japan's Mixi. These are just a few of the more popular Asian social media networks. (Chuang, 2014)

Asian diversities in IT usage reflect inequalities in so many dimensions at once, even statistically. Therefore, it is currently unhelpful to reduce Asian IT use, whether politically or economically, to the moniker of a singular and universal 'digital divide'.

References

Anderson, B. (1991). *Imagined Communities: Reflections on the Origin and Spread of Nationalism*. 2nd edn. London: Verso Books.

Chuang, K.-Y. (2014) 'Reducing Friction in Asia for Growth'. *The Straits Times* (Singapore), 4 February, p.A22.

Index

For Product Safety Concerns and Information please contact our EU representative GPSR@taylorandfrancis.com Taylor & Francis Verlag GmbH, Kaufingerstraße 24, 80331 München, Germany

Batch number: 10725825

Printed by Printforce, the Netherlands